Risking Old Age
in America

‹◆›

A Families U.S.A. Foundation Book

**Families United for Senior Action Foundation
(formerly The Villers Foundation)**

R I C H A R D   J.   M A R G O L I S

Risking Old Age
in America

WESTVIEW PRESS
Boulder ◆ San Francisco ◆ London

Copyright © 1990 by Families U.S.A. Foundation and Richard J. Margolis

Published in 1990 in the United States of America by Westview Press, Inc., 5500 Central Avenue, Boulder, Colorado 80301, and in the United Kingdom by Westview Press, 13 Brunswick Centre, London WC1N 1AF, England

Library of Congress Cataloging-in-Publication Data
Margolis, Richard J.
  Risking old age in America/Richard J. Margolis.
    p.   cm.
  ISBN 0-8133-0939-5—ISBN 0-8133-0940-9 (pbk.)
  1. Aged—United States.   2. Aged—Housing—United States.
3. Aged—Care—United States.   I. Title.
HQ1064.U5M375   1990
305.26′0973—dc20   89-22620
                                                                                              CIP

Printed and bound in the United States of America

The paper used in this publication meets the requirements of the American National Standard for Permanence of Paper for Printed Library Materials Z39.48-1984.

10   9   8   7   6   5   4   3   2

To Diane
for all seasons

CONTENTS

◆

Acknowledgments   ix

Prologue   1

Introduction: The Civic Heart   3

    Progress and Poverty, 8
    Defining the Elderly Poor, 11
    The Book: A Preview, 14

PART ONE
THE SEARCH FOR SECURITY

1   Income: A Tale of Two Programs   21

    Solidarity, 21
    Charity, 23
    Categorical Imperatives, 25
    Social Security: Don't Leave Home
      Without It, 28
    Supplemental Security Income, 37
    Choices, 50

2   Health: The Gift Repossessed   53

    How Medicare Took Shape, 55
    The Many Paradoxes of Medicare, 58
    The Mending of Catherine Cott, 63
    Speeding Up the Clock, 67
    Doing Something, 71

3   Shelter: Bring Us to This Hovel   77

    The Visit, 78

The Status of Elderly Housing, 81
The High Cost of Hovels, 82
Digging In, 85
Letting Go, 90
Elderly Homelessness, 92
The Federal Commitment: A History, 93
Onward, 101
The Lonely Crowd, 103

PART TWO
THE STRUGGLE FOR INDEPENDENCE

4   Home Care: The Dream Deferred   109

"Youth Creep" and "Age Creep," 112
The Caregivers, 115
Home-Care Policy in Absentia, 125
How Do You Spell Relief? 127
Reinventing the Wheel, 128

5   A Personal History   135

6   Exile: The Perils of Institutionalization   147

"Over the Hill": The Past as Prologue, 149
From Social Security to Medicaid, 153
The Way Things Are Now, 156
The Use and Abuse of Medicaid, 163
A Few Suggestions, 173
The Virtues of Not Being Up-to-Date, 176

Epilogue   183

Notes   189
Index   197

ACKNOWLEDGMENTS

◆

There is no adequate way to thank my elderly sources for the gifts they bestowed, other than to declare that this work is for them. It relies on their insights; it attends to their singular accents, the distant cadences of old age. If I have sometimes assigned them fictitious names, it is not because they demanded anonymity—it is because I felt uneasy about invading their privacy.

In retrospect, it seems odd that some of my associates thought it might be risky for me to write about the aged poor. "How will you get through the day?" an acquaintance asked. "Won't the interviews depress you?"

Well, yes and no. The poor people I met in the course of my investigations turned out to be first-rate company. They bore their burdens gracefully; most brought to the interviews an attractive blend of innocence and irony, traits they may have found useful in *their* struggles to get through the day. What saddened me was not the people but their circumstances.

An undertaking like this is the product of countless kindnesses from friends and strangers alike. I was lucky from the start: I got a phone call from Ronald F. Pollack, the talented executive director of Families U.S.A. Foundation (formerly The Villers Foundation), suggesting that I write a book about poverty and old age. Pollack and the foundation stand at the top of my personal, all-time list of altruists. They armed me with the three resources a writer must have to complete a lengthy project: time, money, and the knowledge that somebody cares.

Still, there were occasions when my confidence in the project went on vacation. The research and the writing took considerably longer than any of us had anticipated. At such moments it was chiefly Ronny's steadiness, his serene faith in the book, that kept me going.

The foundation also served as an indispensable supplier of information on old age and poverty. Staff members cheerfully answered my questions and as cheerfully corrected my errors. The following list includes just some of the foundation people who enlightened me along the way: Arnold Bennett, Barbara Campbell, Peggy Denker, Edward F.

Howard, Susan K. Kinoy, Jeff Kirsch, Judith Perez, Marsha Simon, and Phyllis Torda.

There were other institutions that came to my rescue. The Blue Mountain Center, a heavenly way station in the Adirondacks—presided over by that most spirited of angels, Harriet Barlow—took me in for refueling whenever I began to run out of gas. Mine is not the only book to have benefited from Harriet's timely hospitality: She has been an "enabling Muse" for hundreds of writers and artists.

Early on in my explorations, the Institute of Politics at Harvard University's Kennedy School of Government provided me with an office, a copier, and that most precious of artifacts, a library card. Later, when my Harvard library privileges lapsed, Yale University—more precisely, Professor John Simon and the Program On Non-Profit Organizations—gave me the affiliation I needed.

In my research I consulted scores of knowledgeable people, and most of those worthies show up in the course of the book. A few, however, I wish to name here. In the early going, the comments of Fernando Torres-Gil were especially helpful; Tom Joe and Judith Meltzer of the Center for the Study of Social Policy gave me a cram course in the histories of social security and Supplemental Security Income; Chester Hartman, Cushing N. Dolbeare, and Barry Zigas each read and improved my chapter on housing; and Rosalie A. Kane and Joshua M. Wiener did the same for a draft chapter on home care.

My sons, Philip and Harry Margolis, were kind enough to read early versions of several chapters—and brave enough to offer tough-minded critiques. The book is better for their comments. Diane Rothbard Margolis read the manuscript with a shrewd sociological eye and suggested many refinements, especially for the chapters on income and on health. In addition, I have shamelessly purloined certain ideas Diane expressed in her paper "From Our Hearts or Against Our Wills: The Two Faces of Social Welfare" (delivered to the Society for the Study of Social Problems, Washington, D.C., 1985).

As the manuscript grew, I submitted bits and pieces of it to various periodicals. Readers of *The New Leader,* a fortnightly that regularly carries my work, saw tentative versions from several chapters. Thanks are due to my patient friend and editor, Myron Kolatch, for giving me the opportunity to send up those trial balloons. My gratitude also goes to Arlie Schardt, editor of *Foundation News,* for publishing my essay on the federal definition of elderly poverty (see the Introduction); and to Mary Neely Eldridge, who as editor of *Southern Exposure* ran my article on the Social Security Administration's debt collection crusade (see Chapter 1).

I am indebted to Katherine Hall, who retyped much of the manuscript and never once complained about my scribbles and erasures; and to David S. Bruce of the Yale University Computer Center: Somehow he figured out a way to convert my software to something the publisher could use.

Gail E. Ross, attorney-at-law and literary agent, came along at exactly the right moment, as did the publisher she enlisted, Westview Press. My editors at Westview—Barbara Ellington, Marian Safran, Rebecca Ritke, and Jane Raese—have treated me with a considerateness that in the publishing world is far from routine. As copy editor, Marian Safran rates a special thanks for her splendid excisions and discreet explanations.

Notwithstanding all the help I have received, no one but me should be held responsible for the book's content. The buck stops here.

Richard J. Margolis
New Haven, Connecticut

Prologue

Strolling up Sheridan Road in Chicago one March morning, I come upon a silent queue of elderly women and men leaning into the chill wind that blows off Lake Michigan. Nearby, a stern humpty-dumpty of a man, not much younger than the others, stokes a trashcan fire with empty cardboard boxes. The boxes bear a charred warning: "Not to be sold or exchanged—USDA."

The city is getting ready to distribute federal surplus cheese to some of its down-and-old citizens, an exercise made possible by the 1983 Temporary Emergency Food Assistance Program, which allows for the charitable disposal of certain farm products piling up in government warehouses. Today's cheese comes in five-pound bricks. It is yellow, pasteurized, and loaded with cholesterol.

"What's everybody waiting for?" I ask Humpty Dumpty.

"They're waiting for the Police Lady to open up. She's got the key."

I ask if the Police Lady is late.

"She's not late and she's not early," he says. "When she comes, she comes. And please don't ask me no more questions. I'm a part-time person here."

There is some jostling at the rear of the line. A black man with gray hair and a white goatee is feebly defending his turf against an aged newcomer. Humpty Dumpty makes a megaphone of his hands. "Hey, you," he shouts, "you better behave or you don't get no cheese."

Second in line is a woman holding a metal cane. She wears a shabby yellow coat that reaches down to her shoe tops. "I can't hold out much longer," she says to no one in particular. "My legs hurt something awful from the arthritis." She catches my eye and goes on. "I got a good spot here 'cause I woke up early. Been in line maybe two hours. Wish that Police Lady would hurry up."

I offer to stand in her place but she shakes her head. "There's nowhere I could sit. And they wouldn't think you're eligible," she adds, eyeing my tie and jacket. A few minutes later she slips out of line and hobbles away.

The Police Lady arrives soon after. Within thirty minutes everyone has received some cheese and started home. I walk north alongside a small woman who wears a white kerchief on her head. She turns out to be a brisk walker and talker.

"My name is Marie Finley," she says, "and I was seventy-eight last month. It was a very nice birthday. A neighbor made me a small cake. I'm going to give some of this cheese to my neighbors. It's too much for one person, that's for sure. I missed getting the cheese this winter because it was too cold to stand in line. Didn't pick up my food stamps either—afraid I'd catch pneumonia."

"Then what did you do for food?" I inquire.

"That's easy. I went without."

Miss Finley says that all her life she has had difficulty making ends meet. It is not a complaint. "I've never been married and I've always supported myself, till I took sick. I worked mostly in restaurants and I made beds at that college in Evanston. It was hard work but it was a living."

Now she gets $412 a month from social security, or just under $5,000 a year. The total keeps her a shade below the official poverty line while allowing her to collect $25-worth of food stamps each month. She used to get more stamps before Ronald Reagan and the Congress slashed antihunger expenditures by more than $12 billion.

Miss Finley voted for Reagan both times, but lately she has been having second thoughts. "I can't see those cuts," she says. "People need stamps to keep up their strength."

At the corner of Sheridan and Eastwood Marie Finley and I prepare to go our separate ways. She is anxious to get back to her room, to slice up her cheese and give it away. "There are people in my building," she says, "who haven't eaten since Tuesday." Today is Thursday.

◆

The Civic Heart

The social commentator Alvin L. Schorr has noted a paradox of human nature—namely that "we measure decency by our immediate experience and activity but often lack the imagination to project it into policies or administration." The upshot is all too familiar: "Citizens who are good neighbors and give time to charitable activities . . . can also, in concert, behave brutally."[1]

We could say when we behave that way we lack a civic heart. As with social imagination, a civic heart has little to do with one's personal code of behavior; it has more to do with W. H. Auden's sense of pooled "love":

> Hunger allows no choice
> To the citizen or the police;
> We must love one another or die.
> ("September 1, 1939")

That chilly cheese line on Sheridan Road—for which the federal government and the city of Chicago bore joint responsibility—was a pedestrian example of socially cruel behavior. When people go hungry, how are the rest of us to respond? In this case we gave the people cheese, but first we made them stand for hours in the cold. The gift seemed grudging, not gracious. And it *was* a gift rather than a right. As the woman who had waited in line two hours made clear, not everybody was *entitled* to the cheese—only the shabbily dressed. Humpty-Dumpty understood another common characteristic of means-tested philanthropy: "You better behave or you don't get no cheese."

It seems possible, then, to gauge the quality of a nation's support for its dependent compatriots—first, in terms of the benefits it provides and, second, in terms of the dignity it confers. In any sensible social assistance program the self-respect of the recipient becomes as large a consideration as the adequacy of the benefit. Together they constitute a rough index of compassion by which a community can judge how wisely or foolishly it has projected its decent impulses into public policy.

The hope that has prompted this book is that it might amplify the civic heart vis-à-vis a sizable proportion of those 30 million Americans, ages sixty-five and up, whom society calls "old." Herein I consider the elderly poor, who are more numerous than some pretend, along with the elderly middle classes, who are more vulnerable than many suppose. Here, too, I appraise the major national initiatives in old-age support—social security, Supplemental Security Income, Medicare, Medicaid, and sundry housing subsidies—which, taken together, are less adequate than all might wish. To an extent rarely acknowledged, these federal endeavors shape the hopes and spell the fates of millions of elderly citizens, and of millions more approaching retirement.

Our present social arrangements, for all their merit, still hold many of us hostage to the possibility of latter-day destitution. It is not just the ravages of time that can do us in. It is also the ravages of retirement, ageism, medical bills, and institutionalization. Such a commonplace brew may instantly transform middle-aged prosperity into elderly pauperism. To cite a single suggestive statistic, 20 percent of all Americans who make it past their eightieth birthdays end up in nursing homes, where, more often than not, they must rely on Medicaid—the federal health program for poor people—to pay some or all of their bills.

It follows that our present-day policies and attitudes toward older Americans cast more than a humanitarian light: They also cast a peculiarly long shadow—a true foreshadowing—that predicts how we ultimately intend to treat our parents and ourselves. It is that portentous silhouette on which this book will focus.

From a political perspective, this seems a particularly awkward moment for older Americans. Demographics and a king-size national deficit, the latter a legacy of Reaganomics, have combined to paint the elderly into an uncomfortable corner, where they are widely perceived to be too numerous, too affluent, and, in regard to their claims on the federal exchequer, too demanding. "Public subsidy"—that slightly tainted term some use as a synonym for social security benefits—is said to be the elderly's favorite form of income; luxury, their chosen life-style. Even their new-found longevity, a gift of modern medicine, is widely viewed not as a blessing to be prized but as a demographic catastrophe to be feared.

Most of us probably know as much as we need to know about the demographics of aging. They are a form of social weather—easy to predict but difficult to prevent. In a two-line apostrophe to "Old Age," Walt Whitman wrote: "I see in you the estuary that enlarges and spreads / itself grandly as it pours in the great sea." Today, thanks to astonishing gains in life expectancy, old age has itself become a great sea that continues to enlarge and spread.

In 1892, the year Whitman died, only four of every one hundred Americans had made it past their sixty-fifth birthday; today the ratio is twelve in one hundred and climbing. The postwar baby boomers, many of whom have already passed forty, will soon swell the procession. Census projections tell us that by the year 2030 one of every five Americans will be "old."

The numbers strongly suggest that old age need no longer be restricted to the traditional three score and ten; for many it has become a matter of four score and more. In 1820, when Walt was 1 year old, average life expectancy in the United States was less than 40 years; now it is 75 years. Some two-fifths of the 65-plus population have already passed 75, while the over-85 contingent is now the nation's fastest growing age group. Living to be 100 is still considered something of an achievement, but less so all the time. Centenarians in the United States now number about 45,000; by the year 2080, according to the National Institute on Aging, they will number 5 million.

Not just Reagan's disciples but also pundits and professors of all stripes have been busy studying the social arithmetic of aging and computing the possible consequences. The message many appear to favor is two-sided—part Cassandra and part Pangloss. They profess to glimpse a time not too distant when the few remaining young will be forced to toil ceaselessly on behalf of the old with their costly, ever-escalating infirmities. But to that grim portrait of the future, they have appended an oddly roseate snapshot of the present, wherein the elderly poor are nowhere to be found.

Either way, alas, older Americans emerge more as villains than victims. On the one hand, their multiplying numbers are viewed as posing a long-range threat to future generations; on the other, their putative habit of prospering at the taxpayers' expense is seen as placing an intolerable strain on the current national debt.

In such a climate it is hard to see how the aged poor can hope to get a fair hearing. Their very existence has been denied. They are targets of a revisionist assault that would have us dismantle significant stretches of our fifty-five-year-old social welfare system, chiefly on grounds that it is unfair to our young.

A 1980 profile of "The Old Folks" in *Forbes* magazine foretold the line of attack that would distinguish the coming decade from all previous ones. "The myth," declared *Forbes,* "is that they're sunk in poverty. The reality is that they're living well. The trouble is, there are too many of them—God bless 'em."[2]

Such declarations have by now grown commonplace in conservative and liberal circles alike, and not all are so amiably phrased. "Blunt and a tad belligerent" is how *Time* magazine characterized elderly voters, the editors having just discovered that "America's senior citizens are suddenly flexing their biceps."[3]

"In the new America," complained the *Washington Post,* "the old are being enriched at the expense of the young," and "the present is being financed with tax money expropriated from the future." The *Post's* headline said it all: "The Coming Conflict / As We Soak the Young / And Enrich the Old."[4]

Toward the close of 1988 *Forbes* again entered the lists, this time with a blockbuster cover story entitled "Cry, Baby." The apparent purpose of this renewed assault was to attempt a convincing explanation of why the American Dream had turned sour. "This is still a country where a poor kid can rise in the world," *Forbes* declared at the outset. "That part of the American Dream is intact. . . . But the other part— that every generation should live better than the preceding one—is in serious trouble. It is getting harder for the average person to beat his or her parents' standard of living."

Then came the by now familiar rationale: "What is not widely recognized is that the loss of upward mobility is the consequence of an enormous intergenerational transfer of wealth and income that is still going on. . . . The old are getting richer at the expense of the young. . . . Simply put, in economic terms we are consuming our children."

To underscore the point, *Forbes* featured a macabre drawing of an inverted human pyramid with a lone baby at the bottom, on its hands and knees, and a row of elders, complete with canes, crutches, and a rocking chair, perched at the pinnacle. The pyramid's midsection displayed figures from intervening generations—teenagers, young adults, and the middle-aged. On the baby's frail shoulders, *Forbes* seemed to be telling us, rested everyone else's prosperity, especially that of older Americans.[5]

An accompanying U.S. Census chart on federal spending contributed more drama. It purported to show the unfairness of it all. "People over 65," complained *Forbes* in the caption, "comprise 12% of the population but receive 27% of all federal spending." What the chart neglected to note was that nearly all federal spending on the elderly comes in the form of social security benefits drawn from trust funds to which the beneficiaries regularly contributed, each and every payday, during their working years.

What lies behind the recent editorial binge of elderly bashing? Like all scapegoat-type explanations, this one arises out of some authentic discontents. *Forbes* was partly right: The American Dream *has* lost some of its luster; in recent years "an enormous transfer of wealth and income" has indeed occurred—thanks mainly to simultaneous federal cuts in high-income taxes and low-income benefits. The lion's share of that transfer has flowed between classes rather than generations. This new and surprisingly strong current of inequity is not always visible in our daily lives, but it does show up in census totals. Among other things those numbers signal a dwindling middle class, an unprecedented number of citizens living in poverty (31 million in 1989, about two-thirds of them children), and, not least, a growing concentration of wealth among the superrich. Nowadays at least one-third of the nation's wealth is held by those in the top 1 percent bracket.

As it happens, *Forbes*'s own annual roster of "The 400 Richest People in America" unintentionally illuminates some of the real inequities currently plaguing America. The journalist Vance Packard has recently analyzed the numbers behind the list. In 1982, he noted in *The Ultra Rich,* "the cutoff point for inclusion in the list of the 400 richest American individuals was a net worth of $93 million. By 1987 that point had advanced to $225 million. Between 1985 and 1987, the number of billionaires jumped from fourteen to forty-nine. Four of these were entitled to a new phrase in the language—'centi-billionaires.'" The burgeoning wealth of the "*Forbes* 400," Packard pointed out, "equals the savings that all Americans have in commercial banks and . . . is considerably greater than the annual federal budget deficit that has created so much trouble for the nation."[6]

Most of this concentrated wealth, moreover, remains untaxed; hardly any of it finds its way into the commonweal. That is half the open secret that *Forbes* conveniently overlooked in its eagerness to pin the blame on older Americans. The other half pertains to the fiscal consequences. As the late Robert Lekachman, who taught economics at the City University of New York, pointed out:

> The reason we encounter difficulty financing benefits . . . is not to be found in generational conflict but in the ancient war between rich and poor. The fact is that the prosperous, the merely wealthy and the filthy rich do not pay their fair share of taxes. As a consquence, analysts . . . fall into the trap of defining their problem as the distribution of

governmental expenditure burdens among average working families of different ages.[7]

An alternative version of reality will be on display here. It will focus on the 11.5 million elderly poor and vulnerable in our midst; it will underline both the nature of their dilemma and the inadequacy of our communal response; and it will suggest national solutions to which everyone can contribute.

One of our tasks throughout will be to reply to the new mythmakers, whose vision of the world, so different from Auden's, seems to have invaded the nation's civic heart. Seldom now does one hear, in Irving Howe's wistful phrase, "the old cry of American rectitude—*it's wrong, it's unfair.*" In its place, said Howe, has arisen "a peculiar kind of social nastiness" that deems it proper "to revel in . . . indifference to the plight of the weak and the losers."[8]

My own line of argument is more hopeful. It assumes the nastiness will pass. I continue to believe in an America endowed with the blessings, the talents, and the virtues—wealth, inventiveness, magnanimity—requisite to the building of a humane social system. This book presupposes a generous citizenry capable of creating generous institutions to match.

I concede at the outset, happily, that a substantial majority of older Americans are neither poor nor dependent; they are doing just fine—thanks mainly to federal programs their critics would cheerfully discard. But the country's index of compassion makes it impossible to overlook the many still mired in poverty and the additional millions who struggle day-to-day while poised upon that scariest of high wires—the thin edge of economic security. For those so afflicted, public policy is not an abstraction; it is a last chance for deliverance.

The pages that follow prepare the ground—first with a review of the elderly condition, taking into account both the progress made and the poverty overlooked; then with an inquiry into the federal government's peculiar definition of elderly poverty; and, finally, with a brief chapter-by-chapter forecast.

Progress and Poverty

Early on in his pioneering treatise on the American poor, the muckraker Robert Hunter singled out the elderly poor as "the most numerous of all" and noted that they were "insufficiently cared for in all cities—with the possible exception of Boston." He deplored the "derision"—we might call it "ageism"—with which citizens treated their older compatriots. Aged women "who frequent the poorest furnished rooms," complained Hunter, were called such "bitter names" as "scrubs" and "harpies."[9]

By the time Michael Harrington rediscovered poverty in *The Other America,* and despite the flow by then of social security dollars into elderly pockets, the nomenclature had changed far more noticeably than had social conditions. People may "talk of the 'golden years' and of 'senior citizens,'" Harrington scoffed in a chapter on the aged. "But these are euphemisms to ease the conscience of the callous." At bottom, "America tends to make its people miserable when they become old." They are "plagued by ill health; they do not have enough money; they are socially isolated." He estimated that in 1960 more than half of all older Americans were poor.[10]

We have traveled a considerable distance since Harrington wrote his jeremiad, and in the process we may even have peeled a few calluses off our collective conscience: Social security benefits have become more bountiful; Medicare and Medicaid now help the elderly meet their health care and nursing home bills; and the Supplemental Security Income program (SSI), enacted in 1972, guarantees a modicum of sustenance to the aged destitute. In addition, Congress has presented its older constituents with a fulsome grab bag of prizes, ranging from special tax exemptions and retirement shelters to an imaginative menu of social services written into the Older Americans Act of 1965.

At least two of the programs, moreover—social security and Medicare—have vouchsafed assistance in ways that assure a fair degree of dignity to their beneficiaries. That is because the beneficiaries are age-tested rather than means-tested and thus the benefits come relatively free of strings or stigmas. Assisting all, they humiliate none.

That such measures have paid off handsomely seems self-evident. Millions now find it possible to reach a stage and status in life that can be described without irony as "the golden years." If relatively few older citizens attain riches, most enjoy incomes roughly adequate to their needs, and fewer than 15 percent actually live below the federally designated poverty line. Social security alone enables at least half of the elderly population to escape penury.

The record, in short, suggests that our social policies vis-à-vis old age merit two cheers: one for the rescues accomplished and another for the considerateness sometimes shown along the way. A third cheer is yet unwarranted; it awaits our resolve to finish the job. That job turns out to be much bigger than many would have us believe. We still have miles to go before we can soundly sleep.

Census tabulations measure only part of the distance remaining, for they are based on the federal government's somewhat tortured definition of poverty, which both underestimates the number of poor overall and discriminates against the elderly poor in particular. (See below, "Defining the Elderly Poor.") Even so, the official figures are discouraging. Census totals for 1987 place the number of older poor people at 3.5 million. If we include those with incomes only slightly higher—up to 125 percent of the elderly poverty line, or just $130 a week for a single person—the total jumps to 6 million. In other words, at least one of every five older Americans can be said to be suffering from a serious shortage of cash.

Certain groups within the older population suffer more than others. Most of the elderly poor are female (72 percent) and either black (40 percent) or Hispanic (26 percent). To put it another way, one of every four older Hispanic-Americans is poor, as is one of every three older black Americans. To be old, female, nonwhite, and living alone is to bear the heaviest burden of all. An astonishing 55 percent of that multimarked contingent lives *below* the poverty line.

But there is more to the story. To the 6 million aged poor must be added a host nearly as large—the 5.5 million elderly not-now-poor but in daily jeopardy of becoming so. Their incomes reach a level no higher than twice the official poverty rate, meaning a maximum of $209 a week for older single persons and $264 a week for older couples. In the secret army of the elderly vulnerable, any downward turn of fortune—a costly illness, the death of a spouse—can spell instant catastrophe.

Timothy Smeeding, a University of Utah economist, has written at length about the elderly vulnerable. Generally too poor to meet the price of decent housing or sufficient health-care protection, they have been ruled too affluent to be eligible for most essential benefit programs. The bitter lesson they learn, says Smeeding, is that relief comes mainly to those who volunteer for poverty. "When facing economic and/or health problems," he explains, "the only way they can improve their well-being is to spend themselves down to penury and thereby qualify for means-tested transfers [i.e., benefits] in the form of Medicaid and Supplemental Security Income."[11]

Adding up the numbers, then, we get a total of 11.5 million elderly who are either poor or seriously at risk. They make up 42 percent of all older Americans. What such figures suggest is the formation of a two-class system within the aged population, one class protected by subsidies and fortified with cash, the other largely defenseless. Our major old-age support programs have been directing most of their resources toward the former group, the one that needs it less.

The social scientist Stephen Crystal examined this fresh dichotomy in his book *America's Old Age Crisis.* "The good news," he wrote, "is that old age benefits have been successful in eliminating systematic economic deprivation of the elderly as a class. . . . The bad news is that inequality *among* the aged has not been reduced and may in fact be getting worse."[12]

Defining the Elderly Poor

We turn now to the federal government's oddly discriminatory definition of elderly poverty, which for more than two decades has enjoyed near-unanimous acceptance among officials, lawmakers, and social scientists, even among partisans of elderly causes. Defining a suitable poverty threshold is no mere academic exercise. It can have heavy consequences for the poor, whose access to federal benefit programs like SSI and Medicaid may depend entirely on where the line is drawn. The lower the line, the fewer the beneficiaries.

The story of how and where we drew the line is instructive on at least two counts: first, because it underscores the elderly poor's essential political helplessness—they lack the resources to define themselves in ways that might improve their lot; and second, because it demonstrates the policy-making potency of the social sciences, and also their limitations. With the best of intentions, scholars can initiate the worst of practices and then be powerless to intervene.

If we are to credit the federal poverty line, the elderly poor are different from you and me: They need less money. That is because they are alleged to eat less than the rest of us. We define poverty in this country by estimating how much a low-budget family must spend annually for groceries and then multiplying that sum by three, on the assumption that unaffluent households commit about one-third of their incomes to food.

The product of that multiplication becomes the official poverty threshold for a given year, or the level of annual income below which all households are deemed poor. Different allowances are made for different sizes of households and for different ages of household members—and there's the rub. Because the elderly are considered to be relatively Spartan food consumers, the line for elderly poverty has been set below that for other age groups. Depending on which groups are being compared, the difference can run as high as 11 percent.

To put it another way, it is possible for someone to live *under* the poverty line at age 64 and *over* it the following year, even if that person's income has not increased one cent beyond the cost-of-living index. In 1987, elderly poverty lines were drawn at $5,447 for a single person and at $6,872 for a couple. Had the thresholds been squared with those of the under-65 group—$5,909 for a single person and

$7,641 for a couple—at least 700,000 additional older Americans would have instantly become "poor."[13]

We owe this strange state of affairs to certain pioneers of the mid-1960s who invented the poverty line—chiefly to nutritionists and economists at the U.S. Department of Agriculture (USDA) and to statisticians at both the Social Security Administration (SSA) and the Census Bureau. Their prime mover was Mollie Orshansky, a brilliant and admirably single-minded statistician at SSA who had already devoted the better part of a decade trying to devise a scientifically valid and reliable definition of poverty in the United States. At first, Orshansky told me in an interview, she had focused her research on children; later she began to concentrate as well on the elderly poor. "I thought of the old people as my children," she recalled.

By 1965 her efforts had become fortuitously attuned to the politics of the period. Reflecting the Great Society's hopes, and perhaps also its hubris, Orshansky noted in a seminal study that "if we can think bold solutions and dream big dreams, we may be able to ease the problem of poverty even if we cannot yet agree on how to measure it."[14]

As it turned out, agreement on measurements would follow quickly, and the resulting poverty thresholds would become fixtures on our social welfare landscape. From the standpoint of the elderly poor, the permanence has been a mixed blessing. On the one hand, the very existence of a quantifiable definition of poverty has provided reformers with a benchmark by which to assess social progress and retreat. It is now possible to count "the poor" of all ages; it only remains, as Orshansky had pointed out at the start, "to count the ways by which to help them gain a new identity."[15]

Then, too, the poverty line has introduced a certain amount of order into our customarily chaotic national welfare system and thus into the lives of its beneficiaries. As long as we insist on means-tested programs, justice demands a consistent, fair-minded sorting device.

On the other hand, the poor overall and the aged poor especially have been locked into definitions not always relevant to their difficulties. Most Americans, even the poorest, no longer spend one-third of their incomes on groceries. In the two decades since Orshansky did her work, the costs of fuel and shelter have risen much more rapidly than has the cost of food. In consequence, the poverty definition has lost touch with current pricing realities.

If the food-cost formula were to be adjusted downward by eight percentage points—that is, if we were to multiply a low-budget family's annual food expenditure by four rather than three—the resulting threshold would be considerably more realistic. For an older couple in 1987, the poverty line would have been raised from $6,872 to $8,964.

There appears, moreover, to be little evidence in support of the USDA's long-standing belief that older persons eat less than the rest of us. It may be true that caloric demand goes down as age goes up. People in their seventies and eighties, on average, seem to require about two-thirds of the calories they needed when they were younger. But calories are not nutrients—they do not necessarily contain minerals, vitamins, and proteins—and there is nothing to suggest that elderly persons require fewer nutrients. Indeed, nutritionists have paid surprisingly scant attention to the Required Dietary Allowances (RDAs) of older Americans.

In his Pulitzer Prize–winning treatise on growing old in America, Robert N. Butler, the first director of the National Institute on Aging, noted that "the nutritional needs of the reasonably healthy elderly are really little different from those of younger people. They certainly need the same proteins, vitamins and minerals—perhaps in slightly smaller quantities, but even that is debatable."[16]

Robert M. Russell, who directs clinical research at Tufts University's Human Nutrition Research Center on Aging, has gone a step further. In his opinion, "the aged require a higher quality diet" than do members of other age groups. But as Dr. Russell emphasized in our interview, "That is just my guess. The nutritional needs of the elderly have never been systematically examined. It will be decades before we get RDAs for the aged."

Still, Russell's hunch is widely shared by other physicians and dietitians, many of whom not unreasonably suspect that persons afflicted with brittle bones and chronic diseases may require a special dietary boost.

Whatever the merits or demerits of such arguments, it seems clear that the federal definition of elderly poverty is deficient on at least two scores. One relates to the budgets of the poor, the other to the nutritional needs of the aged. It is hard to escape the conclusion that creators of the poverty line, for all their careful formulations, have inadvertently fenced out large numbers of the poor and thus deprived them of essential federal and state benefits.

Mollie Orshansky, now retired from SSA, would be the first to concede the point. Her "lines," she told me, "were really crude estimates of need. They were stated very conservatively." But she added, "Once you have chosen a variable, you have to stick with it. I set it up. That's the way it came out."

The Book: A Preview

The course of this book runs roughly parallel to the course of old age as it negotiates its risky route through the benefit maze, trying always to find a way around the culs-de-sac of dependency and poverty. Barriers are numerous and often nonnegotiable. From an older poor person's perspective the benefits are likely to seem parsimonious, the rules of entry humiliating, and the systems of payment beyond understanding. Those are, in fact, the major elderly discontents that run through the text.

My own programmatic biases can be quickly declared. First, I affirm the natural superiority of universal entitlements—programs for everybody—to means-tested benefits designed exclusively for the poor; second, I view with alarm the growing gentrification of elderly benefits, whereby the rich get richer and the poor stay poor; and third, I deplore the federal drift toward program obfuscation, which is sowing vast confusion among beneficiaries. The elderly poor are particularly vulnerable. Weak eyesight, low-level schooling, jittery nerves—such are the dueling weapons they bring to the bureaucratic lists.

Although the book's format decrees that we treat these programs one at a time, it should be obvious that most older citizens, especially the poor, enjoy no such luxury. An elderly supplicant may have to wrestle more or less simultaneously with a half-dozen different sets of regulations imposed by as many different programs, some of them federally sponsored, others administered by the state, and still others, like Medicaid, of mixed parentage.

I hope to give readers some sense of the technical knowledge and manipulative skills such programs require of their clients, and of the indignities they commonly inflict. Portions of the text will furnish aged poverty with a modest megaphone of its own, taking into account T. S. Eliot's lament: "There is no end of it, the voiceless wailing" ("Four Quartets: The Dry Salvages," II). Some who have long been voiceless will speak eloquently here about old age and its attendant perils.

In addition, an attempt has been made throughout to tease forth the strands of social policy embedded in elderly daily life. Here again I have counted heavily on the aged's own testimony, for when citizens stand in line for benefits, they begin to make connections, for example: "I can't see those cuts. People need stamps to keep up their strength."

Because older Americans must queue up more often than most, it seems important to link the quality of their lives with the temper of federal assistance programs. Wherever those vectors intersect—in the committee rooms of Congress as well as in hospitals, Social Security offices, public housing units, nursing homes, senior centers, and cheese lines—is where we hope to hover.

The journey—theirs and ours—begins with retirement and "The Search for Security" (Part 1) and proceeds to the hazards of decline and "The Struggle for Independence" (Part 2). The first part focuses on income, health, and shelter; the second, on home care and nursing homes.

Chapter 1, then ("Income: A Tale of Two Programs"), explores the complexities of social security and its poor relation, Supplemental Security Income, or SSI. Neither is designed to emancipate the poor from their poverty, yet together they provide virtually all the dollars available to one-fourth of the elderly and to nearly three-fourths of the elderly poor. Although the two programs are managed by a single agency—the Social Security Administration—they present a study in contrasts. Their differences in style and temperament form a striking metaphor, allowing us to savor the advantages of universal entitlements even as we bemoan the faults of means testing.

Like the cheese giveaway effort, SSI has a low compassion index. It is a charity that carefully screens its applicants and vigilantly regulates the lives of its beneficiaries. SSI officials tend to be niggling in enforcing the agency's rules and tightfisted in distributing its meager benefits. Only the poorest of the poor are eligible, and only the most desperate or determined among them—about 1.5 million elderly citizens in 1987— ever bother to apply.

Social security, of course, is for all of us. Its strength lies in the solidarity it engenders, linking the fate of the poor with that of the considerably larger middle classes. If the program has proved politically unassailable, even in the Reagan years, that is because it makes few class distinctions (the lifelong unemployed are alone excluded) and therefore attaches no taint to the beneficiary.

But social security has its weaknesses. It can be said both to prevent poverty and to perpetuate it, depending on who is the beneficiary. The relatively generous benefits that Congress has made possible over the past generation have done almost nothing for the bottom echelon of social security recipients, serving only to widen the gap between the elderly poor and the elderly affluent.

In "Health: The Gift Repossessed" (Chapter 2) I focus on Medicare, a plan of infinite promise but of all too finite fulfillment. Like social security, Medicare is an entitlement rather than a charity. Its mandate is to protect elderly health-care dollars, to insure people against medically induced poverty.

But Medicare, under siege from the Right, has been running backwards. Its reigning philosophy now is cost-containment; its blueprint for reform is to raise elderly premiums and to shorten patient stays in hospitals. As a result, older Americans are paying as much for health care today as they were before Medicare; and some are being prematurely expelled from their sickbeds.

For the elder-bashers, Medicare's painful attrition has an embarrassing side. It casts serious doubt upon their claim that older Americans form an omnipotent interest group capable of expropriating whatever they wish from the public treasury. There are ways to get Medicare moving forward again, but those ways are rooted in a single problematic premise—namely, that a Congress obsessed with deficits will have courage enough to reform the system.

Next we consider the elderly struggle for adequate shelter. In "Shelter: Bring Us to This Hovel" (Chapter 3), after exploring the housing crisis that afflicts millions of moderate-income families, I try to demonstrate its distressing impact on older households. The dramatic difference that decent housing can make in elderly lives—and thus in the life of the larger community—is a point to which we keep returning.

The chapter introduces an historical perspective: Starting with the New Deal, it identifies the peaks and valleys of federally assisted housing. Not long ago the government led the way in providing adequate shelter for older Americans, especially those with moderate incomes. Now, as with Medicare, the government has retreated into a deficit-built cocoon, ceding many of its public responsibilities to the private marketplace.

In Chapter 4 ("Home Care: The Dream Deferred") we address the urgent demand for subsidized home-care assistance among those gamely fighting to preserve their independence. Chapter 5 serves as a bridge between home care and nursing homes. The reader is asked to forgive the intrusion here of "A Personal History." I tell of my mother's long battle to stay in her own house, beyond reach of a nursing home, and of her two sons' helplessness to come to her rescue.

It is an all too familiar story—a private agony arising in part from a public deficiency. The many who summon their last measure of strength resisting the institutional maw could use the community's strength as well. At present, the national community's social welfare arsenal lacks a suitable home-care weapon.

The chapter then recounts my mother's subsequent experience in a nursing home and the responses my brother and I were able to summon. Here again, our personal predicament reflected a nationwide dilemma, one that continues to baffle aged parents and middle-aged children alike.

With Chapter 6, "Exile: The Perils of Institutionalization," the pilgrimage concludes. After tracing the history of nursing homes, we examine their current incarnations. Both the torments of institution-alization and the erosions of Medicaid, the program that makes mass institutionalization possible, get our full attention. If Medicaid has brought unexpected prosperity to the nursing home industry, it has induced widespread poverty among the middle-class aged. That is because one cannot receive any benefits until one has gone broke.

In a brief "Epilogue," I attempt to draw some lessons from all of the above and to point the way toward a speedy overhaul of the system.

To an anxious benefit seeker, that system, with its many opaque enterprises, may appear as stable and enduring as any part of the natural landscape; the programs seem to have been around forever. In fact, they possess no special claims to permanence. They are social artifacts, each one the handiwork of its particular period, history, and political birth pains, and each one vulnerable over time to shifts in the public mood—that is, to improvement or impairment (or even extinction).

Social security is the daddy of them all, an offspring of the Great Depression and the New Deal. Medicare and Medicaid were contributed by the Great Society of the mid-1960s, and Supplemental Security Income emerged six years later as an unexpected product of the Nixon years. The government entered the housing business, with public housing, in the late 1930s—but only to assist the young. Not until the 1950s did federal housing measures make room for old age.

In sum, today's elderly programs are the harvest of yesterday's political plantings. Whichever fields we now agree to cultivate—for instance, elderly home care—will determine what tomorrow brings to all of us who, sooner than we think, will be risking old age in America.

PART ONE

The Search for Security

CHAPTER ONE

◆

Income: A Tale of Two Programs

A program aimed to safeguard old age . . . calls for statesmanship and understanding of a high order.
—Louis I. Dublin, *Health and Wealth*

Modern statesmanship has its limits. Broadly speaking, government has discovered only two ways to safeguard old age: by distributing alms to the few and by establishing entitlement programs for the many. The former emphasizes our individual differences; the latter promotes our solidarity. The policy debate over their proper mix—how much of our resources should be apportioned to each—has proceeded in fits and starts for most of this century. It has never been resolved.

This chapter gets under way with brief examinations of those competing routes to old-age protection. The nation's income support system offers a program to satisfy each school: Social security illustrates the uses of solidarity; Supplemental Security Income, of selective charity. Next we pay a visit to a small-town senior center in Vermont and listen to some who depend on those programs for their sole support. Their stories throw light on where the system works and where it needs fixing. The rest of the chapter is reserved for detailed descriptions and analyses of each program.

Solidarity

Solidarity embodies "social insurance," or—to borrow from Charles Dickens—a system that propels us by means of "a long pull, a strong pull, and a pull altogether" (*David Copperfield*). Another word for

solidarity in the economists' lexicon is "mainstreaming," which, as
Alvin L. Schorr has noted, "is the opposite of means-testing."[1] Our
social security program is an excellent case in point: It encompasses
the whole American community; it asks us all to pull together; it
marches to the reassuring beat of the nation's civic heart.

Thomas Paine understood the importance of mainstreaming. In
proposing to the French government a pension plan for citizens fifty
years old and over—"a sum of ten pounds per annum"—he insisted
that "the payments . . . be made to every person, rich or poor. It is
best to do so," he explained, "to prevent invidious distinctions"
("Agrarian Justice," 1797).

Like Paine, many of the the New Dealers who forged social security
rejected such distinctions. Their aim was to create a universal entitlement, a program for everybody. They hoped to avoid "class legislation"
and to draft "a measure that will benefit the entire public."[2] In many
respects they succeeded. Much of social security's history has been
informed and enlarged by ideals that seek to assist people of all stations
and incomes.

One sign of social security's wide public acceptance, its comfortable
air of belonging in the national picture, is that most commentators do
not even bother to capitalize the two words. The name has become
part of our everyday vocabulary. Understood by few, social security is
appreciated by most and taken for granted by all. Even Ronald Reagan
and his minions were unable to dislodge it, though they did their
worst, mounting an attack the like of which we have not seen since
1936, when Alfred M. Landon, running for president against Franklin
Delano Roosevelt, labeled social security "a cruel hoax" and called
for its repeal. As a Reagan aide conceded, social security is "as American
as mom and apple pie. It might not be the best retirement program,
but it's the one the people know."[3]

Since 1969, when benefits started to climb, social security has wrought
a certifiable miracle on behalf of the country's retired workers. We can
better understand the extent of that miracle by considering the so-
called elderly poverty gap, which calculates the amount of money that
would be required to lift all older Americans above the official poverty
line. In 1986 the gap was $3.6 billion, an astonishingly small sum as
such sums go. Without social security it would have been $34 billion,
and almost half of all older citizens would have been poor. The actual
proportion of elderly labeled "poor" that year was 14 percent.

Late in 1988, the Census Bureau issued its landmark study on federal
programs and their impact on poverty. The report concluded that
"Social Security is the Federal Government's most effective weapon

against poverty and reduces the inequality of Americans' income more than the tax system and more than recent social welfare programs."[4]

Yet for all the good it has done, social security has never fulfilled its ample promise. From the working poor's perspective, the program's ideological reach has consistently exceeded its practical grasp. The reason is no secret: To the notion of equal entitlement, society has appended a typically American extenuation—the idea of just deserts, which tends to reward winners and penalize losers. The ambiguities that undergird social security's philosophy were neatly though unintentionally summed up by the late Wilbur Cohen, who from the New Deal through the Great Society had a strong hand in shaping our income support system. "We need a system which creates no invidious distinctions based on income," Cohen said; but then he added, "—one where an individual is entitled to receive benefits on the basis of his general contribution to society."[5]

In equating a citizen's "general contribution to society" with his or her wage-based payments into the social security trust fund, Cohen overlooked many other kinds of contributions—those of the unpaid housewife, for instance, or of the volunteer worker. In addition, he forgot to allow for widespread discriminatory employment practices, which have sharply depressed the wages of women, blacks, and Hispanics. Cohen mistakenly assumed an invariable connection between one's merit and one's salary.

His assumptions perfectly mirrored those of the social security program, which takes into exact mathematical account one's "general contribution to society." It is designed chiefly to benefit those whose lifetime careers have proven at least moderately successful: Their wages over the years have been sufficient to generate adequate payroll contributions into the social security trust fund, the kitty that keeps the program solvent.

There is, in short, a rough quid pro quo that governs social security arrangements. Those who have never had much "quid"—the low-wage earners, the chronically unemployed—end up getting little or no "quo."

Charity

Congress has long been aware of this fundamental flaw in our elderly income support system. But the lawmakers have been reluctant to tamper with social security's basic structure, which enjoys broad popularity. Instead, they have introduced a second program, one based entirely on the giving of alms. They called it Supplemental Security Income, or SSI. Enacted in 1972, SSI is aimed exclusively at two segments of the underclass: the elderly poor and the disabled poor of all ages (including the blind). And because the program relies on a means test, proof of destitution being the key to entry, it comes replete with those invidious distinctions that Tom Paine and Wilbur Cohen warned against.

That SSI owes a great deal to the Elizabethan Poor Laws of England, with their pitiless provisos, cannot be doubted. The program would have held no mystery for the seventeenth-century philosopher John Locke, who was among the first to grasp the connection between taxing the affluent and giving alms to the poor. Like the Poor Laws Locke analyzed, SSI provides "Title to so much out of another's Plenty, as will keep him from extreme want, where he has *no means to subsist otherwise*" (*Two Treatises of Government*).[6]

In Locke's day as in ours, people believed that supplicants should be required to *prove* their "extreme want"—that is, to submit to a "no-means" test; and, further, that they should be found wanting through no fault of their own, decrepitude or disability being the only recognized justifications for partaking of "another's Plenty." Able-bodied beggars back then were routinely whipped.

From today's fiscally tight angle of vision, we can admire SSI for existing at all. The last of the great safety nets deployed by Congress over four decades of incremental reform, it remains the only federal enterprise to offer poor people direct cash assistance drawn from the national exchequer. (Social security payments flow from special trust funds.) Its payments guarantee that no eligible applicant will be allowed to fall below a specified income level. That level has gone up a little each year; but always, alas, it has hovered at a point between poverty and beggary.

Until recently (before the Social Security Administration bought new stationery) SSI checks were gold to distinguish them from social security checks, which were green. In 1988 the Social Security Administration (SSA), which runs both programs, distributed over $10 billion in gold checks to some 4.4 million individuals, only about one-third of whom were elderly. More than half the aged recipients were also collecting green checks every month. Six of ten were at least seventy-five years old; three of every four were women. Taken together, these 1.5 million make up the bottommost layer of our older population. They have been officially, and permanently, consigned to a status one notch above total impoverishment.

The uneasy coexistence of social security and SSI allows us to compare the two, to examine their disparate strengths and weaknesses, and, in due course, to make some judgments regarding their relative usefulness to society in general and to the elderly in particular. Each is a national program, but the similarity ends there. Whereas social security represents a civic right that nearly all may claim, Supplemental Security Income represents a civic *gift* that only a few—certain certified paupers in our midst—may collect.

The difference is worth pondering. It opposes the traditional, class-ridden politics of almsgiving to the twentieth-century politics of main-streaming. The genius of social security is that no one ever has to ask for it. That is why to most Americans it is more than just another federal program: It is an agreed-upon metaphor for well-being in old age. Still, as we shall see in the following encounters, social security's symbolic value sometimes outruns its actual benefits.

Categorical Imperatives

One summer morning I pay a visit to a municipal senior center in a small Vermont town I shall call Columbia. Some sixty elderly citizens are there, quietly awaiting lunch. "You should have saved Vermont for autumn," I am advised by Christine, the center's young director. "The leaves are beautiful then."

Most of those present are all too familiar with the transformations of autumn, a problematic season in which clinging to life can be a full-time occupation. Nothing in their greener years has prepared them for the uncertainties they now face. Old age and its pauperizing possibilities once must have seemed mercifully remote; there would be plenty of time to make the necessary arrangements. Besides, wasn't the federal government putting aside a fat share of their personal earnings each payday against later, leaner years?

"When you were younger," I ask Harold Milton, a sad-eyed gentleman who grew up on a farm near Columbia, "did you ever worry about how you would manage after you retired?"

"No," he says, "it never entered my mind. You see, I was counting on my social security."

But in the event, social security has disappointed him. His benefits amount to $250 a month, a sum so meager as to render Mr. Milton eligible for Supplemental Security Income. SSI provides him with an additional $86 a month. Between the two Mr. Milton collects $4,032 a year, the most allowed anyone (in 1986) who receives combined assistance. The total falls short of the official poverty line by 25 percent.

Mr. Milton squints at me amiably through thick lenses and states that he is seventy-one years old, has never set foot outside Vermont, and has no plans to do so. "I'm just happy to be alive," he says. "Back a few years I had four operations. That's right—*four*. Two for cataracts and two for cancer. The doctors saved my life."

Somewhat reluctantly, he lets me know he is a semiretired handy-man—"semi," because two nights a week he cleans several offices downtown. Mr. Milton suffers from arthritis in both hands, which he says makes the work "kind of slow. But I don't mind the work and I don't mind the money." The job earns him an extra $100 a month.

He has good reason to be reticent about the extra money. As he says, "The feds, they got all them rules. There's just so much you're allowed to make on your own. After that they lower the boom." SSI comes with the most strings. The monthly ceiling on earned income is $65 (social security's is $500); for every dollar earned over $65 the government reduces SSI benefits by 50 cents. If the feds discovered that Mr. Milton was working, he would stand to lose $18 every month.

Mr. Milton eats here at the senior center every weekday, most days walking the two miles from his rooming house on the edge of town. Lunch costs a dollar—when he can afford to pay. It's "sort of a voluntary contribution," he says.

Today he has the dollar. His social security check came in the morning's mail and he cashed it immediately. He was behind in his rent ($125 for a single room, with a bath down the hall) and in his grocery bill ($94). By the time he had covered the two and purchased some odds and ends—soap, toilet paper, a pair of socks—he was left with $7 in his pocket. "But I'll get my work money next week," he reminds himself, "and my SSI. That ought to come tomorrow."

As soon as the clock on the wall shows noon, we all file into a larger room and take seats at long tables that volunteers have furnished with paper doilies, paper plates, and plastic cutlery. A white-haired woman in an apron says grace: "We thank you, Lord, for these days that You give us. Amen." Then Christine makes three announcements: The exercise group will meet tomorrow in the front room an hour before lunch; today's dessert, baked apple, comes courtesy of the ladies' auxiliary of a local men's club; and, "There's someone here today who does not fit your category. He is writing a book about senior citizens. He may want to talk to some of you."

People here tend to think categorically. Their chances of survival can depend upon which slots they are deemed to occupy.

*   *   *

Stella Roma (one of the persons I talk with after lunch) is a trim sixty-six-year-old widow whose husband died of a heart attack in 1958. "He worked in the quarry," she says, "and he'd never been sick a day in his life. One night he came home and went to bed early. He started complaining of pains in his arm. He was forty-six. I was forty. He was buried twenty-six years ago today."

"Exactly to the day?" I ask.

"Yes. I know because it was my son's birthday. We'd planned a birthday party for him—he was just five years old—and I went through with it. What does a little kid know about such things?"

Within weeks Mrs. Roma and her four children began collecting survivors' benefits from social security. "We were getting about $600 a month," she recalls. "That was pretty good money in those days." She knows what her life might have been like without social security: "My own father died when I was five. He was a baker and his chest was torn open by a bread-making machine. He came from Italy. My mother was left with seven children, and at the time, you know, in 1923, there was no insurance or social security. We kids all had to work our way through high school. College was out of the question—not like with my kids, who all got some kind of degree. My poor mother couldn't even speak English. She never asked anyone for help. She died a long time ago, just after I was married. I don't know how she got through her life."

Mrs. Roma is one of some 5 million widows and widowers who collect social security survivors' benefits. The formula for computing such benefits is complicated. Most survivors without children must wait until they are at least sixty years old before they can start collecting. Mrs. Roma's four dependent children made her immediately eligible and made the benefits relatively generous. But now that the children are married and have children of their own, Mrs. Roma gets only $374 a month, which is the amount her husband would have received had he lived to retire.

"I do without a lot of things. I make clothes last a long time, and I work whenever I can—temporary office work, jobs like that. I have a couple of bachelors in the neighborhood and I do their laundry for them.

"After my husband died I did waitressing for twelve years. It was hard work but I needed the money. I wouldn't do that kind of work any more. Too many hours on my feet. The trouble is, I can't get secretarial jobs. When they ask you your age, you know what the story is. You're over the hill when you're over fifty. No, they don't come right out with it and say you're too old. They just say, 'We'll call you.'"

Mrs. Roma is grateful for the little extra she can earn, about $1,500 a year. (Social security's earnings ceiling is $6,000.) The money helps pay her taxes ($654) on a house that's free and clear, her fire and flood insurance premiums ($750), and her oil bill ($800). That leaves her about $3,800 for everything else—food, clothing, utilities, transportation (no car), eyeglasses, prescriptions, occasional travel, and gifts for her five siblings, four children, and eleven grandchildren, not to mention multiple nieces, nephews, cousins, and friends.

"That's the hardest part," she says, "not having enough to buy presents at Christmas. But I'm not complaining. I have a nice garden and I never think of myself as poor. I guess I'm like my mother—I've never asked anyone for help. God! I hope I never have to."

Social Security:
Don't Leave Home Without It

The social security program has not always cast so wide a net. The original act—at least the part we now think of as "social security"—covered relatively few workers and offered little in the way of recompense. Ida Fuller, a retired law firm secretary, was the program's first beneficiary, and she collected only $22 every month for thirty-five years. (She lived to be over one hundred.) Farm workers and domestic workers were not covered; neither were ministers, physicians, the self-employed, firemen, policemen, or a half dozen other sizable groups, all of whom eventually found their way into the system.

Although the 1935 measure was remarkably wide-ranging (it introduced unemployment insurance and aid to dependent children), its main attraction for the elderly was the old-age insurance program, otherwise known as OAI. Over the years Congress created fresh attractions and added on initials. Survivors and dependents of deceased workers, like Stella Roma, gained protection in 1939 (OASI); disabled workers took shelter in 1956 (OASDI); and the elderly obtained health insurance, or Medicare, in 1965 (OASDHI). Today hardly anyone misses out on the benefactions provided or escapes the obligations imposed by this remarkable program. Virtually every wage earner contributes to its trust funds; nine of every ten retirees collect its benefits, and for two-thirds, the payments are their sole source of support. In 1988 social security checks went to 27 million retired workers and their families, to 4 million disabled workers and their spouses and children, and to 7 million survivors of deceased workers.

Much of social security's political success, and part of its failure to meet the needs of retired workers, rests on its Puritan doctrine, which inspires among many a conviction that they have *earned* their benefits. In effect, workers have been told that if they sow the system with payments during their active years, they will later reap the harvest.

Although payroll taxes are in fact almost immediately passed along to members of the older generation, the illusion of individually earmarked annuities persists, especially among the younger contributors.

As a sociology professor in Connecticut commented to me, "My students believe that somewhere out there a social security piggy bank with their name on it is waiting for each of them. They have no sense of actually supporting their grandparents' retirement."

In reality, social security is less an annuity than it is a pact between generations, whereby younger workers help to support retired workers in exchange for their own future protection. What mainly obscures the pact is the program's tax-and-benefit formula. That formula has varied from year to year, but in general, the higher the wages, the higher are both the contributions and the eventual benefits. The link between what workers pay into the system and what they eventually get out of it has tipped people's frame of reference: They see social security less as a symbol of solidarity than as a reward for individual effort.

The system's leading advocates have reenforced the public's mind-set by repeatedly extolling social security's meritocratic virtues. Robert M. Ball, who as commissioner of social security served three presidents (John F. Kennedy, Lyndon Johnson, and Richard Nixon), has been particularly emphatic on this point. As he observed, "Payments are made to individuals on the basis of the work record, and are part of the reward for services rendered. . . . [I]t is this work connection, the fact that it is earned, which gives social insurance its basic character."[7] (Ball's "reward for services rendered" bears a striking resemblance to Cohen's "benefits on the basis of [one's] general contribution to society."

The "work connection" keeps social security free of any welfare contamination—no charity cases need apply—but it does little for those who have struggled over the years to make a poor living. In consequence, social security and poverty often go hand in hand. For a majority of elderly poor households the program's benefits constitute at least 80 percent of their total income.[8]

Congress, it is true, has tried to strike a balance between just deserts and urgent needs. By fine-tuning the contribution-benefit ratio, the lawmakers have made it possible for low-wage retirees to collect a higher proportion of their past earnings than that allowed more affluent pensioners. Such measures have indeed spread some of the wealth. But a report brought out recently by the Villers Foundation suggests that the transfers have failed to make an appreciable difference.[9]

The study examines the benefits received by two retirees with contrasting career histories. The poorer retiree has earned an average income of $265 per month, whereas the more affluent beneficiary has earned an average of $1,855. Their respective monthly social security benefits of $238.50 and $754.81 do not reflect the disparity of their past wages. Thanks to social security's weighted formula, the career that has earned seven times as much income now collects only three times as many benefit dollars.

The calculations underscore social security's considerable redistributive powers. But they also bring to light the program's inadequacy, which turns poor wage earners into still poorer beneficiaries. The first retiree, after all, ended up getting less than $3,000 a year, while the second was collecting more than $9,000. In a meritocratic world, the discrepancy can be satisfactorily accounted for by the different amounts contributed during the two pensioners' working years; it cannot, however, be considered a victory for the elderly poor.

By the logic of social security benefits, then, job success takes precedence over economic equality. The uneven struggle between the two values constitutes the system's central dilemma. No one has found a satisfactory way of reconciling the gospel of just deserts with the Golden Rule.

Ironically, that dilemma is turned upside down at social security's other end, the payroll contribution part. There, equality eclipses success; yet it is again the affluent, not the working poor, who profit from the arrangements. Unlike the income tax, the social security payroll tax is *flat* and therefore regressive: Every worker—the waitress and the orderly no less than the restaurateur and the orthopedic surgeon— contributes to the system at precisely the same rate of earnings. The affluent are further protected by a ceiling on their taxable income. Thus the higher their earnings, the lower their proportion of contributions. (Contributions are matched by employers; in 1989 each party contributed 7.65 percent.) In effect, the ceiling lowers the tax rates of the rich.

As with the benefit gap, Congress's response to the tax gap has been notably timid. By periodically raising the limit on the amount of earned income subject to a social security tax, it has managed to shift a little of the tax load off low-wage workers. From 1935 through 1950 the ceiling on taxable income held steady at $3,000, after which it started to climb. By 1989 it had reached $48,000 and was scheduled to rise automatically each year hence. The benefits, of course, have gone up proportionately, thus widening the distance between high-wage and low-wage beneficiaries.

Congress could do better. It could simply lift the wage ceiling on payroll taxes and then pass along some of the additional revenues to beneficiaries at the bottom. But the politics of income redistribution is not that simple, or that generous. As Ball observed to me, "We'd be soaking the most articulate members of society, all the commentators and editorial writers who make at least $80,000 a year. They wouldn't sit still for a plan that raises their contributions but not their benefits."

But Ball may have been overestimating the power of our editorialists, or else underestimating their good sense.

The next best thing would be to treat *benefits* as routinely taxable income, thereby linking social security to the more progressive income-tax system. Congress in 1979 passed a solemn resolution pledging never to go that far. But four years later, with social security facing a king-size revenue crisis, the lawmakers reversed themselves. As things now stand, married couples whose net incomes exceed $32,000 must pay taxes on up to half their social security benefits. For single persons the taxable income threshold is $25,000.

Because those thresholds are approximately twice as generous as the thresholds for wages, and because in any case retirees pay taxes on no more than half their benefits, the extra revenues thus far have not amounted to much—just $3.6 billion in 1989. A recent study by the Congressional Budget Office (CBO) has estimated how many more dollars would pour in if benefits were treated as ordinary taxable earned income. CBO's add-on figure for a single year exceeds $13 billion.[10]

All things considered, the notion of fully taxing social security benefits makes sense. Not only would it bring in more dollars—which, Congress and the public willing, might go to assist the elderly poor— it would also tend to silence the means testers and privatizers, who now accuse the program of subsidizing the rich. (For more on this subject, see the next section, "Gentrification.")

One further inequity in the social security system should be noted here. It arises from gender bias in the job market, by means of which the system indirectly enriches itself. The fact that women's average earnings still fall short of men's by 35 percent creates special hardships for working couples facing retirement. That is because social security will pay benefits to just one spouse—the spouse with the higher earnings record—while assigning only about half that amount to the other. The arrangement mocks the program's cherished connection between contributions and benefits, for a spouse can contribute to social security all her working days and never see a penny in return.

At present, a conservatively estimated two million retired spouses and ex-spouses, almost nine-tenths of them women, endure this form of taxation without remuneration. Even if their social security payroll taxes had averaged only $100 a year, over let us say thirty working years, those spouses would have unintentionally donated $6 billion to the program (to say nothing of a like amount donated by their employers). According to at least one study, a commensurate "refund" of earned benefits could bring down the official poverty rate among older couples by eight percentage points.[11]

Gentrification

Congress's natural instinct has always been to improve the lot of its mainstream constituents, no matter the backwater consequences. Ideology and political self-interest have thus combined to shut out the marginal elderly. "Let's keep it as much wage-related as we can," cautioned Wilbur Mills, then the powerful chairman of the House Ways and Means Committee, in a 1960s discussion with Wilbur Cohen.

Cohen, a "founding father" of the program and later Lyndon Johnson's under-secretary of health, education and welfare, had long been espousing a similar doctrine. The wage-based benefit formula, he had earlier explained in congressional testimony, "is part of the system's political sagacity. Since most of the people in the United States are in the middle income, middle class range, social security is a program that appeals to them."

In 1969 Congress set out to make it still more appealing, ultimately legislating what one commentator has described as "a quantum increase in benefit levels."[12] In just three years, real benefits—those adjusted for inflation—rose by 23 percent. For icing on the cake, the lawmakers in 1972 tied benefits to the national cost-of-living index, thereby ensuring that they would keep pace with inflation. As usual at such moments, "political sagacity" triumphed over social equity, with affluent retirees enjoying a lion's share of the gains. Still, we should not lightly dismiss the impact of those 1969–1972 concessions. The "quantum leap in benefit levels" was also a quantum leap in social decency. It made life bearable for millions of older Americans and it prevented millions more from sinking into poverty as they entered retirement.

That very triumph, however, has tended to obscure the program's continuing inadequacies vis-à-vis the elderly poor. With social security as with gentrified neighborhoods, affluence has eclipsed poverty, giving rise to a belief that virtually all the elderly now live on easy street. The upshot has been a widespread gentrification backlash. Instead of worrying about our neglect of the invisible poor, commentators and politicians have fretted over our generosity to the conspicuous affluent.

Not surprisingly, proponents of alms have been quick to renew their fifty-year-old attack on social security, this time on grounds that it distributes money to people who don't need it. Increasingly now, as the Brandeis University economist James H. Schulz has pointed out, "arguments are made that the social security benefits are . . . adequate—maybe even too large."[13]

Those arguments invariably blame social security for our huge federal deficit. For instance, Alan Greenspan, who was Richard Nixon's chief economic adviser and is now chairman of the Federal Reserve Board, told a congressional committee in 1988 that one solution to the deficit problem would be to "reduce the costs of entitlement programs like social security and Medicare."[14]

Another Nixonian, former secretary of commerce Peter G. Peterson, has organized a budget-cutting interest group called the Bipartisan Budget Appeal. In 1985 Peterson assured readers of the *New York Times* that "the real issue is whether we are willing to cut subsidies to middle-income groups through 'non-means-tested entitlements.'" Arguing for a balanced federal budget, he recommended fewer social security benefits and more alms—that is, "beefing up programs targeted directly at the poor."[15]

There is something oddly disingenuous about such critiques. As Peterson and Greenspan surely know, social security is not responsible for the government's deficit. In fact, all of social security's tax dollars are insulated from general revenues: They go into a special trust fund that cannot be used for any other purpose. If we reduced social security benefits, the trust fund would get bigger but the federal deficit would not get smaller.

As it happens, the trust fund is already bulging. Much more money is coming in than is going out. The Social Security Administration estimated a $36 billion surplus in 1988 alone. By 2010, according to SSA predictions, the annual margin of excess income will have reached $400 billion and the trust fund's accumulated reserves will have risen to a breathtaking $4.5 trillion, or almost double the government's total current debt.

Such figures are no secret. They are regularly published by the Social Security Administration, and they have been widely quoted. They were cited recently in a letter to the *Times* written by Orson J. Hart, former chief economist for the New York Life Insurance Company. As Hart noted, "we ought not to be meddling with a program as important to the American people and as successful as Social Security. We should realize that it is not contributing to the deficit."[16]

Then why do the meddlers persist? One guesses they are less interested in reducing the deficit than in diluting the social security program. Some conservative economists have gone as far as to call for the virtual dismemberment of social security by turning it into a voluntary plan: People could either take it or leave it. The poor, of course, would have to take it; the well-to-do, meanwhile, could afford to opt out in favor of one or another private savings plan. The result would be an underfinanced social security program for most and an overemphasized thrift system for some, mainly the rich.

Peter Young, who directs a Washington think tank called the Adam Smith Institute, typifies current voluntarist thinking; and, like many another passionate theorizer—Marx, for instance—he takes it for granted that his particular version of utopia will ultimately become everyone's version. "It is not yet possible to determine who will be the last recipient of Social Security benefits," he has assured a reporter, "but it's fairly safe to say that he or she is alive today."[17]

It is also fairly safe to say that Young's prophecy was dead on arrival. Far from predicting the future, it harks back to a time when growing old was often tantamount to going broke. In the country of the Youngs, only the fortunate few would ultimately be able to cash in. Everyone else would have to rely on means-tested charity—that is, on the sort of measures social security was designed to make unnecessary.

Though unlikely to achieve its objectives, the Right's constant chatter has nonetheless succeeded in blurring our perception of the elderly condition. In effect, the Petersons and the Youngs have been able to define the terms of public debate, thereby deflecting our attention from the 6 million older Americans for whom social security does not work. What follows here, by way of redressing the balance, is an effort to make visible the many who have not been invited to the feast. It is an exercise in de-gentrification.

De-Gentrification

Any discussion of the elderly invisible poor must begin with the "nonmarrieds," who make up more than one-third of all social security recipients. Eighty-five percent are women; nearly all live alone. Defenders of the system seldom mention this group. They prefer to concentrate on retired couples, who fare considerably better in the benefit sweepstakes than do widows, divorcees, and those who never married.

In 1988, retired couples received an average benefit of $814 a month—not a princely sum, to be sure, but still a comfortable 36 percent above the federal old-age poverty line. Single persons, meanwhile, averaged $537, a scant 10 percent over "poverty" and well within the government's own definition of "near-poor."

The numbers further suggest that for many beneficiaries social security stands as a lone but defective agent of rescue. Among the approximately ten million single persons collecting old-age benefits in 1984, almost 40 percent remained poor (under 125 percent of the federal poverty line); among single blacks the proportion of poor rose to nearly 70 percent; among single black women it reached 74 percent.[18]

It can be argued (and frequently is) that social security is not the only resource open to older Americans, nor was it ever intended to be. Thrift was supposed to abet redistribution. Schulz made that familiar point, observing that the program's creators "decided that social security should be only one of many sources of economic protection and that further supplementation, either through group or individual means, would be needed to provide an adequate living standard in retirement."[19]

Indeed, a mixture of social security and "further supplementation" has been sufficient for many. Savings and dividends together rank second in forms of elderly support; then come private pensions, earned wages, SSI, veterans' payments, unemployment benefits, self-employment and welfare assistance. None of those resorts, however, has appreciably elevated the system's bottom half of beneficiaries, who continue to rely on social security for more than three-fourths of their aggregate income.

The figure gives rise to a suspicion that a great many elderly poor people may once have seen better days: Their poverty may well be a function of their age. If true, the claim seriously undermines social security's historic purpose, which has been to help *prevent* poverty. As President Roosevelt told his Economic Security Committee, which he had entrusted to draft the original measure, the main idea was to provide safeguards against "the major hazards and vicissitudes of life."[20]

There is an easy statistical way of assessing social security's power to confound the major hazards and vicissitudes of old age. All we need do is compare elderly poverty rates with those of the next-younger cohort, the group nearest to retirement age. For if social security functions efficiently as a shield against poverty, we can expect comparable poverty rates between the younger and older groups. No individual, in other words, will have become poor simply by becoming old.

In fact, what we get is a sizable discrepancy, as shown by the following Census Bureau figures for 1985:[21]

Age Group	Number Below Poverty	Federal Poverty Rate
55 to 64 years	2,330,000	10.5 percent
65 years and over	3,456,000	12.6 percent

Had the younger group's poverty rate held for those 65 and over (about 27.3 million in all), fewer than 3 million older Americans would have been numbered below the official poverty threshold. The actual total of nearly 3.5 million indicates that about 17 percent became poor after retirement and despite social security benefits.

The discrepancy widens, of course, if the elderly's artificially low poverty line is moved upward to match the line applied to other age groups. In that case, the number of older poor persons rises to 4.1 million, 30 percent of whom can be considered newly impoverished.

The Decline of Mainstreaming

To sum up, then: The gentrification of social security has made it an unlikely source of deliverance for the nation's 11.5 million elderly poor and vulnerable. They will continue to be shortchanged as long as the system's tax-and-benefit structure is framed by the gospel of just deserts. That this marketplace doctrine gratifies the American taste for commerce and individualism, and thus inhibits any major revamping of the system, seems beyond question.

Almost from the outset, the program's staunchest advocates have emphasized its self-serving advantages over its communal ones. As the sociologist Theda Skocpol has observed, "New Dealers after 1935 mostly gave up the rhetoric of collective solidarity as an antidote to excessive individualism, and instead sought to justify New Deal reforms as better means for achieving or safeguarding traditonal American values of liberty and individualism." Skocpol regretted the rhetorical retreat, claiming that New Dealers should have stressed "people's inevitable dependence upon one another and upon a healthy public life."[22]

In choosing to sell social security solipsistically, its creators decisively directed the flow of public opinion. Far from symbolizing the inevitability of interdependence, the program has come to stand for the joys of independent achievement and its natural rewards.

It may be true, as Senator Bill Bradley of New Jersey has proclaimed, that "social security is the best expression of community that we have in the country today." It may also be true, as the Washington journalists Vincent J. Burke and Vee Burke have insisted in their book on welfare reform, that the system represents "the collectivization of the filial commandment" to "honor thy father and thy mother."[23] But the public apparently thinks otherwise. It seems unprepared to endorse any vision of social security that surpasses the limits of self-protection.

Robert Ball conceded as much when he told the House Ways and Means Committee that any steady contributor to the program "would have a right to feel aggrieved if people with only slight attachment to the work force and low social security contributions received benefits as high or nearly as high as those who worked and contributed regularly and substantially."[24]

Still, the question keeps nagging: Is that truly all there is to social security? Didn't its drafters have in mind a larger, more generous framework, one meant to shelter the high and the low alike? Only in recent years has the system appeared to relax its downward reach, to lose sight of the poor and hence of the dream. Thus it is that instead of repairing social security's ragged safety net, Congress has woven a substitute called Supplemental Security Income. We turn now to a closer examination of that alms-giving enterprise.

Supplemental Security Income

SSI's virtues are not hard to assess, nor are its shortcomings. In the debate that led to its passage, Wilbur Mills predicted that the program would "assure that virtually no aged person will have to live below the poverty level." He was wrong. What SSI guarantees to recipients is not deliverance from poverty but promotion to a specified, government-endorsed level of deprivation.

Nevertheless, SSI has introduced a quality of mercy heretofore unknown in the nation's welfare annals. It was designed to expand and to simplify our philanthropic enterprise, and in the main it has done both, protecting many from total destitution and shifting major welfare responsibilities from the states to the federal government. The shift has mercifully curtailed a variety of odious state welfare practices, including the imposition of liens on homes belonging to aged recipients (so that after the client's death the money could be returned to the state).

In my interviews with elderly SSI recipients, what frequently came through was their total dependence on this single form of largess. "Tell your government that my countrymen and I are very grateful for its generosity," Ve Hoang, a seventy-nine-year-old South Vietnamese refugee, instructed me. "I am a Zen Buddhist, if you understand my meaning. I pray when I am thankful."

Mrs. Hoang, who lives in a subsidized apartment in Alexandria, Virginia, is a tiny woman of enormous presence. If in her lifetime she has endured more than her share of storm and strife, her fate now resembles that of most other SSI beneficiaries who have landed outside social security's shelter.

"I belong to a great family," she told me as we sat in her small living room, eating ice cream. "We lost everything in the war. When my children and I were so fortunate as to come to America, we had nothing but the clothes we wore. Here is a picture of my husband; he died in Hue. My niece sent it to me because she understood that I took nothing with me. You can see that my husband was a very wise young man, and a very good doctor."

Mrs. Hoang collects $368 a month from SSI, plus $23 a month in food stamps. "I have no other money. When I want to buy something warm, it is very expensive. Books also cost much but I buy what books I can. I have a French-English dictionary. It does not help because the print is too small to read."

When we parted, I asked Mrs. Hoang if she would like me to send her anything. "Yes," she said, and pointed to her bedroom. "Send me a large map of America that I can put on my wall. I want to go to sleep memorizing your country. Now it is my country, too."

In a village near Gainesville, Florida, I talked with Adeline Jackson, a tall, handsome woman who dresses in sunny fashion. On the day we met she was wearing bright yellow slacks, a green blouse, and a green-and-yellow bonnet. We sat in rockers on her front porch, across the street from the Baptist church, while she reminisced for my benefit. Her life seemed to me to have been no less chancy than that of Ve Hoang's.

"The body I used to work for gave me that rocker," she said, pointing to the chair I was sitting in. "I worked for a lot of people, cleanin' and takin' care of the children, but they all done passed now.

"I was born on Christmas day. Don't know how old I am, but my daddy, he was a slave in South Carolina, and after he was freed he fought for the Union in that Civil War. He was wounded in the foot— two balls in the foot they couldn't take out." His name, she said, was William Chriswell, and some fifty years later he died of infections caused by his war wounds. "I was a little child then, and I was sittin' by the bed when it happened. He just turned around and died."

From that moment on Adeline Jackson had to work for a living: "I been in the fields choppin' cotton all my life, or in the houses workin' for white folks. But now I feels too rickety to work. The doctor told me to slack off a bit, 'cause sometimes I stagger when I walk. Six years ago I had all my teeth took out. A colored doctor pulled them. He dead now.

"No, I don't work no more. I sews some and I goes to church and to the senior center. That's all."

Mrs. Jackson's SSI payments do not always stretch far enough. She's behind on her electric bill and she still owes $149 for a second-hand refrigerator that "ain't worked since the day I got it." But she owns her house—bought twenty years ago with money from her late husband's life insurance policy—and she collects a few dollars' worth of food stamps every month. As she said, "I'm glad to get what I gets."

One guesses that in the American welfare context the daughter of a South Carolina slave and the daughter of a once-powerful South Vietnamese family may not be all that different: Each has been brought low by political hatreds and upheavals that swept all before them; each has been subject to the caprices of caste and class; and each has lived to tell the tale. That both women have gained SSI protection reflects the special compassion of the program. For if social security tends to reward the world's winners, SSI is reserved exclusively for the world's losers. The monthly stipends can be considered a form of affirmative action on behalf of history's often blameless victims.

Regulating the Elderly

Congress created SSI rather absentmindedly in 1972, while it was rejecting Richard M. Nixon's more ambitious Family Assistance Plan (FAP). FAP would have guaranteed a modest base income to every woman, man, and child in the United States. SSI restricts such blessings to three categories of poor people—the aged, the blind, and the disabled—who are getting too little social security or none at all.

In 1989 a maximum SSI benefit for a single person totaled $368 a month, a sum that fell short of the official poverty line by about 29 percent. A couple that year could get $553—still 8 percent below "poverty." It is true that twenty-six states and the District of Columbia supply extra SSI benefits—a throwback to a time when poor people's welfare was a state-owned monopoly. But only in Alaska, California, Connecticut, and Massachusetts are the levels of support sufficient to lift people above the poverty threshold. Overall in 1988, state monthly supplements to the elderly averaged $123.

If SSI does not deliver one from poverty, proof of deep poverty is nonetheless required of anyone hoping to get SSI delivered. A means-tested program, it imposes strict limitations on a beneficiary's income and assets. Although about a quarter of all older Americans endure poverty or "near-poverty," fewer than half of those are considered poor enough to get help from SSI. Elderly black women, who constitute an astonishing 42 percent of the aged poor, would especially gain from a liberalization of SSI benefits. The median annual income for older black women in this country is just $400 above the poverty line, but $1,600 above SSI's eligibility ceiling.

By establishing high entry barriers, Congress has withheld SSI's favors from millions in distress. One troublesome hurdle has been the program's so-called resource limit, meaning the maximum amount of assets a beneficiary is permitted to possess. Congress fixed limits from the start at $1,500 for an individual and $2,250 for a couple, and did not increase either until 1984, even though during that period the Consumer Price Index was rising by 120 percent. The new ceilings in 1989 reached $2,000 and $3,000 respectively, a 50 percent increase over fifteen inflationary years.

In calculating resources, SSI officials do not count the beneficiary's house or automobile. Cash is what they mainly look for, and cash is what they sometimes find—for it is possible to be poor and yet, through sense and sacrifice, to squirrel away a few dollars.

As if these drawbacks were not enough, SSI's myriad regulations seem needlessly complicated, beginning with a twelve-page application form practically guaranteed to discourage the most determined prospect.

The program's increasingly byzantine nature has been the undoing of many an SSI recipient. Violating rules they never understood, these mild miscreants are stretched upon a bureaucratic rack.

For example, SSI strikes an oddly inappropriate blow for self-reliance by granting full benefits only to those who can prove they are "living independently"; in cases of those so rash as to be "living in the household of another"—usually with their children—SSI reduces benefits by one-third. Congress, in other words, has imposed a 33 percent home-care tax on persons unable to take care of themselves, thereby hastening their resort to a nursing home, where Medicaid will bear the freight.

Rules of this sort can lead to all manner of absurdities. In one case, a local Social Security office demanded apartment floor plans from an SSI recipient, so that officials could determine whether he was "living independently" or secretly residing with relatives. Not surprisingly, such petty exercises have turned into an administrative nightmare, possibly costing the government as much in red tape as it wrings from the elderly and disabled poor in savings.

The Baby-Sitting Grandmother

SSI's enthusiasm for independent living has not softened its position on allowable earnings, which remain stuck at $65 a month. The low limit turns the gospel of just deserts upside down, keeping beneficiaries poor (about 9 percent below the 1989 individual poverty line) even when they work. Distressing as this rule can be, Social Security officials have been known to misapply it in ways that hurt still more.

The case of the baby-sitting grandmother, whom I shall call Mrs. Ramirez, seems all too characteristic of SSI's tendency to say no when it ought to be saying yes. A seventy-three-year-old widowed refugee from Cuba who now lives outside Miami, Mrs. Ramirez ran afoul of SSI when she began working as a baby-sitter for her son and daughter-in-law, taking care of her two school-age grandchildren while the parents were at work. For these services the parents paid her $65 a month.

In January 1983, soon after she began baby-sitting, Mrs. Ramirez reported the additional income to her local SSA office. If treated as earned income, the $65 would not have affected Mrs. Ramirez's SSI checks. But because she was working for members of her family, SSA officials decided her baby-sitting income represented a gift rather than earnings and therefore was subject to penalty. They reduced Mrs. Ramirez's monthly SSI benefits by $32.50 ($.50 on the dollar).

Mrs. Ramirez had been living in this country for two decades. She knew her way around and did not suffer bureaucrats lightly. With help from Greater Miami Legal Services she began an assault on SSA's complex appeals structure, beginning with an appeal to an administrative law judge (ALJ). That first venture was not encouraging. In ruling for the Social Security Administration, the ALJ introduced the following argument: "Since Claimant only takes care of her grandchildren, and does not hold herself out to the community as a person who is available for babysitting, this money cannot be characterized as other than unearned income."

It was a peculiar way of viewing matters. Mrs. Ramirez, after all, was in her seventies and not in the best of health. She could not be expected to make a full-time occupation of baby-sitting—to "hold herself out . . . as a person who is available for babysitting"—in order to justify her earnings. Those earnings, in any case, seemed already justified. Her son and daughter-in-law had been in genuine need of her services. Indeed, before hiring Mrs. Ramirez they had purchased identical services from a private child-care agency.

The next step was to go before SSA's Appeals Council, a body that rarely reversed a lower-level decision. But Mrs. Ramirez remained hopeful. By this time her case had attracted allies in Washington and elsewhere, and some were firing off strong letters to the Appeals Council.

The Women's Equity Action League, or WEAL, was one of those. In an eight-page memorandum, WEAL's Maxine Forman and Jeanne Paquette Atkins made some telling points. Women, they reminded the judges, made up 73 percent of SSI's beneficiaries, "many of whom have been *primarily homemakers* throughout their lives, and thus have few skills or retirement resources at their disposal." It was not surprising that these women "may turn to child care as a means of utilizing existing skills to increase their economic security." If earnings from child-care services provided for other family members were not treated as "earned income," then SSI would be penalizing "precisely those women who can least afford a reduction in income."

The Appeals Council rendered its ruling on March 30, 1984: "The decision of the administrative law judge is reversed. It is the decision of the Appeals Council that the claimant received earned income in the form of $65 a month . . . for baby-sitting her grandchildren." We can admire the decision even as we deplore its necessity.

Ways and Means

SSI's capricious ways have not inspired confidence among the aged and handicapped poor, many of whom have simply opted out. Studies have placed the nonparticipation rate as high as 50 percent, and there appears to be a correlation between nonparticipation and age: The number of older recipients has dropped sharply since 1975, from 2.3 million to 1.5 million. The link possibly has less to do with wisdom than with the infirmities that accompany old age, making it more difficult to thread one's way through SSI's regulatory maze.[25]

Small torments are not the only source of public discouragement. SSI's "welfare" stigma, a direct consequence of its means test, is certainly another. Congress had hoped for something better. By putting SSA in charge of the new enterprise, the lawmakers had tried to lend social security's middle-class prestige to a program aimed exclusively at the poor. Senator Abraham Ribicoff of Connecticut declared that SSI would take people "off welfare"; Senator Frank Church of Idaho agreed, rejoicing that adult welfare programs would be replaced by SSI's "new income supplement plan." Writing soon after SSI's passage, the Burkes prophesied, "If Supplemental Security attains the dignity and sense of entitlement of Social Security, recipients of the latter will not hesitate to resort to it."[26] It was a big "if" that did not come to pass. For all the rhetoric about rights and entitlements, SSI from the beginning presented itself to the public as a welfare program, with predictably demeaning consequences for its clients.

A key irritant has been the program's "redetermination" process, which requires beneficiaries to establish their eligibility anew every year. In between, they must keep SSA apprised of any changes occurring in their lives that might pertain to SSI's lengthy list of regulations. The list was not compiled casually. Among other things, it requires that recipients report changes of residence; any gifts they have received; their hospital stays and whether Medicare or Medicaid has paid more than half the bill; their journeys out of the country, including trips to Puerto Rico; spouse separations; new earnings; inheritances; changes in utility bills; and the cash value of their life insurance policies. Failure to acknowledge any of these can lead to termination of benefits.

The heavy reporting obligations stand out in sharp contrast to the much lighter ones imposed by social security, and the difference leaves SSI beneficiaries with few illusions about their status. It is not surprising that people dependent on SSI sometimes say they are getting social security benefits when they are not. It simply sounds better.

Ignorance of the program's very existence may be yet another reason for SSI's failure to reach more aged people. In a 1983 survey of eligible nonparticipants, 45 percent said they had never heard of SSI. (Four of every five surveyed were women.) It is worth remembering that these overlooked "eligibles," whose number approaches 2 million, are frequently deprived of more than SSI benefits. In many states SSI participation opens the door to additional forms of assistance, including food stamps, Medicaid, and help in meeting one's energy bills.

The Social Security Administration, meanwhile, has attempted little in the way of "outreach." Its entire recruitment effort at present consists of mailing out a one-time notice describing SSI to persons newly eligible for Medicare. No follow-up measures are taken, or for that matter contemplated. As Louis Enoff, an acting deputy commissioner, has told me, "I don't see what more we can do. We've looked for supposed eligibles and we haven't found them."

There is in all this, of course, a self-serving element, for the lower the participation rates, the lower will be the program's costs. Yet fiscal prudence alone will not account for the striking unconcern shown by this agency, whose creed has always been "To get the right benefit to the right person at the right time." A fuller explanation can be found in the history of the Social Security Administration's long, uncomfortable relationship with SSI, one defined by bureaucratic confusion and by philosophical misgivings.

Disorder and Early Sorrows

When Congress enacted SSI in 1972—after a debate so cursory that many lawmakers were unaware of what they had accomplished—it gave the Social Security Administration a year and a half to get the program under way. The time span proved too short. The idea behind SSI was to federalize all the state and municipal programs that since 1935 had been providing support to the aged, blind, and disabled poor. Each of the 1,152 jurisdictions cherished its own way of dispensing welfare, its own standards of eligibility and levels of benefits. Now SSA faced the enormous task of homogenizing those motley systems into a single federal blend.

To make matters more difficult, Congress during the tune-up period raised the benefits (those were generous times!) and changed the rules. Worried that in some states poor people would be receiving less money from SSI than they had been getting before, the lawmakers at the last minute provided for the possibility of additional state supplements and by way of encouragement promised to pay for any administrative costs the states incurred. (Maximum federal benefits that first year were $140 a month for individuals and $210 for couples.)

For an agency asked to administer the first means-tested program in its forty-year history, those were days of quiet desperation. An estimated one of every five social security recipients was about to become eligible for the new federal benefits, and SSA didn't have the foggiest idea how to sort them out. In preparation for the program's inauguration, beds were installed at the agency's Baltimore computer center so the employees could work two shifts every twenty-four hours. "Mandatory overtime was a fact of life," John D. Harris, who worked for SSA before joining the staff of his union, the American Federation of Government Employees, recalled in an interview. Even so, he added, "The first year of SSI was a nightmare."

The new program was officially launched on January 3, 1974, amid blizzards up and down the East Coast. In New York City the agency deployed chartered buses—"with heat and toilets," the *Times* reported—to accommodate the crowds of blind, disabled, or elderly poor waiting in snow to have their names shifted from city welfare rolls to those of SSI. Thousands complained they had not received their checks, though "records showed them mailed."[27]

"We had a lot of confusion," remembers Enoff, who had a hand back then in organizing the SSI program. "Probably the error rate exceeded 20 percent."

It soon became clear that confusion was only part of the problem. As the program settled in for the long haul, SSA workers struggled with their new role vis-à-vis older Americans. Whereas before they had seen themselves as dispensers of essential services to all comers, now they were being called upon to screen applicants, to ask embarrassingly personal questions, and even to keep an eye out for "welfare cheats." The transformation would not prove felicitous. By 1979 an SSA study of its own field workers could report one inevitable result: "Our findings show that employees who work primarily in the area of SSI are significantly more negative in their attitude toward recipients than are those working in other program areas."[28]

Cohen's Axiom: A Case in Point

In one of his many defenses of social security's wage-benefit connection, Wilbur Cohen offered a rule of welfare politics that might apply to Supplemental Security. "A program that deals only with the poor," he said, "will end up being a poor program."[29] SSI's frequent outbreaks of nastiness lend a suggestive ring to Cohen's axiom. At question here is whether any needs-tested income support system can in the long run behave responsibly—that is, with a sense of compassion and justice. The query has special force in the case of the elderly poor, who as a group seem least prepared to resist bureaucratic assault.

The Social Security Administration's record on this score has been far from reassuring. A case in point was the agency's "Debt Collection Action Plan," unleashed in 1982, which aimed at collecting "paybacks" from SSI beneficiaries deemed to have received more than their due.

The upside-down crusade, though scarcely noted in the press, paralleled the agency's more widely publicized efforts to push social security recipients off disability rolls. Together these drives brought fresh hardships to millions already in deep distress.

Although the campaign reached peak virulence during Ronald Reagan's first term of office, it was really a bipartisan effort. Officials in the Carter administration had thought they'd discovered a fiscal bonanza in receivables owed to SSI, social security, and hundreds of other federal programs, most of them associated with loans rather than entitlements. In 1979 Jimmy Carter's Office of Management and Budget instructed SSA and other agencies to come up with tough-minded collection plans. "The whole idea," recalls a former SSA civil servant, "was on the drawing board waiting for Jimmy's second term. The Reagan people simply inherited it"—and added some niceties of their own.

The temptation to crack down on the blind, disabled, and aged poor must have seemed natural enough. It arose from the way the agency has been compelled to do business. If an SSI client changes her eligibility status without telling the Social Security Administration— by earning money, for instance, or just by letting savings and interest accumulate—the agency goes on sending her benefits for which she has become technically ineligible. Then, when the mistake is finally discovered, SSA demands repayment.

The sequence seems clear-cut, but in many instances it is anything but. For one thing, the mistake may be the computer's and not the recipients's; for another, the client may not have been aware of the rule she broke—she may not speak English, or be able to read small print, or be mentally capable of decoding SSA's jargon; finally, many years can elapse—and many benefit dollars can be spent—before the agency gets around to asking for a refund. By that time the alleged debt has grown well beyond the client's ability to pay.

None of these complications, however, deterred SSA, which had accumulated an estimated $2 billion in receivables, much of it on SSI ledgers. In gearing up for the collection campaign during the fall of 1981, agency employees were exposed to a variety of goads and blandishments designed to underscore the satisfactions of collecting "debts" from beneficiaries. Several regional offices introduced special awards for "the Collector of the Month." "Dunning notices" were tested in Dallas. From agency headquarters in Baltimore went forth a series of inspirational memos, reminding workers—to cite a typical exhortation—that "the success of our Debt Collection Action Plan is dependent upon a firm commitment by all personnel."

In addition, SSA prepared an hour-long training film for workers assigned to make collection telephone calls. The film, which as late as mid-1985 was still being circulated, stars T. Frank Hardesty, a paid consultant from the Payco American Corporation, a national collection agency based in Columbus, Ohio. Hardesty possesses a bald, egg-shaped head and a penetrating voice that can best be described as nasal-evangelistic. In the movie he tells SSA employees that "a collector's goal is to circumvent the individual's response and collect maximum dollars in minimum time." He advises telephoners to "wait for any break in the discussion and then move in as ladies and gentlemen—and ask for payment in full . . . *today*."

"Control without arrogance" is the name of Hardesty's collection game, which he assures viewers can be "lots of fun." A trainer by profession, Hardesty has published a self-promoting brochure in which he sums up his mission as follows: "to motivate people toward intelligent aggression." At Social Security headquarters in Baltimore, there appeared to be no lack of intelligent aggression. A middle-level manager there, who has requested anonymity, told me that his superiors "looked upon all those people getting checks as welfare cheats. The idea was to figure out ways to beat on them, to get the money back."

In January 1982, the agency took the offensive. From district offices thousands of letters went out informing SSA clients that they had flunked the means test ex post facto and therefore owed the U.S. government money they had already received and spent—as much as $12,000 in some instances. In classic collection-agency fashion, the creditors demanded full and immediate payment, and for the debtor's convenience they enclosed a self-addressed envelope. ("The instant you think in terms of less than full payment," Hardesty admonishes, "you lose control.")

SSA had devised a notice-of-payment format, printed in computer type. Among other things the notice instructed penniless SSI clients to "make your check or money order payable to the Social Security Administration and mail it in the enclosed envelope." But quite a few district offices got carried away and invented more imaginative letters of their own. One missive began with the headline, "NOTICE," in bold, inch-high type. "WE HAVE NOT RECEIVED PAYMENT ON YOUR ACCOUNT," the communication went on. "WE MUST DISCUSS THIS TODAY. PLEASE CALL ME WITHIN 48 HOURS." In Baltimore, SSA staffers were calling such literary efforts "high anxiety notices."

These astonishing letters from a federal program created to befriend the poor caused much pain in the ranks of the aged. Many were too confused to comprehend the tough bureaucratic language and too intimidated in any case to fight back. Nearly all were unable to raise the lump-sum payments demanded, some of which referred to "over-payments" allegedly received seven or eight years before, when SSI was making all those computer errors.

But as an SSA official in Providence, Rhode Island, noted, "some [of the elderly] are really very docile. They'll give you the money right away and then starve to death."[30] Another Social Security worker complained to her congressman that the collection letters were causing SSI clients "so much worry that they have been unable to sleep for several days. . . . Occasionally some 80-year-old recipient dies soon after receiving an overpayment letter for a large amount. It was impossible to prove a direct connection."[31]

In Atlanta an aged woman visited her Social Security office to inquire why her SSI check had not arrived. "I have a little surprise for you," said the man behind the desk. He handed her an overpayment bill for more than $3,000.

"When I understood what the paper was," she told me later, "I burst into tears. I couldn't stop crying for the longest time."

In their eagerness to collect, SSA officials frequently violated their own due process regulations. They failed to inform debtors of appeal procedures and even threatened, illegally, to reduce people's social security payments in order to redress SSI debts. The picture that emerged from thousands of such cases was one of a hard-hearted government bullying a weak and perplexed constituency—folks who were no match for the agency's brand of "intelligent aggression."

"Such heartache the government causes!" exclaimed Helen Johnson, a volunteer advocate for persons attending the senior center in Columbia, Vermont. "When you're old, you're home all the time and you worry about everything because you have nothing else to do. It's killing them slowly, this collection thing."

Mrs. Johnson is a stout, forty-eight-year-old woman who emigrated with her parents to the United States from Norway when she was a teenager. Her speech retains a fjord-like angularity. "It makes me mad," she said, "what the agencies put these people through. But I try not to show it. I have to hide my feelings for the sake of the old ones."

I asked her how she would improve the system if she were granted the power to do so. "Give the old people a set amount to live on," she answered, "and then leave them alone. Yes, leave them alone. O.K., they are old, but we don't have to kill them. They'll die in their own time."

By January 1983, bureaucratic excesses had grown so commonplace that SSA Commissioner John A. Svahn—who later was promoted to the White House staff—felt called upon to send a cautionary memorandum to all employees. "I have recently become aware of instances in which inappropriate notices or other individual acts of overzealousness were used in the collection process," Svahn began. He warned that "our fiscal responsibilities must be balanced by a regard for individuals' statutory rights." But while asking collectors to back off a bit, Svahn in the same memo could not resist calling their attention to what he may have considered a more serious problem. There were a "number of old, relatively large overpayments," he complained, "which are being repaid in rather small monthly payments," even though "it is clear there is little or no likelihood that the current agreement would permit full recovery." To translate, Svahn was deploring the possibility that many aged poor people would die before they had fully paid their debts. His solution was to compel larger monthly payments, or in his more antiseptic language, to "attempt renegotiation under these circumstances."[32]

Despite occasionally voiced misgivings both from within the agency and without, SSA's debt collection riot was allowed to rage unchecked for the better part of three years. Then, late in 1984, Congress intervened. It passed a measure that prohibited the agency from reducing anyone's monthly SSI benefits by more than 10 percent, no matter how much a beneficiary was said to owe the government. The legislation has effectively quelled SSA's worst abuses, but it has not deterred the collectors, who estimate that close to one million overpayments remain outstanding.

Until September 1985, one of those alleged overpayments loomed as a constant worry to a Miami woman named Pearl Battles, a seventy-six-year-old ex-substitute schoolteacher who'd been born and raised in Massachusetts and had moved to Florida in middle age. Pearl's bout with the Social Security Administration resembled many another's, except for the way it ended. She had been prey to her own frugality. So well had she managed her meager income that she'd accumulated $1,538 in savings, which she mentally earmarked for her burial expenses.

As it happens, SSI allows one to maintain a burial fund of up to $1,500 without any of it being counted as assets. But the nest egg must be clearly labeled "For Burial," and no part of it can ever be used for anything else. Pearl was not aware of the rules. Her savings account expanded or contracted according to her needs. Among other things, she enjoyed giving money to her church.

I met Pearl in October 1984, and we instantly became friends. She had bright eyes and an innocent smile, and it was clear she knew how to shop creatively at thrift shops and rummage sales. The day of our first interview she was wearing a black-and-white print dress with a matching scarf knotted at the throat; on her head was a rather rakish bowler bedecked with a wisp of green gauze. "Guess what this hat cost," she demanded of me. "Two dollars, that's what."

We sat side by side on stiff little chairs in the lobby of the Ritz Hotel, where Pearl was renting a room upstairs for $190 a month. The Ritz had seen better days, but Pearl was not given to discouragement. She described it as "a nice family hotel," though later she conceded her room was "not all that spacious" and her stove, bought used for $49, was "usually on the blink."

Pearl had been able to make ends meet on a combined monthly income from social security ($259) and SSI ($75). It was not a great deal, she said, "but I'm a powerful bargain hunter. I don't shop frivolously."

Her troubles had begun the previous May when she had taken a room at the Ritz and had dutifully visited the local Social Security office to report her move. "I met a very nice young Negro gentleman there. He couldn't have been more polite. We were just talking small talk—at least that's what *I* thought—when he asked me how much money I had in the bank. 'Oh, not much at all,' I assured him. 'Just fifteen hundred and thirty-eight dollars,' You see, I didn't *know*. I never dreamed the limit was as low as it was."

The young man seemed reluctant to hear the news. "He put his hands over his ears," Pearl recalled. Then he told her she was over the SSI "resource limit" by $38, and he would have to report the fact to his superior. There followed an investigation of Pearl's bank account, both past and present. In time, examiners discovered "overpayments" along the way that amounted to nearly $2,000. "All those years I've been putting in and taking out," Pearl said. "I mean, the totals keep changing. Lord knows how many times I went over that silly limit."

Aside from the scariness of it all, what troubled Pearl most was that her government did not seem to trust her. As she said, "I'm not one of those people who sponge—I like to be independent. I could have applied for food stamps, but I never did. Not once. Think of all the money it would have cost them if I'd been getting food stamps all these years—much more than they say I owe them now. Why don't they see that?"

I didn't hear from Pearl for quite a while, but her attorney at Miami Legal Services, Cindy Huddleston, kept me posted. They were preparing to appeal to an SSA administrative law judge (ALJ). To get her debt waived, Pearl would have to prove that she was "without fault" because she had not *knowingly* exceeded SSI's resource limit. She would also have to establish her inability to repay the debt.

An ALJ heard the appeal the morning of August 7, 1985, and that afternoon Pearl telephoned me long distance from Cindy Huddleston's office. "We won!" they shouted in unison. "I'm so excited," Pearl added, "I could *spit*."

A final irony: After three years of dinning and dunning, SSA's collection record did not noticeably improve, possibly because it was adequate to begin with. "We've always done well with those overpayments that are truly collectible," William Farrell, a statistician in SSA's Office of Policy, told me. "To be quite honest, the bulk of what we've collected [since 1982] is from the kind of overpayments we would have recovered anyway. We're just not a collection agency and we're never going to be one."

Choices

The collection crusade sheds considerable light on differences between a means-tested program like SSI and a relatively universal one like the retirement component of social security. It is true that the Social Security Administration attempted to recoup perceived overpayments from both sets of beneficiaries, but it focused much more attention on SSI. The reason lay not so much in agency biases as in the contrasting vulnerabilities of the two groups. Universal programs like social security, after all, can manage with comparatively simple procedures: When nearly everyone is eligible, hardly anyone need be closely scrutinized. Means-tested programs, on the other hand, come replete with volumes of fine-print regulations that are hard to grasp and easy to violate. SSI recipients were more likely to be "overpaid" because they encountered more rules to break.

Oh what a tangled web we weave, when first we practice to deceive. The deceit in this case seems related to our reluctance as a society to comfort the poor among us, and to our still greater reluctance to confess the sin. Instead we indulge in political sleights of hand whereby we empower public institutions like SSA to assist the poor and then proceed to erect multiple barriers between those institutions and their targets of mercy. What we get for our ambivalence are the poor programs Cohen warned against, and in that dubious pantheon there is at least a partial niche reserved for Supplemental Security Income. For if SSI beneficiaries were harried and hounded by federal collectors, that was chiefly because Congress had mined the program with niggling provisos and exceptions, all the while calling it a safe harbor for the aged poor. Thus to the gentrification of social security can be added the deceptions of SSI.

It is hard to see how the nation's 6 million older poor people can be substantially helped without our first making sweeping revisions in one or both parts of the elderly income support system. We can do it either through solidarity or through charity. In the first case we would expand the social security net; in the second we would liberalize SSI, wringing the meanness out of its means test. Solidarity is preferable, but both approaches are technically possible. All we need do is summon the "statesmanship and understanding of a high order" that Louis I. Dublin, writing more than sixty years ago, named as preconditions to "a program aimed to safeguard old age."

CHAPTER TWO

◆

Health: The Gift
Repossessed

And just think, Mr. President, because of this document . . .
there are men and women in pain who will now find ease.
—Lyndon B. Johnson addressing Harry S Truman
at the Medicare signing ceremony, July 30, 1965

This chapter examines the strengths and weaknesses of Medicare, a program second only to social security in elderly hearts and also in the amounts of money it collects and distributes. As Medicare goes, so in large measure go both the quality and the quantity of elderly health care; so, too, in smaller proportions, go the integrity of our national budget and the size of our aggregate medical bill. Medicare accounts for 8 percent of the former and about 17 percent of the latter.

If Medicare has brought ease to millions of older Americans in pain, it has also generated some disappointments. The program appears to have lost its way. Its initial rationale has been turned inside out, with considerations of cost containment now largely replacing those of pain containment. The reasons are partly of the program's own making: Its careless reimbursement policies and its bias toward Cadillac-type medicine have boomeranged, serving to inflate health-care prices to a point almost beyond Medicare's abundant means. During its first two decades the program's annual outlays jumped by 1,850 percent.

All this has been occurring within a climate that is deeply deterministic. The health-care system is something we collectively created, but now it appears to have taken on a life of its own. For the most part it has been deaf to our complaints and impervious to our corrective touch.

Looked at through the eyes of an elderly beneficiary, Medicare's present scenario resembles the action that unfolds in a rewinding film: Everything appears to be traveling backwards. We see benefits jumping out of pockets and speeding back to their source; we glimpse the giver repossessing the gift.

The consequences of running the reel backwards have been widely understood but weakly resisted. By now nearly everyone knows that older patients are in some respects no better off than they were during the dark ages that preceded Medicare, when they were spending 15 percent of their aggregate income on health care. Today they are spending 18 percent, or an average of $2,394 per person each year.[1] Some of that personal spending can be directly attributed to Medicare-related charges for premiums, copayments, and deductibles. Uncovered expenditures, including some doctors' bills, account for much of the rest.

The out-of-pocket totals tend to cast doubt on the customarily cheerful assumptions of liberalism. For if progressives in the 1960s saw in Medicare a pleasing example of the incrementalism they had long been preaching—that is, of America's step-by-step march toward social perfection—then it is hard to escape the conclusion that the program is now in danger of becoming its own opposite. Medicare's slippage reflects a "decrementalism" peculiar (one hopes) to the 1980s. Whether it will be permitted to bestride future decades as well depends on what we as a society do next.

Perhaps Congress has already begun to repeal decrementalism. In 1988, with passage of the Medicare Catastrophic Protection Act, the lawmakers liberalized the program in several important ways. Among other things they finally exorcized the demon of medical bankruptcy—a prospect that had terrorized many older citizens—by placing a ceiling on deductibles, copayments, and other personal expenses arising from Medicare coverage. It has been estimated that the 1990 "cap" of $2,146 could reduce out-of-pocket expenses for up to one-fifth of Medicare's enrollees.[2]

In addition, the measure mandated states to pay the Medicare premiums of *all* the elderly poor, not just the poorest among them. And it broke new ground by authorizing partial payments for prescription drugs. But beneficiaries will have to buy the first $600 worth of medicine on their own, before Medicare steps in to share the expense.

One senses, then, that the Medicare program is poised between two philosophies, one bent on cutting costs, the other on expanding benefits. It could go either way. What follows here is a modest effort to keep us moving along incremental lines. I begin with a brief history, largely political, of how the Medicare program assumed its peculiar shape. Next I describe its complex structure, paying special attention to the bureaucratic procedures by means of which the program confounds its elderly clients.

Then, in a section called "The Mending of Catherine Cott," I locate the more serious leaks to be found in Medicare's protective umbrella, and I add up their costs to elderly patients. That is followed by "Speeding Up the Clock," an examination of the Prospective Payments System, that far-reaching cost-containment device enacted by Congress in 1982, and of its effects on elderly patients.

A final section speculates on ways to put Medicare back on "fast forward." I offer a number of specific suggestions.

How Medicare Took Shape

Many of Medicare's problems can be considered congenital in the sense that they were present at birth. The program's unique shape and substance are largely due to compromises its partisans felt compelled to make in order to secure both its passage and its subsequent enforcement. Fear of one failure or the other—a negative vote or a doctors' boycott—prompted heavy concessions from reformers, including their approval of a topless reimbursement scheme that left health-care vendors free to charge whatever they considered "reasonable" or "customary."

If from today's vantage point the consequences seem to have been inevitable, at the time they were far from clear. Few could have predicted that instead of boycotting the program, the nation's health-care professionals would embrace it in an inflationary bear hug—that they would love it nearly to death.

The measure that ultimately emerged was, in the writer Richard Harris's phrase, "a complex but typically American solution to the problem," one notable for the exquisite balance it achieved among disparate interests.[3] There was something in the Medicare grab bag for everyone: The elderly got long-deferred medical coverage; the private insurance industry got a lush new market; and the health-care clan got the keys to the federal strongbox. To cap it all, the American public was handed a new social entitlement without the accompanying annoyance of having to hammer out institutional reforms—for in enacting Medicare, Congress left the health-care industry and its institutions largely untouched.

Still, we should not be ungrateful to the program's beleaguered founders, some of whom had been chasing "The Lost Reform"—comprehensive health insurance for all Americans—for as many as fifty years. Their pre-Medicare struggles merit our attention, if only because the final measure was profoundly influenced by certain anxieties that had accumulated along the way. The difficulties of the quest helped determine the nature of the quarry.

The quest can be said to have begun auspiciously when Theodore Roosevelt's Bull Moose party (in 1912) called for a state-by-state system of universal health insurance. In those days, before ideological lines had hardened, even the American Medical Association (AMA) was on the side of the socialist angels. "The socialization of medicine is coming," the AMA *Journal* cheerfully announced in 1914. "The time now is here for the medical profession to acknowledge that it is tired of the eternal struggle for advantage over one's neighbor. . . . Medical practice withholds itself from the field of science as long as it remains a competitive business."

World War I and its reactionary aftermath changed all that. By 1918 the AMA membership had shoved aside its progressive leaders and replaced them with officers more likely to view medical practice as a competitive business. A resolution passed that year declared the organization's steadfast "opposition to . . . any plan embodying the system of compulsory contributory insurance against illness . . . [which is] provided, controlled or regulated by any state or the federal government."

With the onset of the Great Depression public support for just such a plan increased dramatically, as did the respect accorded it by politicians. For one brief moment, in fact, Franklin D. Roosevelt seemed ready to include universal health insurance in his social security package. But then, in a fateful decision, he yielded to protests from the AMA and from his own White House physician, Ross McIntyre, who solemnly warned the president about "the deep anxiety of physicians on the health care issue."

What Roosevelt may have feared was a full-scale doctors' revolt fomented and financed by the AMA, whose leadership equated federally sponsored health coverage with a form of "Sovietism for the American people." The fear was probably justified—or so insisted Harvey Cushing, a distinguished neurosurgeon who was also the father-in-law of the president's son James. Whatever measures Roosevelt might choose to recommend to Congress, Cushing pointed out in a gently worded caveat to FDR, "no legislation can be effective without the good will of the American Medical Association, which has the organization to put it to work."

In ensuing decades the AMA lost neither its deep anxiety nor its sense of moral certitude. But over time the doctors had to contend with a formidable new challenge: Their older patients were increasing in number and growing in political restiveness. One of many harbingers appeared in 1959 when the Senate's newly formed Subcommittee on Aging (itself a harbinger) held hearings around the country to learn more about the concerns of older Americans. "The old folks lined up by the dozens every place we went," a staff member later recalled. "And they didn't talk much about housing or recreational centers or part-time work. They talked about medical care."[4]

Leaders in Washington began lining up alongside their elderly constituents. John F. Kennedy, and then Lyndon B. Johnson, became figures in the lengthening procession. "Many of our older citizens are still defenseless against the heavy medical costs of severe illness and disability," President Johnson pointed out in a special 1964 message to Congress, adding that only a massive federal initiative could reverse the miserable odds. His top-heavy electoral triumph over Barry Goldwater later that year virtually assured the enactment of some such initiative.

When Medicare finally materialized, in July 1965, its margin of victory was surprisingly wide (313–115 in the House and 68–21 in the Senate). But Medicare's friends could not have achieved such a broad consensus without first surrendering significant stretches of fiscal and ideological turf to Medicare's enemies, many of whom had resisted the measure to the very last. Only a month before passage a group even further to the right than the AMA—the Association of American Physicians and Surgeons (AAPS)—had again raised the specter of boycott. In a nationwide mailing to doctors, the AAPS had exhorted "every . . . ethical physician in the United States to individually and voluntarily pledge *nonparticipation* in . . . the socialized hospitalization and medical care program for the aged."[5]

In the face of so much resistance, Congress failed to establish firm federal controls over the health-care business. Medicare's peculiar design favored self-determination among vendors: Hospitals remained free to set their own rates; doctors could either sign up for the program or turn their backs on it, just as they pleased. Much of Medicare's subsequent history can be read in the light of those original decisions, which preserved certain balance-sheet freedoms but virtually guaranteed rampant inflation.

Increasingly now, Congress has been having second thoughts, albeit timid ones. If the lawmakers have been eager at times to grasp some of the powers they forswore in 1965, they have been reluctant to bite the essential bullet—that is, to redesign the basic program. We turn now to a detailed description of that program.

The Many Paradoxes of Medicare

Out of its accommodating past flows Medicare's paradoxical present. The program today is both free spending and parsimonious, voluntary and compulsory, easy to enter and difficult to find one's way through, publicly financed and—in certain key respects—privately managed. Resisted by doctors at the start for the "socialistic" poisons it was sure to spread, Medicare has learned how to present to the world, and in particular to its beneficiaries, a capitalistic face: Its corporate surrogates wield enormous power over the elderly and reap substantial earnings in the bargain. Hailed early on for its promise of "comprehensive" coverage, the program's benefit package has proved so porous that private insurers have rushed in with a whole new species of allegedly leak-proof protection, called "medigap," which has grown into a $6 billion industry.

At least one additional contradiction should be listed here, and that pertains to the nature of Medicare's benefits. They are oddly off-target. It may be that the old, frustrated dream of providing health-care insurance for everyone blinded Medicare's creators to the new, restricted reality. The measure they drafted seemed designed for a younger constituency. It sharply circumscribed many elderly-type benefits and omitted others altogether. Medicines appeared nowhere on the program's roster of reimbursable items. (As we have seen, they were added on a limited basis in 1988.) Neither did such old-age staples as eyeglasses, dentures, and hearing aids—items an acquaintance of mine has described as "the spare parts us oldsters run on."

Even more telling were the measure's medical biases. Benefits relating to acute, short-term care loomed larger than those targeted for chronic, long-term care; exotic high-tech procedures eclipsed sensible preventive ones. The statute specifically banned payments for "routine physical checkups," eye, hearing, and dental examinations as well as most immunizations.

The inappropriateness of all this, and its costliness, plague the program and its beneficiaries to this day. As an aged resident of Los Angeles remarked to me, "Medicare doesn't cover routine anything."

Two Faces

Medicare is really "Medipair." The long debate in Congress between those loyal to The Lost Reform (the universalists) and those committed to business as usual (the free enterprisers) ended in a Solomonic solution: Medicare was split in two. Part A became a plan for Hospital Insurance, Part B for Supplementary Medical Insurance (SMI).

To this day the two plans have little in common. Broadly speaking, Part A works on social security principles, whereas Part B runs along more market-oriented lines. The hospital plan aims at universality: All are taxed that all may benefit. Virtually every worker contributes to Part A's exchequer via regular payroll deductions, and virtually every elderly and disabled American—some 32 million in all—has a place on its rolls.

Part B, which covers physician and outpatient care, reflects a different philosophy in deference to a different interest group, the nation's 490,000 doctors. For openers, the plan exacts payments from those at risk, not by means of payroll deductions, but through insurance premiums charged directly to the elderly. In 1989 the premium came to $31.90 a month. It was just $3.00 when Medicare got started.

Although Part B was designed as a "voluntary" program for both doctors and patients (*nobody* had to participate), nearly all the volition has been on the doctors' side. Few patients see themselves as having a choice. Not only do they need the plan's protection, but Congress has also devised a compelling method of collecting their premiums: Unless a person specifically objects, her monthly premium is automatically deducted from her social security check. That may be why on any given month only about 100,000 of the 30 million eligible participants opt out of the program. (The revenues collected provide about one-quarter of SMI's essential funds; Congress has had to supply the other three-quarters through yearly appropriations.)

That Medicare works as well as it does can partly be ascribed to its liberal rules of entry. The program imposes few of the indignities, the means-testiness, commonly associated with social welfare endeavors in the United States. In Part A, at least, it runs along a single track for all classes. Its popularity is broad because its arithmetic is actuarial. Winston Churchill could have been referring to Medicare (he wasn't) when he spoke of bringing "the magic of averages to the rescue of millions."

In 1989 Medicare assisted in some thirty-three million separate rescues at a cost of almost $96 billion. About four-fifths of the rescues, but only two-fifths of the dollars, helped Part B beneficiaries pay their doctor and clinic bills. Nearly all the rest went to hospitals, with the residue reserved for nursing homes, home-care specialists, and hospices for the dying. (About 6 percent of Medicare beneficiaries die each year.)

The high number of Medicare reimbursements does not imply an equally high number of recipients, for it appears that most older Americans are well most of the time. Among Part A's elderly enrollees, some 22 million received no benefits at all in 1986; for Part B, the number of unbenefited participants exceeded 8 million. Seven of every ten Medicare beneficiaries in 1986 got less than $500, and as a group they accounted for a scant 3.3 percent of the program's twelve-month outlay. At the other end of the spectrum were the 18 percent who each received more than $2,000 in benefits. They represented nearly 90 percent of Medicare's total disbursements.

Mystifications

In both structure and ideology, then, Medicare has the look of a centaur, with a compulsory pension program at one end and a semi-voluntary, pay-as-you-go insurance plan at the other. The nature of the beast and the incompatibility of its parts have caused considerable confusion within elderly ranks. Hardly anyone on the rolls has been able to figure out how the program works.

Medicare's reliance on third-party interventions has compounded the confusion. The agency that is supposed to run the program is known as the Health Care Financing Administration, or HCFA (pronounced "hicva" by those in the know). But from the beneficiary's angle of vision, HCFA is both invisible and unaccountable.

Instead of dealing directly with the public, HCFA appoints corporate surrogates in every state or region to sort out claims and make payments. (Part A's surrogates are called "intermediaries" and Part B's are called "carriers.") Blue Cross and Blue Shield affiliates do most of the work for Medicare, but a number of private insurance companies—Aetna, Equitable, and Prudential among others—also hold contracts. Although they sometimes claim otherwise, the surrogates seem adequately paid for their services. In 1985 carriers and intermediaries together grossed $933 million.[6]

The beneficiaries and the corporations seldom meet, but they do correspond. Corporations send to beneficiaries sheets full of gray, computerized type, each sheet said to contain an explanation of Medicare benefits, or EOMB for short. Although the clarity of EOMBs varies from state to state, the average is not high and the overall effect has been one of vast befuddlement among elderly patients.

It doesn't seem to help to be exceptionally bright or well educated. One woman I interviewed, a sixty-eight-year-old editor in New York City, had spent her entire career deciphering esoteric copy for technical publishers, yet the EOMBs she received from Empire Blue Cross and Blue Shield defied her understanding. She sent me a copy of one. It had been accompanied by a mysterious check for $95.58. Her note to me bespoke the sort of resignation that receipt of an EOMB can easily inspire.

"I don't know what the amounts refer to," she wrote. "I don't know why they sent me a check for $95.58 nor one to Dr. Jacobson for $23.74. . . . I've never put in a claim that says I've paid him anything. However, I've given up trying to figure it out; I'll just deposit their check, send an equivalent amount to the doctor, and forget it."

A less jaded beneficiary might have attempted to telephone her carrier. But this woman had tried that before and had never succeeded in talking to anyone: Either the line was busy or else she was put "on hold" for so long that she finally gave up. Nearly all the beneficiaries I talked with recounted similar experiences. One woman told of an afternoon call she'd placed to Medicare's intermediary in Boston. A recorded message assured her she would be answered "momentarily" and urged her not to hang up. Then came lots of static and violin music. The woman listened to this for what seemed a long time, after which she placed the receiver on her night table and went about her business. She had dinner, read a magazine and went to bed. When she woke up the next morning, the first thing she saw was the receiver off the hook. She put it to her ear. The violins were still playing.

At first I was skeptical of such tales, so I conducted my own unscientific survey, making it a point to dial a surrogate's number in each city I visited. I must have made dozens of such calls, but I never reached anyone. In the end, my picture of Medicare came to resemble that of "the Castle" in Kafka's famous novel. The elderly were like the villagers who live in the valley below. "There's no fixed connection with the Castle," explains the village mayor, "no central exchange that transmits our calls farther. When anybody calls up the Castle from here, the instruments in all the subordinate departments ring, or rather they would ring if practically all the departments—I know this for a certainty—didn't leave their receivers off."

Medicare's failure either to speak clearly or to listen attentively— its essential dumbness and deafness—has kept the elderly in a steady state of nervousness. I was able to eavesdrop on a few of their anxious moments when I went to Arcadia, California, with Eileen Harper and Bess Bratter, young lawyers who worked for the nonprofit Medicare Advocacy Project in Los Angeles. They served as circuit-riding answer-women for beneficiaries caught up in the coils of Medicare; one of their jobs was to visit different neighborhoods and suburbs and try to untangle the knots.

Harper and Bratter set up shop one morning in the Arcadia Town Hall, using the auditorium stage as their office and a long conference table as their desk. People seeking help filed in all day long; many needed the table's full length to accommodate the thick bundles of Medicare documents they had brought with them.

Most of the questioners revealed only a scant knowledge of how the program functioned. They could make no distinctions between Parts A and B, and they often seemed unaware of Medicare's multiple imposts—the deductibles and copayments that the program exacted from beneficiaries. Quite a few, in fact, had the impression that Medicare paid for everything, including prescriptions and "spare parts."

Mary Berlin walked in with a cane and needed help mounting the two steps to the stage. The year before, she told Harper and Bratter, she had gone twice to the hospital—once for "an operation on my innards" and again "because I was full of adhesions from the first operation." While there the second time, she had suffered a stroke. Now the hospital was dunning her for $870 that she didn't think she owed. She thought Medicare had paid for everything.

"I don't have the money," she said. "All I get is the social security and the union pension." Her social security benefit was $499 a month; her monthly pension, the reward of forty-eight years as a seamstress in the garment industry, came to $88.

Scanning the EOMBs Mrs. Berlin had brought along, the attorneys could not be sure who owed what to whom. They suggested she call Blue Cross, the local intermediary, but Mrs. Berlin said she had done that already: "I had a hard time getting through, but one time I did talk to someone up there. I gave him my number because he said he wanted to call me back. Well, the next day the phone rang but by the time I got there the party was gone. It takes me about ten rings to get from the kitchen to the phone. Maybe they were in a hurry."

Bratter and Harper made an effort to explain Medicare's complex benefit rules, emphasizing the deductibles and the copayments. "Yes," said Mrs. Berlin, "those things you're telling me seem right. But when I get home I'll forget them. I'm eighty-four years old and I'm getting funny in the head."

In the afternoon there arrived a "snowbird" couple from Michigan's Upper Peninsula who wintered each year in southern California. This winter they were renting a two-room trailer in space #22 of a camp on Live Oak Street in Arcadia. "We can't afford a real house," the wife explained, adding that her husband had worked "in the woods and in the mills all his life," but now he was retired. "We get a check for $266 from social security every month," she said, "and that's all we see."

She wore a short-sleeved gray dress; her arms were brown and muscular. Her husband seemed smaller and considerably older, but he looked resplendent in a purple jacket, red-checkered shirt, and multihued trousers. The cap he carried matched his jacket and bore a John Deere imprint.

She did most of the talking at first. "He's 69 and he's hard-of-hearing," she began, "so you'll have to talk loud. The left ear is his good one. He's not what you'd call sick. It's just that last summer he was feeling weak and the doctor put him in the hospital for lots of tests. We're still paying for them tests."

The husband spoke up. One series of tests, he said, "was when the doctor put me under these machines. I believe we paid for that one." He also must have been given blood tests, because "we are getting these bills from some doctor we never seen. He calls himself a hematologist." The hematologist's bill was for $953.

They had received several checks from Medicare and had passed them along to one doctor or another, never certain they were paying the right amount to the right creditor. "Medicare don't say who the checks are for," the wife complained, holding up a packet of papers. "It's supposed to all be in here but I can't make it out. They keep sending us forms and we keep sending them back. Our cousin in Michigan helped us fill them out."

She spread the papers on the table for the attorneys to read. One paper in particular caught Harper's attention. "It looks like you bought medigap insurance from Union Fidelity and Globe," she said, "and you're paying them $46 a month. Is that correct?"

"Sounds right," the husband answered. "Fellow got me out of bed to sell me the policy. We got no phone so he just come one night and knocks on the door. We were asleep."

"Have you put in a claim to Union Fidelity? Have they sent you any money?"

"Can't say for certain. Don't think so."

Nobody that day in Arcadia questioned Medicare's mission, only its mystery. With all its faults, the program remains an essential and deeply appreciated ally of the aged. Somehow Medicare stumbles on; somehow its constituents stay more or less in step.

Catherine Cott is one of those constituents. Her story underscores both sides of the Medicare paradox: On the one hand, its damnable deficiencies; on the other, its abiding indispensability.

The Mending of Catherine Cott

Catherine Cott is a small, white-haired woman with a quick smile and an easy manner. She loves company but is accustomed to living alone. Never married, she worked for thirty-nine years as a secretary at one San Diego insurance company, retiring in 1973. She will soon be eighty. Miss Cott's entire support comes from social security and amounts to less than $700 a month. She never goes to the movies and she rarely eats at restaurants. For recreation she dons yellow slacks and a red sweater and takes early-morning walks along the ocean beach, relying on tiny steps to carry her a long way. (In politics her mode of progress would be called "incrementalism.") When bored, she sometimes goes on a cleaning rampage, vacuuming rugs and washing down walls. The apartment, she has assured me, is usually "squeaky clean."

One morning not long ago Miss Cott slipped on the kitchen floor and broke her hip in two places. As she recalled months later, "I had arthritis in both knees—still do—so my pins were extra-shaky. But I was bound and determined to mop my kitchen floor. It was filthy. Well, you see where it got me."

The accident set in motion a perfectly ordinary train of medical and economic events, which on inspection seem to typify both the shame and the glory of our everyday health-care arrangements. Miss Cott went through all the customary stages of trauma, treatment, and recovery. She was hospitalized, operated on, and sent home after twelve days; physical therapy came later, as did the bills. Since much of this chapter is about our medical system's defects and the hardships they impose on older citizens, it seems fair at this juncture to specify some of the system's strengths, at least two of which were on display in Miss Cott's case.

To begin with, the doctors made her whole again, and they did so by applying the remarkable skills and technological resources that American patients have come to take for granted. Apparently Miss Cott's surgeons were also master carpenters and engineers; the hipbone X-rays I saw six months after the accident—by which time the breaks were nearly knit—revealed a veritable fretwork of steel screws, bolts, and wires. I had the impression I was gazing into one of those subcutaneous miracles that modern American medicine routinely performs.

As Miss Cott can attest, moreover, orthopedic technology was not the only miracle mender in her life. The Medicare program, with its timely infusion of dollars, also worked wonders. We tend to forget the blessed difference Medicare can make in elderly lives, especially in the lives of people with limited incomes. Before Medicare, almost half of all older Americans lacked any kind of hospital coverage. After Medicare, with 99 percent of the elderly gaining protection, medical decisions could more often be made on the basis of need rather than wealth. Hospital admissions shot up 29 percent during Medicare's first ten years; the number of cataract operations doubled.

The new accessibility of health care contributed to several demographic marvels, not least, to a precipitous drop in annual mortality rates among the aged—by an average of 1.5 percent for older men and 2.3 percent for older women. Life expectancy increased accordingly. It had been gradually rising all century, but in Medicare's initial decade the pace of longevity quickened, accounting for one-third of all gains made during the seventy-five-year ascent.[7]

If Medicare did not necessarily lengthen Catherine Cott's life—and who can say for sure?—it certainly restored her mobility. Without the program's support it is unlikely she would ever have walked again; by herself she could never have met the five-figure price of surgical deliverance. The total bill came to $12,293.87, of which Medicare paid $10,136.51.

But here, alas, the glory ends. For the protection Medicare afforded Miss Cott fell short of the mark. It left her with a king-size bill of her own, amounting to between $2,100 and $2,500, depending on the method of computation. Either way, the bill threatened to swallow up at least a quarter of her $8,000 yearly income. In order to get out from under her medical creditors, Miss Cott was compelled to shoulder one additional debt: She borrowed money from a local bank, at 17 percent interest. (All this occurred before the 1988 enactment of Medicare Catastrophic Protection, but for Catherine Cott the measure would have been a difference without a distinction: Its lid on out-of-pocket expenses was pegged too high to have helped her with her bills.)

Most of Miss Cott's financial woes stemmed from the many extra tariffs that Medicare levies on beneficiaries. These have always been a part of the Medicare package, but as the price of health care has climbed, so have most of the tariffs. For elderly patients with low incomes the additional costs have been hard to bear.

Part A, for example, imposes a substantial deductible that the patient pays up front. Along with just about everything else relating to Medicare, that deductible has been soaring. In 1981 it was pegged at $204; by 1989 it had climbed to $560, a jump of 175 percent. The hospital deductible accounted for about one-fifth of Miss Cott's total out-of-pocket expenditures.

Unassigned Obligations

At the doctor's end of the centaur (Part B), the required deductible is relatively modest, currently $75 per year. But Part B can be expensive in other ways. For starters, the most it will pay is 80 percent of the total bill, and then only if the charges conform to Medicare's official fee schedule—or, to use Medicare parlance, only if the physician "accepts assignment." Here is where the program's "voluntary" philosophy can enrich doctors and impoverish patients. Although those physicians who choose to participate must set their fees with Medicare's price list in mind, the rest are free to charge whatever they wish, and it is the patient who bears the additional freight. Pity the patient whose doctor does not accept assignment.

Catherine Cott was lucky in her two surgeons, both of whom adjusted their fees downward—by almost $500 between them—in order to stay within Medicare's assigned limits. Even so, the two reduced bills came to $2,183.90, and Miss Cott was responsible for 20 percent of the total, or about $437.

Some of her other doctors were not so obliging. The bookkeeper's ballet danced by Medicare, Miss Cott, and her anesthesiologist shows what can occur when a doctor does not accept assignment. The anesthesiologist charged $396 for his ministrations at the operating table, whereas Medicare's approved maximum fee for that service was $254. So Medicare paid $204 (80 percent of the assigned fee) and Miss Cott paid the rest—$192. Had her doctor accepted assignment, the cost to Miss Cott would have been just $50.

Such shortfalls are as much the rule as the exception. In their billing practices seven of every ten doctors sometimes exceed Medicare maximums. According to 1986 tabulations made by HCFA, about one-third of all SMI claims—there were 299 million that year!—topped Medicare's assigned ceilings. HCFA's deadpan way of expressing this is to speak of "balanced billing," meaning that patients in such instances are required to pay the "balance" of the bill. Beneficiaries often prefer another term: They call it "excess billing." In recent years excess billing has accounted for more than one-fifth of the elderly's out-of-pocket medical expenses.

The excess billing, the deductibles, and the coinsurance payments—not to mention the Part B premium of almost $400 a year (in 1989)—all become part of the painful reckoning. For Catherine Cott they constituted a tab of over $2,100.

But the reckoning was not complete. An additional expense arose from the program's exclusion of medicines from its list of reimbursable items. Miss Cott estimated that in the months following her operation she spent about $250 on prescriptions. (Here again, the 1988 measure, with its $600 deductible for prescriptions, could not have helped.)

Medicare's tendency sometimes to reject legitimate claims created yet another expense for Miss Cott. In effect, the program outfumbled her for several checks. The problem centered on two types of billing items, one for ambulance service and another for personal equipment. Medicare was willing to pay for the ambulance that took Miss Cott to the hospital but not, unaccountably, for the one that took her home. The charge for that ride was $36.

Once home, Miss Cott needed a wheelchair, which she rented, and a commode, which she bought. Later she required a walker and a cane. Medicare was obligated by law to pay 80 percent of all four bills, which came to $289.52; in fact, it paid only $105.56 and stuck Miss Cott with the rest of the check.

The 36 Percent Solution

Congress did not intend to make life more difficult for older Americans down on their luck. When the lawmakers enacted Medicare, they also created Medicaid, which they billed as a health insurance plan for the poor. The assumption regarding patients like Miss Cott, who happened to be both poor and old, was that Medicaid would rush in where Medicare disdained to tread—for instance, in meeting the costs of prescriptions. In the event, however, Medicaid has proven almost as unsatisfactory as its more prestigious sibling, and more demeaning to boot. Means-tested and states-administered, the Medicaid program serves to remind us why most older Americans, all things being equal, would prefer to rely exclusively on Medicare.

It may be easier for a poor woman to pass through the eye of a needle than to enter the kingdom of Medicaid. That is because in their testings for eligibility many states have demanded something more than mere poverty—or something less, for what they have required is utter destitution. A disproportionately large share of Medicaid's elderly support goes to those already pauperized by long stays in nursing homes, while much less goes to those who are poor but still live at home. In 1986 only 36 percent of all such elderly poor households enjoyed Medicaid protection.[8]

The Medicare Catastrophic Protection Act could partially correct this problem. In effect, it would compel the states, via Medicaid, to purchase Medicare coverage on behalf of all older Americans whose incomes fell below the poverty line. It also would liberalize the Medicaid "assets" test by doubling the dollar limit permitted for eligibility.

Those welcome improvements, however, would be of no use to Catherine Cott, whose income remains slightly above the poverty line. She is one of many caught between the rock of Medicare and the hard place of Medicaid.

Speeding Up the Clock

In addition to a shortage of Medicare cash, Miss Cott also endured an odd abridgment of Medicare time—that is, of her allowable length of stay in the hospital. At what seemed a critical juncture in the healing process she was suddenly sent packing. The expulsion underlined Medicare's extraordinary powers to intervene in the lives of elderly patients.

The way Miss Cott subsequently described her discharge, it seemed not only premature but mysterious. For as so often happens in matters pertaining to Medicare, no one bothered to explain to her the intricate rules that governed her life as a patient. All she could do was speculate— inaccurately, it turned out—on the reasons why she had been sent home before she could even stand up.

"I came home right before Christmas. I think they were anxious to clear everyone out for the holidays, because at the time I could hardly move. They put me in an ambulance one morning, and when we got to my place the driver carried me in. He lugged me upstairs, right into my apartment, and sat me down in a chair. After he made sure I could reach the phone, he just went away and left me. It was awful. I couldn't stand up or put on a shoe or even bend over. I just sat there and cried. I think I cried for a whole week."

Catherine Cott's predicament that morning arose from budget-cutting measures that Congress had taken in 1982 and 1983, in particular from a reform known as the Prospective Payments System, or PPS. This was an ingenious device aimed at resetting the Medicare clock wherever hospitals treated older patients. PPS altered the climate of reimbursement for both sides. It made Medicare stingier with its payments and the hospitals leaner and meaner to their older patients. There may be no better example of the invisible cord that binds elderly lives to federal policies, for it was PPS, not the holiday rush, that left Miss Cott stranded and weeping in her own living room.

Before PPS, hospitals billed Medicare the old-fashioned way, that is, on a cost-plus basis for each elderly patient. They simply toted up the dollars spent and factored in a generous markup for profit. Medicare seldom questioned the totals; in effect, it provided the hospitals with a blank check on every billing occasion. That way of doing business probably encouraged inefficiency and avarice in about equal parts.

PPS has reduced the inefficiency if not the avarice. Now Medicare *predicts* how much a patient's care will cost and then reimburses the hospital for that predicted amount. The forecasts are based on categories of ailments called DRGs, which is short for diagnostic related groups. Every patient is supposed to fit into one DRG or another—at last count there were 470 on HCFA's list—and thus to call forth a set, nonnegotiable payment from Medicare.

The new system has unnerved many a hospital administrator. Every elderly admission has become a fresh gamble, the bet being that the cost of the patient's care will not exceed the amount of Medicare's reimbursement. (To lose the bet too often is to go out of business.) Miss Cott's fractured hip, for example, placed her in a DRG entailing no more than twelve days of hospitalization, at a cost of about $7,500. It would not have mattered to Medicare if she had stayed two days or two months: Its payment to the hospital would have been exactly the same. But it would have made a world of difference to the hospital: In accounting terms, it made sense to get Miss Cott out of there "on time."

The record thus far suggests that PPS may be dollar wise and pain foolish—and even the "wise" side of the equation is suspect. It does appear that PPS has cut down on the amount of time older patients spend in hospitals; their average lengths of stay dropped from about ten days in 1982 to about eight in 1987. Medicare's hospital bill, or at least the rate of increase, dipped accordingly, leveling off from an average annual rise of 17 percent during the preceding decade to one of 5 percent by 1987.

But such numbers may conceal as much as they reveal, for the savings seem far from consistent. A Johns Hopkins University study, which examined records for 57,000 Medicare patients in six hospitals, concluded that the new reimbursement method, while underpaying certain hospitals, actually overpaid others. Not surprisingly, the ones most frequently shortchanged were those serving poor people, whose ailments were more likely to be multiple and complicated.[9]

The system's baneful impact on older patients has been widely publicized. Increasingly now, people like Catherine Cott find themselves stranded in what Carroll Estes, a gerontologist at the University of California, has shrewdly named "no-care zones." A three-year study conducted by Estes and her associates, covering thirty-two communities in eight states, suggested not only that Medicare patients are being released "sicker and quicker," but that many have nowhere to turn for help.[10]

Several other investigations, including one undertaken for Congress by the General Accounting Office, have come to similar conclusions. It may be true, as the Reagan administration used to insist, that much of the evidence remains "anecdotal" rather than "scientific." But the anecdotes keep piling up, and the patterns they form do not inspire confidence in the new system's capacity either for moderation or compassion. To certify the presence of a social disaster, one need not count each and every tear—and Miss Cott in her weeping has had plenty of company.

Some of the victims have found an attentive ear in the House Select Committee on Aging. Their stories flow darkly through a committee report entitled "Out 'Sooner and Sicker': Myth or Medicare Crisis?"[11] In that almanac of botched treatments and premature discharges, the account of one Milwaukee couple, Dorothy and Harrison Seeley, can easily stand for the whole. Mrs. Seeley's testimony encapsulates many of the torments that Medicare now disburses along with the benefits— not least, the torment of medical recidivism: Many a hasty discharge has led to relapse and return.

Mrs. Seeley was seventy years old, her husband was seventy-two, and neither was in the best of health. Her bone disease had occasioned two spinal fusions and the artificial replacement of half a knee. Mr. Seeley, a semiretired carpenter, had suffered for years from severe back pains. But, as Mrs. Seeley told the committee, their big troubles did not begin until May 1985, when her husband went to his doctor for a routine checkup: "The doctor spotted a small tumor on Harrison's bladder, which was later removed under spinal anesthesia. He spent one week in the hospital." While there, she said, "His back became flared up. I thought that the spinal anesthetic caused his pain. . . . They sent him home from the hospital even though he had trouble walking because of the pain. Nobody tried to find out what was causing it."

Mr. Seeley "recovered just fine" from the bladder surgery, but the pain in his back persisted and he had difficulty walking. "Enough is enough," Mrs. Seeley finally said to her husband. "I'm taking you to the doctor." They went to the orthopedist who had treated Mrs. Seeley the year before, and he promptly sent Mr. Seeley to the hospital, but "not the same one where he had the bladder surgery." It was in this second hospital that the term "DRG" took on new significance for the Seeleys. What the initials came to mean was: *Don't Recover—Go.*

"The doctor put Harrison in traction, and after six days the doctor came into his room—I'll never forget it. He stood at the foot [of the bed] and said Harrison had to go home. He told us that Medicare's DRGs would pay for only seven days of traction.

"I told him I couldn't handle Harrison at home, and I said he's not ready to go home. He said, 'Dorothy, I have to put on a different hat now. The hospital administrator is on my back, and Harrison has got to leave. I know he is not ready to go home and you know he is not ready to go home, but he has got to go.'

"Well, Harrison went home on Saturday by ambulance. Can you imagine? I drove him to the hospital so that he could have his back pain treated. Yet when the hospital let him go, he had to be taken in an ambulance."

The pain in Mr. Seeley's back grew worse. In desperation Mrs. Seeley called the doctor again, and this time he recommended a CAT scan.

"So on Tuesday, just three days after he was discharged from the hospital, Harrison went by ambulance for the scan at the same hospital. Then the ambulance brought him home."

Two days later the doctor got the CAT scan results: Mr. Seeley had cancer of the spine.

"The doctor said he had to go to the hospital right away to begin radiation therapy. . . . The ambulance came to the house and took him to yet another hospital. That was the third hospital in about four weeks and his fourth ambulance ride in five days. . . .

"Mr. Chairman, that week, going from hospital to hospital . . . was an ordeal that still brings tears to my eyes. . . . After we got over the initial shock, however, we got angry and worried.

"We asked ourselves why in the world didn't the doctors at the first hospital look at [Harrison's] spine when he went for bladder surgery. He complained about his back. Why wasn't the diagnosis made before he was sent home in pain? Why was everyone so much more anxious to get him out of the hospital than to find out why his back hurt?"

Mrs. Seeley concluded her testimony with what was surely an understatement. "There is something wrong with DRGs," she declared. "The people that we trusted to take care of us seemed to put Medicare payments first. To them, the cancer hiding in Harrison's spine was secondary."

It was not only the betrayal of trust that worried Mrs. Seeley. In her view the system that had been created in the name of cost containment was squandering the taxpayers' dollars. "I think a lot of Medicare's money is being wasted. Medicare paid for Harrison's three hospital admissions in a four-week period. Medicare paid for five ambulance trips. I think the money Medicare paid out would have been much less if Harrison's cancer had been diagnosed when he had his bladder surgery. No matter who is paying the bills, unnecessary expenses are unfair.

"This should not have happened to us," Mrs. Seeley told the lawmakers. "It should not happen to anyone. Please do something about it."

Doing Something

In his flirtations with the world, confessed Augie March, the hero of Saul Bellow's picaresque novel, *The Adventures of Augie March,* he had displayed "a weak sense of consequences." Congress and HCFA have shown a similar weakness in their flirtations with Medicare. Each official act has portended a later embarrassment of unlooked for complications, and those in turn have inspired fresh rounds of half-considered erasures and revisions. (The move to repeal the 1988 Catastrophic Protection Act is but the latest example.)

It is not hard to see how the chain reaction got started, only to know where it will end. The logic of incrementalism seemed to call for political compromise, a dilution of the gift; compromise led to health-care inflation, inflation to cost containment, and containment, finally, to today's shabby decrementalism that bids fair to repossess the gift.

As so often happens in the wake of intellectual negligence, those measures have come to resemble steps in a cycle of no one's making and beyond everyone's powers to break. The pessimism implicit in all this both defines the process and becomes one of its major constraints.

It may be true, as Bernard De Voto remarked, that "Pessimism is only the name that men of weak nerves give to wisdom" ("Mark Twain: The Ink of History"). But is not optimism only the name that persons of weak faith give to social reform? Here I shall argue for a more hopeful approach to Medicare's chain-link history, suggesting that what it really represents is not the triumph of determinism but the correctable failure of political vision.

It seems a shame that no preamble, no bold declaration of intent, graces the original Medicare Act. For what has been lacking all along is a framework of pro-beneficiary principles within which our leaders can fashion policy. In the absence of explicit precepts has come improvisation: Congress has simply lurched from crisis to crisis.

What follow here are intimations of an outline for the preamble that Congress never wrote, mixed with a sampling of programmatic suggestions that seem consistent with Medicare's original purpose.

Easing the Pain

To begin with, Congress should declare its intention to restore and enlarge the gift. In returning to old incremental habits, the lawmakers will have to deal imaginatively with both ends of the inflation riddle—with the patient's out-of-pocket expenses as well as with the health-care industry's out-of-this-world prices. On the patient's side, no one enrolled in the program should feel compelled to go into debt to meet her health bills.

Congress could start by widening the beachhead it established in 1988. It could announce a moratorium on increases for all Medicare-related charges, including deductibles, copayments, and Part B premiums. It could also design a long-range plan and set long-range goals for rolling back the costs. We need a "Gramm-Rudman" for elderly patients, a way of systematically reducing their personal health-care budgets from year to year.

In addition, the Prospective Payments System should be declared a failure and given a decent burial. The miseries it spreads easily outweigh the savings it may generate. At bottom, PPS reflects a maldistribution of cost containment responsibilities: It asks too little from hospitals and too much from older patients. There are more humane devices at hand for subduing hospital prices, and I shall mention one of those in a moment.

The doctors, too, should be asked to play a deflationary role in these complex proceedings. If 1914 turned out to be much too early a conversion date for the AMA, then surely "The time now is here for the medical profession to acknowledge that it is tired of the eternal struggle for advantage over one's neighbor." Congress could make doctors more neighborly (and beneficiaries less worried) by requiring them to accept Medicare assignments in all cases. It works in Massachusetts. Why not try it in the other forty-nine states as well?

Medicare's benefit package, which has hardly been touched since the beginning, could stand a thorough overhaul. Here again, Congress's obligation is not to do everything at once but to commit itself to getting the job done over a period of years. The idea is to phase in new benefits that square more sensibly with elderly needs, starting with "spare parts" like eyeglasses and hearing aids and moving on eventually to long-term care both at home and in nursing institutions. (For more on long-term care, see Chapters 4 through 6.)

Taken together, all of the above suggestions might spare older Americans many dollars and as many griefs. They might also have a mercifully diminishing effect on the need for Medicaid; for by reducing out-of-pocket expenses and by expanding the range of medical benefits, the new measures could shorten the list of elderly poor who need extra help. In the meantime, Medicare would be that much closer to becoming what its originators meant it to be: a class-blind program.

A "Prevent" Defense

In reshaping the Medicare package, Congress should reserve ample space for preventive care, with special emphasis on checkups and monitorings by primary-care physicians. It makes no sense—and saves no dollars—to keep insisting that Medicare's beneficiaries are too old or too disabled to get any value from preventive medicine. As Anne R. Somers, the distinguished health-care commentator, has pointed out, "the most useful health practice for any Medicare enrollee is to seek early detection of suspected illness and immediate treatment." No one, she added, has taken the trouble to assess the cost effectiveness of early detection, "but we know very well the cost ineffectiveness of the current overuse of highly fragmented, technology-oriented specialty care."[12]

Here looms one promising way to restrain Medicare's unruly hospital bills, a large portion of which reflects precisely those exotic strains of medical practice that Somers thinks can be abated. "Far from transferring additional funds from low-technology primary care to high-technology tertiary care," she writes, the Medicare program "should now move . . . in the opposite direction."

The payoff could be substantial, even if the low-tech checkups actually headed off costly illnesses in only a small proportion of cases. As Somers has noted, Medicare's reimbursements are remarkably concentrated, with most of the dollars flowing to the few who are very sick. She asks us to consider the following 1982 figures: "Under the existing benefit structure, 39 percent of elderly Medicare enrollees received no reimbursement at all;. . . 54 percent received less than $100 and accounted for 0.4 percent of all reimbursements. At the other extreme, 14 percent accounted for 70 percent of the total reimbursements." (The few, in other words, were helped by the many, which is what social insurance is supposed to be all about: It brings "the magic of averages" to the rescue of those already on the far side of prevention.)

Whose Program Is This?

Congress also may wish to consider ways of restoring to older Americans their sense of personal connection with the Medicare program. The principle at work here—to amend Thomas Jefferson's famous dictum—should be as follows: That agency that communicates worst governs least. Over the years, Medicare has shown an amazing knack for alienating nearly everyone it speaks to, the vendors no less than the enrollees. Part of the problem has been all the cost-containment tampering. New systems like the DRGs only serve to widen the gulf that separates Medicare from its numerous constituencies. The patients especially are made to feel more like pawns than participants.

Both Congress and HCFA could do a lot to simplify and demystify the Medicare process. For instance, Congress could boldly slay the centaur by merging Parts A and B into a single, straightforward program. Few older Americans understand the distinctions anyway; they are a major source of confusion. And if the doctors' end of the centaur were no longer voluntary, then why preserve it as a separate entity?

HCFA, meanwhile, should resolve to speak plainer English and to make certain its surrogates do likewise. The explanations those contractors send to beneficiaries are anything but user friendly: Many read like a blend of kindergarten English and advanced calculus. HCFA could strike a blow for lucidity by tossing out the current batch of EOMBs and starting over from scratch. New formats should be pretested on a generous cross section of older Americans, including folks like the Arcadia snowbirds from Michigan.

People's anxieties might be further allayed if Medicare and its private contractors would answer their phones. Surely that is not too much to ask of a program meant to serve the old and the handicapped. HCFA is justly proud of its low administrative costs, which in 1985 amounted to only 1.3 percent of Medicare's total expenditures. But the lean budget contains a hidden price to beneficiaries, and *their* currency is time and worry. A 2 percent cost would still be acceptable—insurance companies commonly spend 7 percent of premium income for administration—and it might silence the busy signals. As things now stand, Medicare is putting millions of older Americans on hold.

Who, finally, will bear the costs of a resurgent incrementalism? As I have tried to suggest, the responsibility belongs to everyone—to vendors and consumers alike, to the young as well as the old. Like social security, Medicare is a kind of river in which all of us swim: In exchange for future protection the young keep providing for the old, and in time the upstream givers become the downstream takers.

But comparisons with social security are not entirely suitable. For the nature of Medicare decrees that the downstreamers must continue to carry a portion of the load. Besides, the whole arrangement ultimately depends on the behavior of a profit-oriented health-care industry whose avarice must somehow be moderated, if not radically transformed, into an unaccustomed altruism. We need the industry's healing hands even as we deplore its grasping ways. What we should strive for is not a dismantling of the health-care system but a more equitable distribution of the financial burden.

It is not that older Americans expect miracles from their government. On the contrary, as a group they seem unusually aware of the limits of federal largess. The pollster Louis Harris found in 1987 that nearly 40 percent were willing to take a cut in social security benefits if it meant that Medicare could then afford to offer more complete coverage. The widespread recognition that some such trade-off might be necessary underscored the elderly's many health-care anxieties; it also testified to their sense of shared obligation in making Medicare work better.

Many of the people I interviewed tended to worry out loud about the large amounts of money they felt they were costing the Medicare program. Like Dorothy Seeley, they believed that "no matter who is paying the bills, unnecessary expenses are unfair," and they seemed at least as protective of the federal treasury as they were of their own pocketbooks. In more than one instance I encountered beneficiaries who had voluntarily forsworn certain reimbursements on grounds that the charges were exorbitant—not for themselves but for taxpayers.

Irving Wolfe, a poor widower I met in Los Angeles, was one of those benefit-abstainers. Just turned eighty and gradually going deaf, he had been taking lip-reading lessons from a speech therapist twice a week at a neighborhood senior center. The lessons were important to him because, as he told me later, "I kill a lot of time at home watching TV. But what's the good of watching when you can't figure out what they're talking about?"

Medicare was paying 80 percent of Mr. Wolfe's bill and the speech therapist had agreed to forgo the remaining 20 percent. All the invoices went directly to the senior center's bookkeeper, who passed them along to Medicare, and Mr. Wolfe never saw the charges—at least not until the time a secretary got mixed up and sent him an invoice. It was a costly error.

"I couldn't believe my eyes," he said later. "That speech person was getting $100 an hour just for moving her lips. Can you imagine the government paying all that money? I felt terrible."

I asked Mr. Wolfe what he did then.

"What *could* I do?" he replied. "I cancelled the lessons."

CHAPTER THREE

◆

Shelter: Bring Us to This Hovel

> Kent: *Gracious my lord, hard by here is a hovel;*
> *Some friendship will it lend you 'gainst the tempest. . . .*
> Lear: *The art of our necessities is strange. . . .*
> *Come, bring us to this hovel.*
> —Shakespeare, *King Lear*

Although nearly 3 million older Americans now reside in some kind of federally subsidized dwelling, at least as many could instantly benefit from similar forms of assistance, were they available. It is mainly the ill-housed elderly on whom we shall focus here. Some have literally been left out in the cold: They belong to the ranks of America's homeless. Others have had to settle for makeshift dwellings beyond repair, and often for rents beyond belief. Still others are homeowners trapped in an inflationary cycle of taxes, upkeep, and utility bills.

The trap has many springs for renters and homeowners alike, the most terrifying of which is institutionalization. An aged resident may be too poor or frail to stay put but too scared to move. The authors of a study on older residents of Manhattan's West Side report that many occupy "semi-abandoned buildings lacking heat and hot water," yet they "live in constant worry of eviction. . . . Like a line of dominos, a lost check or a mugging can result in institutionalization."[1]

The elderly, of course, are not the only sufferers. If their residential needs are in some respects unique, they also reflect a national housing malaise that discriminates less by age than by class. The young as well as the old have been victims of a system widely assumed to be capable of healing social ills with profit-oriented remedies. Speculation,

77

inflation, and gentrification have all had their innings, and all have contributed to an alarming shortage of decent, reasonably priced housing.

Bulldozers have widened the affordability gap by toppling old neighborhoods to make room for shopping malls and luxury condominiums. It has been estimated that 2.5 million households are displaced each year, "some through publicly or privately financed redevelopment, others through abandonment."[2]

The White House and the Congress, meanwhile, have done little to intervene. Instead of inventing programs more suitable to the times, they have simply gutted the federal housing budget. Since 1981, Congress has given the Department of Housing and Urban Development (HUD) fewer and fewer dollars to work with. Incredibly, HUD's budget authority over the decade has been cut by 76 percent.[3]

The sharply reduced outlays have turned a vexing problem into a full-blown emergency. As we shall see, it was the elderly who had most to gain from earlier federal housing iniatives. Now, with inertia replacing initiative, it is the elderly who have most to lose.

A bit later in this chapter I shall present an overview of elderly housing conditions nationwide, paying particular attention to strains on the pocketbooks of the poor. Then, in tandem segments called "Digging In" and "Letting Go," I rely largely on elderly voices to recount the hazards of both entrenchment and displacement. A penultimate section traces the history of federal housing programs for the aged, taking into account the breakthroughs achieved as well as the hopes still to be realized. Finally, I consider what is to be done. Solutions are at hand; they only await a firm national commitment.

To begin with, though, it may be helpful to examine the difference that decent housing can make in the life of someone who is old and poor, and by extension, in the life of the general community. Edna Morrison lives in a subsidized apartment in Alexandria, Virginia. The apartment helps her stay productive, not as a job holder, but as a grandmother and a churchwoman. What she mainly produces are vital services to family and friends, considerations of the sort we all rely on to hold things together.

The Visit

"Would you like to see my place?" It is a pleasant May afternoon. Edna and I are sipping coffee at a picnic table beneath a flowering dogwood outside St. Martin's Senior Center. We have just met, and although we have hit it off instantly—"You call me Edna and I'll call you Dick"—her invitation surprises me. Few of my new acquaintances have appeared eager to let me see where they live. The quality of their housing has governed the extent of their hospitality.

Edna Morrison is a large black woman who wears leg braces and uses crutches. Locomotion is painful. "You just go ahead," she says as we inch toward my car. "Don't you worry none about me. I came into this world like you see me now: oversize and crippled. I had what they call the rickets. The doctor told my mother it was brought on by soft bones."

In the car she tells me more about her life. She was born in Alexandria in 1915, the youngest of seven children. "We never had money but we didn't think we was poor. My mother took in washing. She was a church person, just like me. She would give away her own money to the poor for food on Christmas and Thanksgiving, just like me. She belonged to the Love and Charity Club.

"All I knew growing up was church and work. I was born again when I was seven, and Mama wouldn't let me go to no parties after that. My father worked on the roads, when there was work. After I finished the eighth grade I went to work, too, 'cause nobody in the family didn't help out. I got a job in the laundry."

Edna married twice and had three children by the second marriage. "Joyce is the oldest and Robert is next—he's thirty-nine. Cindy is my baby. She was the late late show. I have eleven grandchildren. Think of that: *eleven.*"

She is warming to her subject. "I didn't have what you'd call a bad life," she says, "just a complicated one. My first marriage was to a minister, but he turned out already married. So I divorced him. My second marriage was to a smooth talker. He'd come home at three in the morning and I'd ask him where he'd been all night. He'd say, 'I ain't been nowhere but window shoppin' to see what you want for Christmas.' I divorced him, too. Well, after eighteen years I was fixin' to marry him again, but the Lord knew best. He took him away."

Edna lived in the same place—"a little house on South Alfred Street"—for forty-eight years, and paid off the mortgage with money she earned working in laundries and kitchens. "But when I got my heart condition I couldn't work no more to keep up the taxes." She sold the house in 1981, and most of the proceeds went for back taxes. Edna gave her children a share of what was left and banked $2,000 against a rainy day.

Then, for the first time in her life, housing became a problem: "At first I moved in with Joyce, but that didn't work out. We kept bumping into each other. Then I found a room on the other side of town and I stayed in it two years. I sat in that dark place and watched the roaches crawlin' around the linoleum. I didn't call nobody and nobody came to see me. I got sicker and sicker. Well, I'd been waitin' for one of those government apartments to open up, and when it did, I moved there quicker than a cockroach. 'Cept for my children getting born, that was the happiest day of my life."

We park in front of a development I shall call Maple Manor, a large brick complex made up of 2,300 apartments. Most of the units command luxury-style rents on the open market, but 300 are subsidized through a federal program called "Section 8," and Edna lives in one of those. She pays $90 a month (30 percent of her income) plus utilities.

We walk through a lilac-scented garden. Edna unlocks a door and we make our way painfully up a concrete staircase. She lives on the second floor. "Well," she says as she ushers me in, "this is my place."

The apartment overlooks the courtyard and gets the afternoon sun. Edna gives me a fast tour. There is a small, carpeted living room full of stuffed furniture, framed family photographs, and electronic devices—a TV set in one corner, a huge stereo in another. "My grandson gave me that stereo," Edna says, "so when he visits he can listen."

A formica-top counter separates the living room from the narrow kitchen, which features a large refrigerator, a gas stove and oven, and a double sink. Edna opens the refrigerator to show it off. It is gleamingly clean—and empty.

"And here's the bathroom," she goes on, opening another door. "I like the shower but I could use a tub." In the bedroom Edna calls my attention to her large closet. She also points out "my new bedroom suit," which she bought with the $2,000 she'd been saving. There is a gorgeous purple-and-orange quilt on the bed, and I ask her where she got it. "That's one I made myself," she answers. "I'm thinkin' of givin' it to this old lady I met at St. Martin's."

Back in the living room Edna invites me to "sit over there on my new couch. I want you to try it out." The couch seats four and is upholstered in a scratchy tweed. I remark on its stylish look.

"I gave the old one to Joyce's first-born when he got married," Edna tells me, "—something to get them started with, you know. And then I went out and got this new one. It cost me over $1,000, but the man lets me pay $73 a month and I don't mind. I needed to buy something beautiful to cheer me up. It gives me a new zeal on life. And it's where my grandchildren sleep. Two of them are coming tonight. They're in their teens, so they don't get on too good at home."

Edna is sitting next to a shiny green telephone. When it rings, she answers without saying hello. "That you, Carla? Thought so. When y'all comin'? That soon, huh? No, but I ain't cleaned yet."

"That's my church club," she explains as she hangs up. "We meet every month and it's usually here 'cause here's the best place. Yesterday I got cookies. Today's the day."

I ask Edna if she ever runs out of money, and she laughs. "Uh-huh," she says. "I got the rent and the couch and the 'lectric and the gas and all the medicines I got to take and the fire insurance and the cable TV, and I ain't even mentioned food. Yah, I runs out of money lots of times, 'specially 'round the birthdays and Christmas. That's when I'm hurtin', when I can't give no presents to my grandchildren."

A social worker has told Edna she is not eligible for social security because her employers failed to keep records or put money aside. But she could probably collect Supplemental Security Income if her son Robert, an officer in the U.S. Navy, consented to stop supporting her. At Robert's request the Navy sends Edna $300 each month out of his paycheck. She is proud of his loyalty: "When Robert was in his teens, he said to me, 'Mama, you took care of me when I couldn't take care of myself, and now I won't let you down.' And he never did." But she worries that she has become too much of a burden to Robert and his family. "He has a wife and five little children to feed," she says. "The money should be going to his babies."

I visited Edna several times, and each time I came away with a strong impression that the money we as a nation were spending on her housing—it amounted to about $5,000 a year—bought something very like her salvation. She may have exaggerated the dreadfulness of the room she lived in before moving to Maple Manor ("I sat in that dark room and watched the roaches"), but surely she did not exaggerate her feelings of depression during that difficult time. In her eyes, and perhaps in the eyes of her friends, the room diminished her. Very likely, too, its tawdriness discouraged her grandchildren from coming to see her.

Edna's present apartment affords her a view of the garden, a "pad" for the grandchildren, and a gathering point for friends. What such assets finally signify, to use Edna's own word, is her "place"—not only a place of residence but also a place of purpose within the larger community. By assuring Edna's continued usefulness to others, by preserving her social identity, the apartment makes it possible for her to keep on struggling.

But not everyone has been so fortunate as Edna Morrison.

The Status of Elderly Housing

Housing is a serious problem for a sizable minority of older Americans, who as a group occupy 21 percent of the nation's 88 million dwellings.

Among the poor overall, the elderly face disproportionate risks: They make up two of every five low-income households nationwide. To alter the terms slightly, HUD has identified close to 4 million elderly households with incomes below the official poverty line and another 1 million whose incomes exceed that threshold by less than 50 percent— the so-called near poor.[4]

About three-fourths of all elderly residences are said to be owner occupied, but in many such cases ownership is no guarantor against hardship, as can be seen from HUD's market-value estimates. Elderly dwellings account for 34 percent of all units valued at less than $40,000—this in a real estate market that is generally booming. The age of the houses, like that of their occupants, seems inversely related to their perceived worth: About two-thirds of all elderly residences were built at least forty years ago.

HUD has also tabulated some of the housing deficiencies that beset elderly owners and tenants alike. For instance, more than 1 million of their dwellings lack electrical wiring; about .5 million are without decent plumbing facilities; and some 3 million have no central heating. The elderly account for a third of all households using unvented room heaters.

In sorting out winners and losers among older households, we can discern a rough pecking order. Broadly speaking, rural residents fare worse than do metropolitan residents; renters worse than owners; and single persons worse than couples. At the lower depths are black older women who live alone and rent, and they account for 17 percent of *all* black elderly households.[5] If the nation ever decides to clean up its elderly housing act, it can begin here, where the keenest sufferers reside.

The High Cost of Hovels

For the losers, shelter expenses can be hard to bear. HUD's figures suggest that 2.6 million elderly poor households must spend 50 percent or more of personal income on housing. One way of assessing the scariness of that number is to express it as a proportion of older households that are eligible for, but not privy to, federally subsidized housing. In those terms, 56 percent of all unassisted elderly poor households consume at least half their incomes on shelter.

What money remains usually goes for food and medicine, and for little else. As a number of researchers have demonstrated, just the daily expense of keeping warm can overwhelm an aged resident already near the end of her rope. One study focused on households whose sole support came from Supplemental Security Income. Researchers found that in forty states, during the year's three coldest months, home fuel costs consumed nearly one-third of a person's maximum SSI benefit; in nine other states, more than half the maximum benefit; and in Maine, 71 percent of the maximum benefit.[6] The figures underscore the absurdity of the federal definition of poverty, which assumes that groceries, not rents or fuel, are the poor's biggest budget item.

According to Edwin Rothschild of the Citizen/Labor Energy Coalition, some 2.8 million older Americans "who live alone and are in poor health" risk succumbing to hypothermia, or loss of body heat caused by constant exposure to the cold. In Connecticut, the risk loomed so large that sympathetic citizens began knitting "hypothermia kits" consisting of blankets, slippers, hats, and scarves. In Colorado, Rothschild reported, "low-income elderly are living in bathrooms, huddled around kerosene heaters, because they cannot afford to turn on their furnaces." He said his coalition had received "numerous letters from people who spend winters in bed, wrapped in blankets and clothing, because they cannot afford heat."[7]

People who live in the Sun Belt have their own kind of energy problems. Here is Ruth Carlyle, a senior citizen from Tampa, Florida, testifying at the same hearing:

> I will tell you about my energy experience. . . . Last year, while waiting for a bus, I was overcome by heat. My electric bill was only $18 during the winter because we are very lucky, we don't need very much heat. . . . But [that summer] my electric bill went up from $18 to $92. I found myself keeping cool by going to the shopping malls and sitting in ladies' lounges in department stores. I am not going to wave the flag. This country has been very, very good to me, and I don't expect it to support me, but on $289 a month . . . I find it very hard to pay $90 a month [for electricity].[8]

Many of the elderly I interviewed were paying sacrificial sums for the most wretched of shelters. From them I learned just how strange "the art of our necessities" can be, and how much it can cost in courage as well as in dollars. Three sobering examples, plus one that is relatively cheering, must stand here for the whole.

Ivar Peterson, Eighty-six. Income from social security: $357 a month; rent: $135 (38 percent of income). Mr. Peterson lives in a small, spare room in the basement of a brick apartment building near downtown Minneapolis. An iron cot and a narrow wooden chair are his only furnishings. The bathroom, which he shares with three other tenants, is down the hall. There is a large steam radiator bolted to his ceiling, but "it doesn't give much heat," Mr. Peterson says. "I had two coats on yesterday." The only entertainment he can afford is "taking a walk some days." But he complains that the landlord does not always clear the walkway of snow: "I feel a little wobbly sometimes. Once I fell in the soft snow. I didn't want to get up."

Walt and Evelyn, Both in Their Seventies. Combined SSI income: $472; rent: $257 (54 percent of income), plus $40 a month for gas and electricity; total housing expenses: $297 (63 percent of income). Walt and Evelyn live in Hartford, Connecticut, where they occupy cramped quarters—four dirty walls and a damp ceiling. One end of the double bed has been shoved into an open closet: The bed is too long for the room. Walt, a retired janitor, has a cheerful manner. "Most of the pipes leak," he tells me. "When we sit on the toilet, we have to hold a newspaper over our head to keep dry. It's good exercise. Another way I stay fit is killing roaches."

"What do you kill them with?" I ask.

"My fist," he says with a smile and pounds the wall.

Alfonso and Elizabeth Gutierrez, in Their Late Sixties. Income from SSI and Elizabeth's part-time jobs: $478; mortgage, taxes, and insurance: $219 a month (46 percent of income), plus $30 for electricity, $25 for gas, and $20 for water; total housing expenses: $294 (62 percent of income). Mr. and Mrs. Gutierrez are Cuban refugees. They live on the outskirts of Miami in a four-room cinderblock house their son helped them purchase in 1973. In those days both parents did seasonal work in the tomato fields. Now Mrs. Gutierrez finds occasional factory work. The house is close to adequate, but the roof leaks in three places. Mr. Gutierrez cannot fix it himself—he suffers from emphysema—nor can he afford to hire someone. They are four months behind in their mortgage payments, and Mrs. Gutierrez fears they will lose the house. "We have no extra money," she says. "My husband needs medicine. I did not think being old like this would be so hard."

Susan Williams, Seventy-four, and David Williams, Seventy-five. Income from social security and a veteran's pension: $519; house taxes, utilities, heat, and insurance: $160 (31 percent of income). The Williamses live on Bloom Street in Jackson, Mississippi. Their low-lying area, misnamed "High Towers Neighborhood," is subject to frequent flooding. "Back a few years we had five feet of water in the house," Mrs. Williams says. They bought the house in 1947 for less than $3,000. It is of the type known in those parts as a "shotgun bungalow"—so named, I have been told, "because you can shoot through the front door and the bullet will come out the back door. Nothing but a hallway between doors." Eight persons besides Mr. and Mrs. Williams live there: two daughters, a son-in-law, four grandchildren, and an older brother of Mrs. Williams. At night, with everyone home from work and school, the house gets crowded.

Still, the roof is tight, the rooms are dry and warm, and the mortgage is paid. The difference between this family's circumstances and those of the others is in part due to Mr. Williams's veteran's pension (he fought in World War II) and in part to the job he held at Union Hose Corporation for twenty-nine years. His wages never exceeded $3 an hour, but they were enough to pay off the mortgage before he retired.

Digging In

The Williamses' long tenure on Bloom Street reflects another important trait of many elderly residents: No matter how inadequate the dwelling, they prefer to stay where they are. According to Leo Baldwin of the American Association of Retired Persons (AARP), "Seventy percent of all people who reach the age of 65 will die with the same residential address as the day they reached 65. So we're not talking about a very mobile market."[9] Thoreau would not have been surprised. "Our lives," he commented, "are domestic in more ways than we think."

A prospectus published by the Commonwealth Fund, a New York–based charitable foundation, offers a precise summary of the elderly's domestic attachments: "Most elderly people prefer to remain at home even if their ability to maintain independent life declines. . . . For them, home is the place where families grew and friendships flourished. It is the center of things accessible and familiar. It is the key to a lifetime of feelings and memories."[10]

In Chicago I was told a story by Jerry Riemer, a young, soft-spoken Lutheran minister who runs a neighborhood center called the Uptown Ministry. Most Uptown residents are old and poor. There are eighteen nursing homes in the area.

"There was an old woman," said Riemer, "who was going to be sent to a nursing home in an ambulance. She had been making a fuss—she definitely did not want to go—so I was asked to come along and help smooth the way.

"Well, before we'd gone very far she insisted that we turn around. 'I have to get my things,' she kept saying. 'There is a letter I want to take with me.'"

The place they returned to was a tiny room with four bare walls, and what few things of hers remained did not fill a small paper bag. But she found the letter and she seemed content.

"Did you get a look at it?" I asked Riemer.

"Yes. It was a Christmas card—from a local bank."

It is not surprising that younger Americans change their residences three times more frequently than do older Americans. In youth we turn outward, impatient to spread our wings. In old age our bones demand more predictable consolations: the rosebush in the yard, the family photographs on the shelf, the cat at our feet. Our very walls take on new meaning. In the language of gerontology, we prefer to "age in place," and at times the preference shades into obstinacy. It is then that we dig in for the duration, whatever the cost: We shall not be moved.

But for many older Americans, to age in place is no simple task. The poor in particular must struggle for a firm purchase and then hang on tight. That is why any discussion of elderly housing conditions must take into account the fear of expulsion as well as the solace of stability. The two are part of a single dilemma.

Sisu

The Finns have a word for it—*sisu*—which means to "keep on going," or just "guts." There are quite a few Finns in Houghton County, Michigan, where the elderly make up about 10,000 of the 40,000 residents. As in other parts of rural America, most of the county's aged (four of every five) own their dwellings, but some of these are hovels that lend scant friendship against the tempest.

Houghton County is part of the state's northern peninsula, separating Lake Michigan from Lake Superior. Once it was rich in copper and lumber, but the mines are shut down now and the logging isn't what it used to be. The old people there were never prosperous, not even in their prime; and because the logging bosses they worked for commonly paid them in cash, with no written records to show for it, their minimal social security benefits keep them poor. The housing reflects the poverty.

Michael Aten, a young man, has been living up there for six years, working for the local branch of an international care-giving organization called Friends of the Elderly. One of his responsibilities is to help people move out of their freezing backwoods shacks and into warm, subsidized "senior housing" available at modest rents in towns like Hancock and Laurium. It has not been easy.

I interviewed Aten by telephone the day after Christmas. He said he'd been cutting wood all day and delivering loads to those on his "most in need" list. "It's going to be tough this year. People are running out of wood before the winter's half over. We've had 150 inches of snow this month alone."

Yet none of Aten's clients seemed ready to move. "Rural people like their independence," Aten told me. "There was a man I knew—he must have been in his nineties—who actually had a stroke and still wouldn't leave his place. I found him one day chopping wood *on his knees*. He couldn't even stand up, but he refused to switch to an apartment in town where all he'd have to do for heat was flick the thermostat. I can't really blame him. He knew what he wanted."

Mayme Kemppainen is seventy-six. The house she has lived in much of her life is falling down around her. Part of it caved in after the blizzard of 1984, when she had felt too weary to climb up and shovel the heavy snow off the roof. It took longer for the other side to go— it just seemed to rot away. Now Miss Kemppainen is confined with her dog and two cats to a single room, ten feet by twelve, where she does all her cooking, eating, and sleeping.

The mechanical facilities are not the best, but in Houghton County neither are they the worst. A kerosene space heater works some of the time. Thanks to Aten's diligence, the house has both electricity and running water, though the water is not for drinking because the new well is shallow and sandy. For potable water Mrs. Kemppainen must travel twelve miles to a public restroom, where she can fill up her six half-gallon milk jugs. She ties the plastic jugs together with string, for easier carrying to and from the bus.

But transportation has proved a problem ever since her arthritis got so bad that she had to start using a walker. The bus won't stop for her any more because the walker slows her down and the driver grows impatient. Now, when she runs out of drinking water, she must wait for Aten or a neighbor to come by in a car.

Every winter Aten reminds Mayme Kemppainen that she doesn't have to endure the isolation, the temperamental kerosene stove, the sagging remnant of a house: She can move into the senior project at Laurium. All she has to do is say the word. And every winter she agrees, promising that this will surely be her last winter in the woods. But then comes the thaw, and with it second thoughts. What will become of her dog and her cats if she moves to town? And what will happen to *her*, tucked away among all those strangers in a citified building with long hallways a person could get lost in? She can name people like herself, folks getting on in years, who tried that peculiar way of life and didn't last two weeks. Quicker than you'd think they'd packed up and gone back to their little cabins. Too much noise, they said. Too many rules.

Well, maybe she won't go to Laurium just yet. Maybe she can tough it out just one more winter. *Sisu.*

A Little Piece of the United States

Thelma Poole was born in Sweden in 1910 and has lived in the same house in Minneapolis for more than half her years. It is a two-story, wooden-frame "fourplex," just a mile south of downtown, which she and her husband bought in 1938 for $2,700. The down payment took all their savings. "My husband was a chauffeur and a gardener for a very rich family," she told me. "We didn't have much money but my husband was smart with his hands. He fixed our house just right."

Her husband died in 1978: "I miss him terrible. Nothing seems to matter any more. All I cared for was . . . was . . . I can't think of the word. It's something like 'togetherness' but that's not it."

I had come to Mrs. Poole's house one wintry afternoon at the suggestion of Julie Gamber, a young woman who worked for the Minneapolis chapter of Friends of the Elderly. "It's not a pleasant place to spend time in," she had warned.

"This lady stays forever in one room. She never goes out. The other three apartments are empty, so it's not as if she gets any rent money. A few months ago a woman on welfare moved into some of the rooms downstairs. She didn't pay rent, she just squatted there with her children and her boyfriend. They played music all day and all night—the kind that thumps. It drove Thelma bats. When you're very old, you're helpless. People can just invade your space and do anything they please. The city finally got them out of there, so now the place is empty again except for Thelma upstairs. I'll take you there."

The front door is unlocked. We walk up the groaning staircase and enter a shadowy room that smells of stale food and urine. My feet find trash at every step—twisted cans, plastic dishes, crushed paper bags. Accidentally I kick something large and round, and it rolls across the floor. It is an empty bird cage.

"I used to have canaries." The voice is Scandinavian and lilting. "Oh, what music they made! Not like those tenants and *their* music. That wasn't music at all—just crazy crazy sounds."

Thelma Poole is lying beneath blankets on a bed in the far corner, her white head resting on a dingy pillow. "Oh, you are a tall one," she says to me, extending a skeletal hand in greeting. She must have been a beautiful woman. Even now her large eyes hold me. They are a deep blue.

Julie says, "Thelma, this gentleman is writing a book. He wants to know how you are getting along in your house."

"Getting along? Well, you see me here. It is a good house. When we bought it, it was just a ramshackle. I said to my husband, 'This house looks like an old pirate's nest, but to us it's a palace.' My friends,

oh, how they made fun of it! They wanted to know how in the world
we could buy such an old ramshackle. But later they kept quiet. *They*
didn't have anything, you see, and we had this house, a little piece
of the United States, and when I woke up I could step out on my
own little lot."

Mrs. Poole doesn't step out anymore. The doors to her kitchen and
bedroom seem permanently shut, and the room we are in, the living
room, is indeed the one in which she does all her living. For food
Mrs. Poole depends on Meals on Wheels, which delivers two meals
each weekday. She does not eat on weekends. Her monthly social
security check is mailed directly to the bank where she has a checking
and savings account, as are her fuel and tax bills. Mrs. Poole is not
much bother to the rest of us. She has outlived all her close relatives;
she has no telephone. People from Friends of the Elderly and other
agencies look in on her from time to time, but beyond cheering her
up and making her comfortable, there seems little they can do.

The house, meanwhile, is slowly reverting to its ramshackle state.
There are leaks in the pipes and holes in the plaster. Minnesota storms
have cracked several windows and torn away some of the roofing as
well as many of the gutters. Nothing gets repaired. One sees a reverse
symbiosis at work here, in which house and owner simultaneously
deteriorate, growing less and less capable of protecting each other. It
is not an uncommon condition in America. Among persons seventy-
five years old and older, some 70 percent still reside in their own
homes and nearly half the owners have incomes below the poverty
line. In tabulations made during the late 1970s, about one-quarter of
such dwellings were found to have "persistent deficiencies" such as
leaks, unvented room heaters, and inadequate plumbing or electrical
wiring. Deficiency rates in rural areas reached 35 percent.[11]

We lack the programs and institutions needed to allow these determined homeowners to age gracefully in place. In Thelma Poole's
case, where helpful measures seem feasible, none has been taken.
Surely tenants could be found for the vacant apartments downstairs;
surely portions of their rent could be paid in essential services—in
maintenance work around the house, for instance, and in home care
for Mrs. Poole. Such a plan does not appear farfetched, yet it would
require initiatives and arrangements for which no agency at present,
not even Friends of the Elderly, seems prepared to take responsibility.

So Mrs. Poole remains trapped in her cage. Her alternative—the
only real option society has granted her—is to surrender body and
soul to a nursing home. It is a recourse at which I gently hint as we
take leave. Wouldn't she receive better care, I wish to know, in a
different kind of place?

The question astonishes Mrs. Poole. "Why should I want to leave my house?" she finally asks, her eyes opening very wide. "No, I think I die here."

Letting Go

People cannot always choose their dying places. A few years ago Mary Chambord, now an Uptown resident, wished to stay forever in the West Side apartment she and her family had called home for more than two decades. "It was really the only place I wanted to be," she told me. "I figured sooner or later I'd die in my kitchen. And you know what? I almost did." More recently, she just wanted to die, period—it didn't matter where. There are tales more dramatic than Mrs. Chambord's, but few more representative of her working-class generation's search for a safe harbor amid the geriatric storm.

She is a seventy-year-old Chicagoan, a large red-headed woman whose bifocals keep slipping down her nose. In the summer of '84, desperate for a place she could call her own, she took a single room in a "retirement residence" I shall call Balfour House. It is an old-fashioned stone building with a gilded lobby, an enormous dining room, and a "TV lounge" that Mrs. Chambord likes to frequent. Balfour House is a proprietary enterprise licensed by the state, with a twenty-four-hour telephone switchboard and a trained nurse always on call. For revenue it depends on the tenants' social security and public assistance checks.

Mrs. Chambord went there directly from a nursing home, where she had spent eight years recuperating from a number of serious maladies. Her older brother, she said, had taken a nearby room in the same nursing home.

"I'd been wanting to leave the institution for some time. I kept saying to my brother, 'You make arrangements to get out of here and we can both live together somewhere cheap. We'll manage.' But he never made the arrangements.

"One day the hospital called and told me my brother had had a heart attack, in fact two of them, and they had tried to save him but they couldn't."

The next week she moved into Balfour House. Her tiny rectangle on the fifth floor bulges with massive, dark-brown hotel furniture. The books atop her dresser are piled ceiling-high, covering up a wall mirror; more books lie scattered on the gray linoleum floor. The walls, painted a dull yellow, are bare except for a drugstore calendar hanging from a nail beside the entranceway. There are cans of juice on the windowsill, along with a hot plate and a little pile of pink Sweet 'n Low packets. (She suffers from diabetes.) The day I visited—a very cold January morning—the radiator was bubbling hot and the windows were wide open.

Mrs. Chambord shares a bathroom with her neighbor in the adjoining room. "It's a nuisance," she said, "but I can't be too particular for what I pay." Her rent is $325 a month, which includes three meals a day served in the congregate (communal) dining room. She collects $299 in social security and gets "extra help from welfare" ($103 a month from the state). The $77 that's left after she's paid the rent is "enough to keep me in cigarette money."

She made instant coffee for us on her hot plate, and she was gracious throughout; yet something in her manner struck a melancholy note. Her speech dragged noticeably, like a tape played at too slow a speed.

"My husband was a construction worker from Canada," she told me. "He spoke better French than English, so we never talked much to each other. That was OK. We kept busy."

She had married soon after graduating from high school. They set up housekeeping in a one-bedroom apartment on the West Side, "but after Leonard was born we moved to a bigger place on the same block. When Nicky came along we didn't move. We'd been paying rent so long we felt like it belonged to us. There were sixteen years between Leonard and Nicky. He was what you'd call a surprise child."

Her husband died on Thanksgiving Day, 1975, and some months later Nicky joined the army. Leonard had long since married and settled in Arizona. Suddenly Mrs. Chambord was gazing at an empty nest.

"I began to put on a great deal of weight. I weighed 225 pounds. I had difficulty walking and breathing. The doctor was giving me medicine—I don't know what it was, tell you the truth. Anyway, this is what they tell me: Somebody from the church came over to see me—a woman. They found me on the floor. At the hospital they told me I'd had a heart attack, and after I got better the doctor said to me. 'We don't think you can take care of yourself. We think you ought to go into a nursing home.' So I went to the same one my brother was living in. We always got along, you see.

"That's when I lost all my things—my pictures, my letters, my books, my dishes, my furniture. I just walked out and left everything behind me, because I didn't have anybody to store them with. I imagine the landlady kept most of it; some of the things I had were in very good shape. I always saw to it that the children took good care of their things. There was a sled in the basement that still looked brand new. All the furniture you see here belongs to the hotel. None of it's mine."

Toward the end of our interview I asked Mrs. Chambord how she liked living at Balfour House. Her answer was more than I had bargained for. "There's something I ought to explain to you," she began.

"At first everything was going along fine. Then my other brother died, my younger brother, and I took that very hard. And the woman I shared the bathroom with, she died too. I liked her. We used to sit around evenings and talk about people in general, and I would give her my books to read. Her name was Mary, too.

"Well, one time I sat here—it was in the evening—and I went over to the drawer, got a knife and began sawing on my wrist. I also took an overdose of pills that I had, and I don't remember anything else. However, a nurse found me—we have a nurse here on duty all the time—and I asked her afterward how did she know I needed help. She said, 'because you called me.' I don't remember calling her. Maybe I wanted to live after all."

In the lottery that often determines housing for the elderly poor, Balfour House seems neither the best nor the worst of draws. For Mary Chambord it became a timely haven, a way to shake free of institutionalization's chains while being assured warm shelter, daily sustenance, and even a measure of care. Its round-the-clock nursing service probably saved her life. On the other hand, the dreary and expensive cubicle to which she was consigned, and the loneliness it must have engendered, doubtless deepened her bereavement and contributed to her own brush with death.

Elderly Homelessness

If some displaced older Americans have managed to find more agreeable quarters than those afforded by Balfour House, many have had to settle for considerably less.

One rainy morning Dorothy Lykes, not knowing where else to turn, telephoned the Gray Panther office in New York City.

Mrs. Lykes was 78, terminally ill with cancer, and weighed 70 pounds. Her husband was in the hospital, also terminally ill. Most of their Social Security was going for his hospital bills. The city had taken possession of their Bronx home, which they bought in the 1950s, because they could not pay the property taxes. Nor could they pay the $300 a month rent the city was asking from them for living in their own home. Mrs. Lykes asked: "Is the next step for me to move to Penn Station?"[12]

Increasingly now, our older residents are being forced to move out of their single rooms, their rented apartments, even their own homes—

places and neighborhoods they have lived in for generations. And in more cases than is generally recognized, these refugees have no place to turn. Thus to the pain of relinquishment is added the nightmare of homelessness.

One study of states in the northeast concluded that elderly people there make up about 30 percent of the homeless.[13] An analysis by Mary Ellen Hombs and Mitch Snyder (of the Community for Creative Non-Violence) noted that those who "populate our city streets" are mainly "the old, the sick, the mentally ill, the unemployed, the disabled, the displaced and the disenfranchised." It is not unusual for a single individual to embody all seven traits. Hombs and Snyder emphasized still another characteristic of street people—their invisibility: "Thus, the older woman next to you on the bus may be going nowhere in particular, riding only to keep warm or dry or seated. . . . In the world of the streets, invisibility equals access, and those who can pass unnoticed into public places . . . suffer less abuse and harrassment."[14]

The elderly's street-wise invisibility has been matched by a calculated myopia on the part of federal officials; they have doused the homeless aged with vanishing cream. In 1984 a HUD functionary named Carol Bauer assured a congressional committee that "our current programs are adequate to provide a coordinated package of housing choices designed to prevent the elderly from entering the homeless category."[15] (Bauer's title at HUD would have delighted Nicolay Gogol. She was executive assistant to the deputy assistant secretary for policy, financial management and administration.)

In fact, the range of choices available to poor people of all ages has been shrinking for at least a decade, along with the federal resolve to lend them a helping hand. Certainly for older citizens there is no such thing as "a coordinated package" of affordable housing, only a forlorn heap of once-promising programs lately eviscerated.

But I am getting ahead of my story.

The Federal Commitment: A History

It would not be difficult to imagine a rough topographical "picture" of the federal commitment to low-income housing as it has developed over the decades. In the background we might place a large desert to represent the arid years prior to 1937. The desert would yield gradually to more fertile stretches that climb toward the green uplands of the 1960s; then a sudden descent into an almost forgotten valley known as "Nixon's Rest Area" (1973–1974), followed by another hill, which peaks at decade's end. The gulf that yawns beyond could be called "Reagan's Ravine."

But the size of our picture may be misleading, for in the larger scheme of things all the elements would appear as little more than a brush stroke. The truth is that America has never quite accepted the idea of decent housing as a universal right or entitlement; year after discouraging year federal assistance to people in urgent need of shelter has constituted less than 1 percent of the national budget and reached fewer than 25 percent of the poor.

Of this mouselike portion, however, it must be said that older Americans have enjoyed a lion's share. Today they occupy 39 percent of all government-subsidized housing. Only the rural programs, those supported by the Farmers Home Administration, appear to have short-changed the older population relative to other age groups. Of the 1.9 million households assisted by that agency, just 207,000, or 11 percent, are elderly.

The other programs present a very different picture: In public housing, 541,000 older households make up 45 percent of the total; in the two rent supplement programs known as "Section 8," 983,000 elderly units constitute 48 percent of the total; and in the "Section 202" program, which offers building loans to local nonprofit sponsors, older households (188,000) and handicapped households (12,000) make up the entire roster of beneficiaries. The numbers overall suggest that elderly assisted housing is now a large fish in a very small pond.[16]

There was a time when the elderly were nowhere near the pond. The public housing program started in 1937 with passage of the Wagner-Steagall Low Rent Housing Act, and its target was not the elderly poor but the millions of younger families displaced and made destitute by the Great Depression. Reformers back then had a tendency both to identify with and to romanticize the poor. Eleanor Roosevelt characterized the homeless of her day as "the finer people" who had "adventure in their souls." She was struck by "the beauty of some of the children" and their "bright minds."[17]

Early beneficiaries of public housing were seen not as dependents but as people temporarily down on their luck. In Alvin Schorr's words, they were "families who voluntarily sought to improve their housing but could not afford private rentals."[18]

It was not until the massive urban renewal and slum-clearance projects of the 1950s, which dislocated huge numbers of poor people, that the program—to cite the social commentator Chester Hartman—came to be viewed as "'last resort' housing for the economy's cast-offs."[19] The upshot might have been expected but wasn't: an increasingly affluent, largely white America started insisting that public housing projects be placed in neighborhoods far from their own, where they had the effect of augmenting the very slums they had been meant to replace. The sociologist Nathan Glazer would later observe that public housing in the popular mind became "a graveyard of good intentions."[20]

The Greener Uplands

At that critical moment the federal housing pendulum began to swing sharply toward older Americans. In 1956 only 2 percent of the nation's public housing units were occupied by elderly tenants. The proportion rose to 19 percent by 1964 and to 46 percent by 1984. In the interim several new housing programs had been inaugurated, one of them (Section 202) aimed almost exclusively at assisting older tenants. As Jon Pynoos, a University of Southern California gerontologist, has pointed out, "In spite of the limited resources of their interest group, . . . the elderly have been a prime beneficiary of federally subsidized housing programs."[21]

What lay behind the elderly's remarkable gains? Society's interests seemed partly political, partly demographic. To suburbanites who had been rejecting proposals for low-income projects in their towns, the presence of *older* poor people appeared less threatening a prospect and, in the bargain, a convenient appeaser of uneasy consciences. In addition, people had already begun to take note of the old-age population boom and to wonder out loud where all the new senior citizens could find places to live. As far back as 1950 delegates to the First National Congress on Aging had pointed with alarm to the growing demand for elderly housing and had called for swift federal action.

In fact, a handful of pioneer thinkers in the field had been recommending such measures for more than a decade. Among them was a remarkable woman named Marie C. MaGuire (later Thompson), who in many respects can be considered the founding mother of federal housing for older Americans. Her story neatly encapsulates the evolution of elderly housing, both the victories scored and the setbacks endured.

Mrs. MaGuire staked much of her distinguished career on finding ways to build decent shelters for older Americans. The career began in Houston, Texas, where in 1942 the local Public Housing Authority hired her as manager of a new project. She was thirty-eight years old. Early on, she noticed that many of the project's applicants were considerably older than the conventional portrait of public housing tenants had led her to expect. Quite a few were widows or widowers, and their applications were perforce rejected: The law in those days specifically barred single persons from tenancy in low-rent projects.

Those few older applicants who did gain entrance soon discovered that their new apartments had not been designed for the likes of them. "The floors were bare concrete," Mrs. MaGuire recalled when I interviewed her in her Washington, D.C., apartment. "All the old people complained about the cold floors. And there were many accidents. The shelves were too high—people had to stand on chairs, and sometimes they fell off. The frailer tenants couldn't get out of their bathtubs because there were no grab bars. One woman actually drowned in the tub."

Mrs. MaGuire resolved that one day she would plan a project to answer the special needs of older tenants. She edged closer to that goal in 1949, when the city of San Antonio asked her to direct its Public Housing Authority. Now, at least, her voice would be heard in decision-making councils. But she had to wait until 1956 before Congress cleared the way. In that watershed year the lawmakers lifted restrictions on single-person occupancy of low-rent housing and instructed local housing Authorities "to give preference to admission of the elderly. . . . This preference is to be prior to any other preference." Congress also recognized that older residents might require extra amenities: It earmarked an additional $500 in project construction money for every elderly household.

Mrs. MaGuire did not need to be pushed. In an application fired off to Washington, she pointed out that the elderly population in Texas had increased by an astonishing 20 percent in just five years. In Greater San Antonio they numbered 37,000, and nearly one-quarter were living with their children or with other relatives. She proceeded to give Washington officials a short course in housing's role vis-à-vis the elderly. "At varying chronological ages," she wrote, "old age ceases to be academic. Old age is a condition that demands individual attention. Society must provide the setting for such attention." She held out the hope that "enlightened communities" would provide housing that permitted "the aged to live independently, insuring that privacy which equates with personal dignity."

Apparently Washington got the point. The result was a six-story, 184-unit project named Victoria Plaza Apartments, the nation's first low-rent housing complex designed and built exclusively for older citizens. It opened, amid much fanfare, on July 2, 1960, with rents starting at $25.50 a month.

"From the first," noted the authors of a special brochure published eight months after the opening, "the residents were joyful about their new homes." It was easy to see why. The new building was equipped with many of those age-targeted niceties Mrs. MaGuire had found lacking elsewhere: ramps, nonskid floors, grab bars, an elevator with a bench, storage space that required no reaching up or bending down, even "sit-down" showers where one could take one's sudsy ease. (The glass was shatter-proof. The seats were made of Alaskan birch, a wood impervious to water.)

The project, moreover, was within easy walking distance of stores and churches. Mrs. MaGuire had been "aghast" at the placement of some earlier projects: "They were sitting in the middle of meadows, far away from everything." The prime location of Victoria Plaza paid off in tenant morale as well as convenience, a dividend that earlier had been identified by the Senate Committee on Labor and Public Welfare in its ten-volume *Studies of the Aged and Aging.* "Not only do older persons want to be in the center of things," the committee had observed, "but they want to feel they are an active part of community life."

For Victoria Plaza tenants, some of that community life would occur on the premises. The building included a community activities center on the first floor, where a number of city agencies quickly set up shop—for health, recreation, and library services, among others. Here was "the setting" in which elderly people could receive "individual attention."

Less formal activities took place in the lobby. "That's when I found out how important it was to have a large lobby with plenty of seating," Mrs. MaGuire recalled. People enjoyed coming together: "They would start waiting for the mail an hour before it was due to arrive. It wasn't just the mail they wanted—it was the social life." The lobby represented something of an aesthetic triumph as well. Mrs. MaGuire had been able to raise an extra $100,000 from local philanthropists for the purchase of artwork. "I wanted to introduce the thought of beauty," she said.

Victoria Plaza appears to have been a turning point in the development of housing for older Americans: It converted an abstraction into bricks and mortar. Housing officials from cities with problems identical to San Antonio's made pilgrimages there to look and learn. The parade grew so long that Mrs. MaGuire began passing out printed guides. She also mailed out some three hundred architectural blueprints to planners who had written in for information. The seeds thus planted, some of them started to sprout, with Victoria Plaza replicas springing up in many places.

The project was also a turning point in Marie MaGuire's career. The following year she went to Washington to serve as President Kennedy's commissioner of public housing, a position she held through 1966. When the Public Housing Administration became part of the newly created Department of Housing and Urban Development, she stayed on as HUD's special adviser on problems concerning the elderly and handicapped. She retired in 1972.

Mrs. MaGuire's time in office happened to coincide with elderly housing's golden years. The signs could not have been more favorable. Congress had already given its blessing to Section 202 (in the Housing Act of 1959), which helped nonprofit sponsors to build rental and cooperative housing for older Americans. (The law was amended in 1964 to include the handicapped.) In 1963 President Kennedy promised major new housing initiatives for the elderly. Not surprisingly, federal investments in elderly housing quadrupled between 1961 and 1964, and the number of elderly units actually completed during those years increased ninefold. Few doubted Moses J. Gozonsky, a federal housing official, when he boasted, "Housing for the elderly has become a growth industry, but its future growth should dwarf all previous records."[22]

The advent of the Great Society only confirmed the obvious. In a message to the Congress delivered in March 1965, Lyndon Johnson declared his intent "to ensure a steadily increasing supply of federally assisted housing for older Americans." He was as good as his word. By 1968, the annual total of public housing units under construction had risen from 35,000 to 103,000; about one-third were earmarked for older tenants. The new Section 202, meanwhile, had already accounted for 45,000 additional elderly units.

It was a moment worth savoring: Twelve years before, we had falteringly begun to confront the critical shortage of affordable housing for older citizens. Now we were well on our way toward a solution. All we had to do was keep pushing—or so it appeared.

Nixon's Rest Area

In fairness, Richard Nixon did not hold a patent on the ensuing retreat. In 1968, with Johnson a "lame duck" in the White House, HUD decided to phase out all new construction under Section 202 and replace it with a less age-oriented program. The substitute enacted by Congress that year (Section 236) assisted tenants of all ages rather than just the elderly. The 202 program lay buried in HUD until 1975, when Congress exhumed it, rewrote it, and put it back to work. The good repute it enjoys today, however, belies its surprisingly limited impact. Less than 3 percent of poor older households enjoy 202 housing subsidies, yet the Senate Special Committee on Aging has called this form of assistance "the flagship of federal housing programs for the elderly."[23]

At the start of his second term (January 1973), Richard Nixon made a deteriorating situation still worse by announcing a freeze on all shelter construction subsidies, including those for public housing. The moratorium would last nearly two years and would deprive nearly one million low-income households of their chances for adequate shelter.

"I could never understand the Nixon moratorium," Marie MaGuire said in our interview. "They claimed it was to give them time to think up new ideas, but I suspect it was just their way of saving some money. In any case, it was devastating."

HUD's two years of enforced meditation were not entirely wasted. Besides the eventual disinterment of the 202 program, the interlude's happiest effect on older Americans was the drafting of Section 8 legislation, which Congress passed in late 1974 as part of its landmark Housing and Community Development Act. The Section 8 measure came in two parts, one for new or rehabilitated housing and one for old housing. In both instances, low-income tenants were charged rents at below-market levels, with HUD making up the difference through payments to landlords.

As we have seen, the elderly poor have made considerable use of this program. But in 1983, at the Reagan administration's urging, Congress threw out the program's new-housing component—so now the poor must settle for half a loaf. (A wit who works on the Hill has suggested that the program's name be changed to "Section 4.")

As was the case with quite a few other social welfare measures passed in the mid-1970s, the 1974 Housing and Community Development Act marked the end of a more bountiful era. Henceforth, lawmakers would shrink from making further programmatic leaps, while presidents would call for withdrawals along a wide front. In Jimmy Carter's time the federal housing commitment fell off noticeably, dropping from 517,000 newly completed assisted units in 1976 to 206,000 in 1980. In Ronald Reagan's era the descent grew even more precipitous.

Reagan's Ravine

The chief goals of Reagan's housing policies were "to shrink the growth of programs as far as possible and to replace the solutions . . . with cheaper options."[24] In this he succeeded admirably, but not half so well as he seemed to wish. Congress on the whole temporized, yielding to some of the president's demands while elsewhere digging in its heels. During the last seven years of the 1980s, the White House and HUD requested $465 million in housing assistance; Congress appropriated $62 billion.

The administration may well have felt free to press for wholesale elimination of essential housing programs only because it was certain that Congress would not go along. There is something unappealing about using such a tactic. It brings to mind the little boy who relies on his parents to stop him from being naughty. Before they can intervene, of course, considerable damage may be wrought.

The damage in this case, as Struyk has noted, "is absolutely clear: the poor have lost." In HUD-sponsored programs, "The actual number of newly assisted households was only one-third to one-quarter of that during the Carter years." For the first time in recent memory annual totals of subsidized housing starts dipped below six digits. The drop was dramatic: In 1980, HUD started 183,000 subsidized units; in 1983, 81,000; in 1988, 10,000. Low as those numbers were, they would have been much lower had Congress simply rubber-stamped the president's recommended budgets.[25]

The steep decline in new construction reflected the administration's customarily sanguine view of the marketplace and the miracles it could achieve. Despite a large body of evidence to the contrary, HUD had concluded that there was sufficient housing out there for everyone, even for the poor, who had only to seek in order to find. Neither the record-low vacancy rates being reported by cities from coast to coast nor the alarmingly long lines of applicants awaiting housing assistance were enough to alter the official version of reality.

With an eye to opening up the private market, the administration urged Congress to enact a system of federal housing vouchers that low-income tenants could exchange for a portion of their rent. The plan in due time was supposed to replace what was left of the much-bloodied Section 8 program. Congress responded unenthusiastically, providing demonstration money for only 15,000 vouchers in 1983 and for 42,000 more in 1985.

Congress was more receptive to a rent-hike recommendation that had been on the table since the Carter years. In a characteristic move to make subsidized housing more "cost effective," the lawmakers raised rents from 25 percent of a tenant's income to 30 percent. The seemingly small increment occasioned much distress in federally assisted households, as I learned when I interviewed elderly public housing tenants in New Haven.

Fred Stancill's plight was typical. A seventy-seven-year-old tenant of the Elm Haven public housing project, Mr. Stancill now had to pay $105 a month instead of $87.50. He said the extra $210 a year came directly out of his food budget. "But to tell you the truth," he added, "I'm behind in my rent right now. I got two months owing."

Mr. Stancill was not the only tenant in New Haven to fall behind because of the rent hike. Things got so bad that the Public Housing Authority announced it would impose a $20 penalty on residents who did not pay their rent by the tenth of the month. In the past, wayward tenants had been assessed only 50 cents a day, with a ceiling of $10.50 per month. But the new rule did not appreciably improve collections, and a few months later it was quietly dropped. As one of the commissioners observed, "If a tenant can't pay $10.50, how is he going to pay $20?"

Onward

As we bid Reagan's ravine a not-so-fond farewell, we should bear in mind that the hardships it engendered were part of a much larger catastrophe. Reaganomics, after all, did not discriminate among generations or types of deprivation: It exacted tribute from the poor of all ages and along a wide front of public assistance endeavors.

Still, the virtual abandonment of time-tested housing programs represented an especially shabby page in our social-policy annals. For in housing, as perhaps in no other category of elderly support, we had been learning how to do things right. We had found ways of making a positive difference in the quality of elderly lives.

Our newly summoned will to fail can be readily understood if not wholly excused. As with Medicare, inflation has been the problem perceived and cost containment has been the solution attempted. We have allowed our federal housing programs to become indentured to the private market with its soaring rents and out-of-sight land prices. The $5,000 that Edna Morrison's rent supplement cost us in 1986 would in 1976 have been sufficient to subsidize *two* low-income households.

The marketplace may be able to supply us with a plethora of luxuries—it can gentrify vast stretches of America—but one thing it appears unable to supply is adequate housing at affordable prices. If we are serious about finishing the job we began fifty years ago, we shall have to invent a new system of housing and financing that works independently of the old. We need a national housing institution whose functions combine those of a bank with those of a foundation. In the best of all possible worlds that institution would be capable of making construction grants and low-interest loans to churches and other local nonprofit groups prepared to rebuild their communities along compassionate lines.

To make possible the rebuilding, we shall also require measures that can remove selected land parcels from speculative arenas and earmark them for what Chester Hartman has called "social ownership." By social ownership he means "housing that is operated solely for resident benefit and is subject to resident control."[26]

If the initial cost of all this seems excessive, consider the billions to be saved over the long haul from less speculation, lower interest rates, and a more watchful community involved in the housing process. The real issue, one guesses, is not how much it will cost but how much we shall consent to spend on behalf of the poor. Right now we are spending enormous sums on the nonpoor, chiefly in the form of tax deductions for mortgage interest payments and property taxes. Between 1976 and 1990 those accumulated deductions cost the national treasury about $58 billion, which is more than all moneys spent on government-assisted housing programs since the inception of public housing in 1937. Three-fifths of the benefits went to taxpayers in the top 10 percent income bracket.[27]

For the older poor as for the younger poor, much depends on the nature of our priorities. But the elderly, in addition, have uncommon burdens that require special attention. There are, to start with, the diggers-in, the millions like Thelma Poole who will not be moved. Many of them could use a combination of home care and house care, a program that will hold together body and soul and domicile. Several federal agencies do sponsor home repair programs for the elderly (as do some states and municipalities), but their reach is short and the list of suppliants is long. Besides dollars, what is missing from these scatter-shot efforts is a *plan,* a thoughtful federal home repair and maintenance policy aimed at helping older Americans stay where they are. The money saved in Medicaid reimbursements that won't have to be paid to nursing homes may justify the expense—if the lives saved will not.

Much more will be required on behalf of the elderly displaced, who still await the realization of HUD's phantom "coordinated package of housing choices." A genuine package would offer something other than wrappings: It would contain useful options for the frail and the hardy alike, choices ranging from Edna Morrison's no-frills residence at Maple Manor to complex, multiservice versions of Marie MaGuire's Victoria Plaza in San Antonio. The rule should be special facilities for some, decent dwellings for all.

It is not only a question of money. Poor or affluent, many older citizens lack the strength to fend wholly for themselves—to cook their own meals, to drive a car, even to get up in the morning. An assumption that informs this chapter concerns the importance of bringing home-based care and services to the frail and forgotten—not the "total care" that nursing homes are supposed to provide (and usually don't), but the kind of day-to-day support that may help someone retain a measure of verve and independence.

"Congregate housing" is the term experts use to describe such residential arrangements, whereby many essential services can be enjoyed right on the premises: meals, health care, transportation and housekeeping assistance, to name a few. Gerontologists and housing commentators have been extolling the virtues of congregate housing for at least forty years. Here is Charles E. Slusser, President Eisenhower's Public Housing Administration commissioner, speaking on the subject in 1956: "Livability for the elderly must go beyond handrails in bathrooms, low-hung cabinets, non-skid floors, and ramps instead of stairs. It should also look to the social and recreational needs of our elderly residents and provide facilities for them."

Slusser's early hopes remain largely unfulfilled, especially for people of limited means. The dream is barely kept alive nowadays by a scattering of federally funded demonstration projects—authorized in the Congregate Housing Services Act of 1978—which together serve fewer than 30,000 older residents.

The Lonely Crowd

If congregate housing were to do no more than dispel loneliness, it would be worth the price. Elderly loneliness has many causes, but to judge from Edna Morrison's experience, much of it seems a function of place—the place one lives in and the place one is asked, or not asked, to fill in the community. We are dealing here with a sense of uselessness as well as a sense of isolation.

Some of the consequences were spelled out for me by an eighty-year-old Minneapolis widow named Rose Darling, whom I interviewed in her small, neat apartment in a subsidized senior housing development: "I wake up in the morning and start to get up. Then I ask myself: What for? Because I have nothing to do any more—no dog, no garden, nobody to take care of. And I don't eat. I cook something for the evening and when it is ready, I say ach! I don't want to eat it, and I put it in the refrigerator.

"The other morning I was alone and I thought at least I wish somebody would call me. I sat there waiting for the phone to ring. And then it actually rang. 'Hello, Hello,' I said. They wanted to speak to someone named Steven. It was the wrong number."

What did she do then, I asked.

"I switched on the TV. A game show."

There are well-meaning experts who counsel new kinds of clusterings as alternatives to living alone—small-group housing, retirement villages, and the like. "What has to be done," said Leo Baldwin of the AARP, "is . . . create an atmosphere where we can help older people understand that it is appropriate to move into conditions which will serve them better."[28]

But given America's love affair with self-reliance, it is hard to see how we shall ever succeed in persuading a majority of our older citizens to apply that theoretical truth. And even if we could, the elderly poor would scarcely benefit, for it is a truth beyond their means.

In Minneapolis, at the Cedar Riverside People's Center, a dozen older women were gracious enough to meet with me one morning and speak frankly about their lives. All but one were renting small apartments like Rose Darling's, in the multistory, federally assisted senior developments that dominated the neighborhood landscape. I asked them if they would prefer living in a small group (not necessarily with each other) to living alone. No one welcomed the suggestion. One woman, a retired secretary, seemed to speak for all when she remarked, "I like what I got, and what I got is privacy."

"It's true," another concluded, "that living alone can make you selfish. But don't us oldsters deserve a little peace of mind?"

In place of group living, some of the women proposed more comfortable ways of opening up their lives. They wished for gardens to cultivate in common, more shared space in which to entertain friends and relatives, and more timely transportation services—"to help us get up and get going," one of them said. Not least, they yearned for smaller residential buildings in which each tenant could be recognized by name. "In a big building," complained the ex-secretary, "you're nothing but a number."

The lesson seems clear. If we hope to be helpful to our older friends and relations, we shall have to listen to their expressed needs. What those women definitely did not want was anonymity and isolation. What they did want was independence-plus—plus mobility, plus conviviality, plus beauty.

No one expects Congress to accomplish such miracles overnight, but Congress *could* resolve to start anew, and this time to finish the job. In gearing up for a fresh start, the lawmakers should plan in an affirmative-action mode, giving priority to those most grievously deprived of shelter. An emergency program for the elderly homeless would be an essential first step, to be closely followed by measures to assist the next-worst-housed contingent—poor black women who live alone and rent.

If the ultimate goal—decent shelter for all the elderly—seems discouragingly distant at times, we should bear in mind that a mere 2 million additional units would finish the job begun thirty-five years ago. The main thing is to restore our sense of urgency, to keep pressing ahead with all deliberate speed. For as Robert N. Butler reminds us, "The old can't wait for housing."[29]

* * *

Edna Morrison is not well. Soon she will require services that surpass those offered at Maple Manor. She may need help in transportation, in provision of meals, in housekeeping, and in on-the-premises health care. Where will she live when she cannot entirely fend for herself, and who will assist her in ways that preserve her independence and prolong her usefulness to others? These are among the questions we shall next address.

PART TWO

The Struggle for Independence

CHAPTER FOUR

Home Care: The Dream Deferred

*I am done with great things and big plans, great institutions
and big success. And I am for those tiny invisible loving human
forces that work from individual to individual, creeping through
the crannies of the world like so many rootlets, . . . yet which,
if given time, will rend the hardest monuments of human pride.*
—William James

The purpose of this chapter is to sketch the dimensions of what
amounts to a national home-care emergency. Its millions of victims are
in no position to march on Washington or otherwise call attention to
their difficulties. The struggle to fend off dependency is nearly always
waged behind closed doors, in the privacy of one's home and in the
teeth of one's panic. The public does not bear witness; neither, in
most instances, does it bear any part of the home-care burden.

"Every morning I wake up in pain. I wiggle my toes. Good. They
still obey. I open my eyes. Good. I can see. Everything hurts but I
get dressed. I walk down to the ocean. Good. It's still there. Now my
day can start. About tomorrow I never know. After all, I'm eighty-nine.
I can't live forever." Thus begins Barbara Myerhoff's remarkable portrait
of the elderly Jewish community in Venice, California.[1] This woman's
name is Basha, and "Basha wants to remain independent above all."
But independence is never a permanent asset. Each day it must be
pursued and captured anew. Basha devotes all her waking hours to
the struggle.

As Myerhoff notes, Basha's "life on the beach depends on her ability
to perform a minimum of basic tasks. . . . She must shop and cook,

dress herself, care for her body and her one-room apartment, walk, take the bus to the market and the doctor, be able to make a telephone call in case of emergency."

But each of these routine tasks turns into a complex challenge:

Her arthritic hands have a difficult time with the buttons of her dress. Some days her fingers ache and swell so that she cannot fit them into the holes of the telephone dial. Her hands shake as she puts in her eyedrops for glaucoma. Fortunately, she no longer has to give herself injections for her diabetes. Now it is controlled by pills, if she is careful about what she eats. In the neighborhood there are no large markets within walking distance. She must take the bus to shop. The bus steps are very high and sometimes the driver objects when she tries to bring her little wheeled cart aboard. A small boy whom she has befriended and occasionally pays waits for her at the bus stop to help her up. When she cannot bring her cart onto the bus or isn't helped up the steps, she must walk to the market. Then shopping takes the better part of the day and exhausts her. Her feet, thank God, give her less trouble since she figured out how to cut and sew a pair of cloth shoes so as to leave room for her calluses and bunions.

A community committed to long-term caring could make life easier for Basha. Transportation would probably head her wish list—not those lumbering metropolitan buses with cranky drivers and nonnegotiable steps, but vans and minibuses with easy access, convenient schedules, and patient personnel. Regular home visits by a nurse practitioner might be next on Basha's agenda—someone to help her with the eyedrops, to remind her about the medicine, and to make sure she is eating the right food. In addition, occasional foot care would surely not be amiss, nor would a modest exercise program aimed at keeping the arthritic swelling in check.

These are not extraordinary measures. Millions of older Americans receive just such timely services. Yet millions more miss out. It is not that they are beyond help, only that they seem beyond the reach of our one-armed home-care system. As with Basha, their solitude and their poverty have been thrust upon them.

Much of the material presented here will be from the poor's special angle of vision—not the elderly poor alone, but the millions of younger poor as well, mainly women, who have undertaken to minister to the needs of their parents, their in-laws, their relatives, and their neighbors. It is caregivers such as they who provide more than four-fifths of all the home care currently available to older Americans. They do so at a personal cost we can only begin to appreciate and cannot hope to measure.

But to speak of poverty in this context is to beg the question. Home-care imperatives mock middle-class affluence, too: Hardly any of us can afford for very long to buy essential services that cost as much as $1,800 a week. With home care now, as with elderly health care prior to 1965, need and neediness go hand in hand. That is because nearly all home care, even the medical kind, remains an uninsured benefit. Only about 3 percent of Medicare's $96 billion expenditure in 1989 went for home care services. Medicaid contributed even less—1.5 percent of the $61 billion it spent that year.

Medical assistance in any case constitutes only one corner of a complex mosaic of home-care needs. They include personal hygiene, laundry, cooking, shopping, transport—whatever it takes to preserve independence and deflect or delay institutionalization. As these needs have gradually come to light, and as their status has evolved from one of private distress toward one of public concern, many new actors have entered the arena. Government agencies, senior centers, churches, and volunteer organizations all have added their strength to that of the original home-care corps—the wives, daughters, and neighbors whose unseen labors remain paramount. The new money and the new energy have helped, but not nearly enough. No one has yet figured out a way to organize so vast and customized an endeavor, or to get the job done without bankrupting the elderly and their children.

Are politics and bureaucracies capable of organizing our tenderest impulses? Can love be legislated and caring be funded? Such riddles underlie all discussions about the politics of elderly home care, including this one.

Our exploration opens with an assessment of elderly home-care needs, along with a comment or two on nonelderly attitudes. In both instances we take note of the critical role played by that mysterious force scholars call demographics. From there we proceed to encounters with some of the principal participants in the home-care drama—the family and next-door caregivers who shoulder much of the responsibility and upon whom our rickety home-care system largely depends.

There follows a brief section on federal home-care policy, still a skeletal presence, but one awaiting its chance to take on muscle and heart. (A more detailed discussion on federal support of long-term care will be found in Chapter 6.) The chapter closes with an example of one type of federally subsidized effort that seems to work—the provision of transportation to the halt and the homebound. Strictly speaking, of course, transportation is not "home care." But for millions of older Americans, especially for the rural poor, it looms as a key element in the home-care portfolio. What every teenager knows instinctively, many elderly have had to learn again: Independence is a thing on wheels.

"Youth Creep" and "Age Creep"

"All would live long," remarked Benjamin Franklin, "and none would be old." Increasingly now Americans must cope with that cussed contradiction. The new elderly conspicuousness has worked a powerful influence on the rest of us, bringing to the surface long-buried feelings of dread and hope, resentment and compassion. More and more now we worry about the consequences of growing old—not just in terms of our own dimly perceived prospects, but also in light of our immediate responsibilities. "The subject of our lunchtime conversations has shifted," wrote the columnist Ellen Goodman about herself and her middle-generation friends. "Once they leaned heavily toward pediatrics. Now they include geriatrics. . . . In middle age, most of us are flanked by adolescent children and aging parents. We are the fulcrum of this family seesaw, and expected to keep the balance."[2]

Sometimes, in considering these matters, we give into a heavy fatalism that recalls Seneca's dismissal of old age as "an incurable disease." At such moments we see only the darker side of longevity: increasing feebleness, helplessness, mindlessness. The evidence, of course, is all around us. At other times we may effect a studied cheerfulness. Then, with the media, we conspire to find good news everywhere. "Age Improves Intellectual Activities, Creativity," my local newspaper, the *New Haven Register,* informs me. Atop the same page the outlook seems brighter still: "Sex Doesn't End When Social Security Begins."

As with our fears, there is evidence at hand to support our hopes. For even among persons in their eighties and beyond—the group some gerontologists have taken to calling the "old old," as distinguished from the "young old" in their sixties and seventies—the need for assistance varies markedly, from constant to hardly ever.

"People should not be so condescending about the over-85 cohort," cautions Dr. Charles F. Longino, director of the Center for Social Research in Aging at the University of Miami. His analysis of 1980 census data indicates that fewer than one-quarter of that age group live in nursing homes, while another 11 percent live with their children. Nearly all the rest (55 percent) maintain "independent households."[3]

Some of the old, even the *very* old, do seem remarkably independent. They lead lives of quiet exhilaration. Beneath a headline that portrays "Oldest Americans" as "Not So Frail," the *New York Times* features a ninety-nine-year-old Californian named Ethel F. Nixon, a former librarian, whose life seems to affirm Sara Teasdale's definition of an optimist: "one who makes the most of all that comes and the least of all that goes." Mrs. Nixon "drives regularly to Mexico or north along the coast to visit her two sons, her five grandchildren and her six great-grandchildren. . . . Rarely ill, she feels the key to longevity is 'staying active and looking at things in a positive way. . . . I thank the good Lord every day for the blessings I have.'"[4]

One guesses that Mrs. Nixon's admirable vigor lends credence to our own secret dreams—not of immortality, alas, but of the next best thing: a care-free independence in extreme old age. Is it so wild a dream, after all? Are not the aged acting younger all the time? "Youth creep" is the oddly disturbing term Longino has coined to describe this apparent miracle. "The old group seems younger as the decades pass," he assures us. "The old old seem like the young old of a few decades earlier."[5]

Other researchers have been swimming in the same soothing waters. Calling its work "life-span analysis," a whole new school of behavioral science apparently believes we have reached a moment in history—to quote a *Newsweek* headline—"When Age Doesn't Matter." "The major assumption behind life-span analysis," said *Newsweek,* "is that after adolescence, age is no longer a reliable factor in how people feel or act." A leading life-spanner, University of Chicago gerontologist Bernice L. Neugarten, has spoken of an "age-irrelevant society" and argued that it is already here. "Our society," she claimed, "is becoming accustomed to the 28-year-old mayor . . . the 50-year-old retiree, the 65-year-old father of a preschooler and the 70-year-old student."[6]

Yet something in all this seems gravely amiss. For neither the wonders of youth creep nor the nostrums of life-span analysis can explain away the inexorable aches and confinements of old age. Indeed, to study the elderly condition in the United States today is to be less impressed with youth creep than with its opposite number, "age creep," and with the home-care revolution that age creep plainly demands but thus far has failed to produce.

Nine of every ten disabled older Americans are not in nursing homes. They are candidates for home care. But fate and poverty have played their customary roles here, for those who need home care the most usually can afford it the least.

The demographer Beth J. Soldo has noted that "the prevalence of home-care need among black elderly is 44 percent higher than the white rate." Other high-risk groups include "the very old, . . . women, those living with relatives and [the] low-income elderly."[7] Soldo cited studies that suggest an astonishing rise in elderly home-care requirements overall. Between 1966 and 1979 the need ratio may have jumped as much as 50 percent, going from 80 to 121 per 1,000 elderly. For elderly blacks, the 1979 ratio reached 168 per 1,000; for elderly women, 141; for older persons with incomes under $4,000, 215.[8]

Even so, the estimates seem surprisingly low. In their treatise on Medicare policy, Karen Davis and Diane Rowland refer to "the 4–7 million elderly Americans needing long-term care assistance."[9] We know that some 11.5 million older Americans suffer from arthritis, 9.4 million from hypertension, 7 million from hearing impairments, 6.9 million from heart disease, 4.6 million from chronic sinusitis, 3.4 million from eyesight troubles, and 2 million from diabetes.[10]

In all, "Approximately 86 percent of the elderly report some sort of chronic condition." Among the seventy-five-and-over group, almost 5 million complain of some difficulty in walking, climbing, or bending; among the very old (eighty-five and over), about 800,000 say they need help with such ordinary tasks as eating, bathing, dressing, and using the toilet. Finally, at least 10 million older Americans either do not own a car or else can no longer drive.[11]

Note that the numbers focus almost exclusively on *physical* needs. There appears to be no place in these annals for such widespread elderly afflictions as loneliness, isolation, lethargy, despair. Yet such strains of anguish are precisely the sort that can often yield to home-care-type remedies.

Consider the following "thank you" letter, written by a grateful octogenarian couple in rural Michigan to Friends of the Elderly (sometimes called Little Brothers), that peerless home-care organization whose sole mission appears to be cheering up the aged. The letter merits our attention both for its poetic eloquence and for what it reveals about the differences between LTC (long-term care) and its less-technical first cousin, TLC. Note how few of the many kindnesses celebrated here can be found on any standard listing of "LTC Needs."

Dear Little Brothers,

You have helped us along over so many rough spots in our Older Lives—Melvin and Mine. You have cheered us with your cheery smiles, hugs and kisses.

Two months ago today was Christmas. . . . Neither one of us dressed. A sick husband, and I had fallen twice, before Christmas. A real northern Copper Country blizzard raged Christmas Day.

I didn't cook anything, but was about to open a can of Campbell's Chunky Style soup, when a knock came at the door.

There stood a youthful tall man, with two Christmas dinners for us from Little Brothers. . . . That day I was real hungry, which for me is unusual. At some points my fingers were more agile than knife and fork. Imagine!

And how we thanked God, for those who came to ailing Oldsters. Too, the Brothers take my husband to the doctors and [to] Marquette General Hospital. Words can't convey our gratitude. . . .

When last summer arrived, and I found it to be too hot with our storm windows on, at my request they came and took four main ones off. And put one new pane in. In the Fall they replaced them.

Many a phone call from them to see how we are sustains us in knowing there are hearts that care. We have no children or kinfolk near. Second cousins twelve miles from here, but I can hardly remember what they look like. . . .

Over all is the concern, and the bit of chit-chat—conversation is so good—the smiles, the oft times hugs [that are] so warmly good!

Thanks be to God for Little Brothers. . . . Fondly, in deep gratitude,

Gwyneth and Melvin

To sum up thus far: The home-care needs of older Americans are as varied as they are insistent, surpassing by far all scholarly and political measures. Having underestimated the challenge, it is not surprising that we have also underestimated the ways and means required to meet it. By and large, we have been content to leave long-term caring to those who by blood or by temperament seem to care the most. They are the ones who find world enough and time to sustain elderly lives. Only recently has their story begun to be told.

The Caregivers

Although families and older neighbors constitute the two main sources of home care for the elderly, most experts have recognized only the former source. Aged-to-aged strains of assistance lack status among researchers and policymakers alike; they remain largely unexamined. We begin this caregivers' profile, therefore, with a brief look at elders who take care of elders.

Especially in elderly housing projects, where the frail and the not-so-frail live side by side, do neighborly ministrations seem bountiful. The most frequent gainers are the many without money or family. One-fifth of the elderly are childless, and most of those are female, poor, and alone. In 1980 only 39 percent of all older women lived with a spouse, in contrast to 74 percent of older men. The single women's median annual income was below $5,000.[12]

The psychotherapists Melody Anderson and Leora Magier, who founded Resources for Midlife and Older Women, Inc., in New York City, have told us: "Two-thirds of the approximately 18 million women over the age of 65 [will] die alone. . . . Many women may be diagnosed as suffering from senile dementia when in fact they are lonely and isolated." The only solace afforded millions of such loners is that of caring neighbors who may be just as old and just as poor.

Minnie Olson, whom I interviewed in Minneapolis, is a typical care-giving neighbor. She lives in a subsidized two-room apartment on a social security income of $438 a month. Mrs. Olson is eighty-one and has suffered three heart attacks in the last six years. "I never sit still if I know somebody who needs me. I have a lady on the seventh floor. I do different things for her, like washing her hair and making lunch for her. She loves peanut butter. Every night I walk her up and down the corridor so she gets her exercise. If she don't exercise, she'll get sick and be sent to a nursing home. I also do her laundry when she's not feeling up to it, which is most of the time. This lady is only seventy-two years old. She could be my little sister. But she has no family, no one to look in on her. The people in this building, we're her family."

Sometimes a neighborhood agency comes along and organizes older residents into volunteer care-giving associations. Minnie Olson belongs to one of those. But it hardly seems to matter: The care that she and her friends lavish on others flows naturally and continually; it requires no urging, no staffing, no funding. It can, however, entail considerable effort, even risk. The perils of elderly selflessness should not be underestimated, for the givers are as vulnerable as the takers.

Ella, a friend of Mrs. Olson's, told me she broke her arm while attempting to deliver a bouquet of marigolds to a sick friend: "I picked them myself because I knew Becky loved flowers and she was feeling down-in-the-mouth. To get to her apartment you have to walk down steps. Well, it was drizzling and slippery and I should have been more careful. I was in the hospital three weeks. My arm isn't right yet." Ella is eighty years old; her friend is eighty-six.

Aged-to-aged home care knows few boundaries or inhibitions. Its repertoire includes bedtime reading, windowbox weeding, spoon feeding, special pleading—whatever it takes to enliven, gladden, or nourish. Its emanations can be conventional or creative, depending upon the occasion. In a rooming house in Denver an elderly tenant, her fingers swollen with arthritis, patiently trims her bedridden neighbor's plastic Christmas tree. In Chicago, the ninety-year-old widow whom George F. Wills interviewed in her shabby hotel room refuses to look for better quarters because "she wants to stay near the elderly man down the hall, who has cancer."

Madeleine Corry is a seventy-one-year-old widow who lives in Burlington, Vermont. She survives on a monthly $372 social security check. Mrs. Corry has appointed herself a kind of postal Miss Lonelyhearts of her senior housing project. Each morning, in bathrobe and slippers, she pads down to the lobby and writes notes to all the tenants who have not been lucky enough to receive mail that day. "I am thinking lovely thoughts about you," she may write. "Hope your back is feeling better. Love & Kisses, An Admirer."

I tended to dismiss her pen-pal efforts as too obvious to make a difference—until I talked with some of the other tenants. It turned out they couldn't wait to get Madeleine's messages. "Madeleine has spoiled us," said a woman on the second floor. "I don't think I could bear facing an empty mailbox any more."

Numerous as these useful citizens may be, they do seem a breed apart: Their spirits are willing even when their flesh is weak. Money and prestige may have eluded them all their days, yet in their aged extremity they have made themselves indispensable—not only to the elders in their care, but to all who share in the commonweal. One thinks of the advice W. B. Yeats gave "To a Friend Whose Work Has Come to Nothing": "Be secret and exult. / Because of all things known / That is the most difficult." Older caregivers may be secret exulters. Certainly they seem happier than most. In this they differ markedly from their care-giving counterparts, the family members on whose attentions millions of older Americans continue to rely.

All in the Family

On August 8, 1985, in New York City, the Governor's Task Force on Aging held public hearings that focused on "The Harsh Economic and Health Problems of Aging Women." Many caregivers came forward. From their accumulated testimony emerged a table of emotional contents to a book that America's female caregivers seem never to finish writing. The inferential headings included Grief, Anguish, and Desperation, along with Love, Loyalty, and Obligation. In the three representative accounts presented here, the helpers are crying for help.

*   *   *

"My name is Agnes Sullivan. . . . My husband and I just had our forty-second anniversary. I was twenty-two, my husband twenty-three when we were married. He had quit school at sixteen to help support his family. We met at our church in the Bronx. We had a daughter and two sons."

After they were married her husband went to night school and earned a master's degree in hospital administration. In time he became a Medicare coordinator for the federal government. "My husband did not want to retire until he was seventy. We both love to travel and we were planning to enjoy a lot of that.

"[But] seven years ago my husband started forgetting things. The first thing I noticed was the difficulty he had making small decisions. He also started to arrive home later than usual. He began to lose weight, lose money. . . . He had always loved crosswords. Occasionally I would notice one around the house missing even the simplest words. I felt he was actually aware of his own deterioration and was trying to hide it. He couldn't recognize places or make decisions."

They tried different doctors and different remedies. After three years of searching they finally got a diagnosis: Alzheimer's disease. Now, "my husband is not hostile but he requires constant attention. He cannot converse, cannot express what he wants. I consider myself very lucky that my three wonderful children live close by and help me. My sons give my husband his showers, a task very difficult for me to do alone.

"Essentially I am on-call twenty-four hours a day. My husband is up every hour all night. Often I am at the point of sheer exhaustion. Lying awake at night, I think about the future. I ask myself, will this go on forever? . . . The thought of putting him in a nursing home is very painful to me, but very shortly it will be the only solution."

Mrs. Sullivan worries a lot about money. If her husband should die before her, she will get 55 percent of his pension, plus her own small social security stipend. "I could never afford my current rent," she says. "And if my husband enters a nursing home, I am afraid I won't be left with enough money to live on. I fear impoverishment."

* * *

Grace Anderson is a caregiver no longer, but her ordeal continues: "When my husband got cancer, I took care of him. When he died, we had used up our life savings. I have barely enough to live on and am terribly worried about my future."

Her husband battled cancer for ten years. "Even with the chemo-therapy he kept working. It was amazing. . . . But one day he said, 'Grace, call up the store. I can't make it no more.' And that was the last day he worked.

"I kept him at home, and our savings began to go. My children said, 'You've got to remember yourself, too, Ma.' But I said to them, 'My husband is the one who worked for it, and my husband is the one it will go to help.' I took care of him twenty-four hours a day.

He died eleven months later, on my birthday. . . . After my husband died my blood pressure just went crazy."

Mrs. Anderson's monthly income comes to $318, most of it from her husband's veteran's pension and union fund. Her rent and utilities amount to $218, "and I am left with $100 to live on." Like so many women of her generation, Mrs. Anderson was able to accumulate very little social security. As a teenager she had clerical jobs, "but I stopped working for thirty years, while I raised my children." A long bout with phlebitis interrupted her return to the work force, and "after six months of disability, I got a Special Delivery letter telling me I was fired. . . . I have no savings whatsoever. If it wasn't for babysitting jobs, I'd be in deep trouble."

*   *   *

"My name is Mary Hladek. Like several of my friends, . . . I am a full-time caregiver for my elderly mother.

"I am sixty-four years old and my husband is seventy. My mother is ninety-two. My husband and I live in First Houses [a Public Housing project] on Avenue A and 3rd Street; my mother lives in . . . a project two blocks away.

"She lives alone in a one-and-a-half-room apartment. She is very deaf and is also losing her sight. She is alert but frail. Because of her frailty my mother cannot use the telephone; if anything should happen to her, she would be unable to let anyone know. She can't . . . take care of her daily needs.

"Five times a day I go visit her. I start at 7:30 when I help her out of bed and get her dressed and give her breakfast. I come back at 10:30. . . . At two o'clock and again at five I come back to check up on her, and I get her dinner and help her eat. In the evening I come for a final visit and help her get ready for bed.

"This has been my routine for four years. Weekends, holidays, are all the same to me. My mother cannot go without help for a single day. . . . My husband and I raised three boys. After they were grown I hoped to go back to work. But then my mother started failing, and my plans changed. This has been the worst time of my life. It takes so much out of me. Sometimes I am so tired I fear for my own health."

But Mrs. Hladek was not asking for respite. Her one request to the task force was aimed at extending her care-giving hours: "If I could get a larger apartment for my mother, it would be possible to stay over on nights when she is not well. As you can imagine, her room is very crowded. She lies in bed, while I sit in the chair. The room is filled with her wheelchair, a commode, her walker, and other equipment. We have no privacy.

"I am terrified to leave her alone. Once I found her on the floor, lying in waste. If she's not feeling well, I can't stay with her. That's why I would like to find an apartment with an extra room."

Several months after the hearings I telephoned Mrs. Hladek and arranged to meet her on a Saturday morning in front of her mother's building on the Lower East Side of Manhattan. Among other things, I was hoping to learn what kept Mrs. Hladek going and whether any assistance from the community might make her life easier.

Mary Hladek is a small, sturdy woman with lots of energy and a preoccupied manner. "The one good thing that came of those hearings," she says as we rush into an elevator, "is that my mother is finally going to get a bigger apartment. You'll see in a minute why I kept asking for one."

Forewarned, I am nonetheless surprised. The wheelchair, the commode, the recliner, and the walker are all present as advertised, along with some items not previously mentioned—large potted plants, shopping bags filled with clippings, a carpet sweeper, a scale. Somewhere to the rear of all this lies Mrs. Hladek's mother.

"Her name is Sandecki," I am told. "Louise Sandecki. I'll let her know we're here, but you'll have to shout. She's very hard-of-hearing."

We thread our way to the bedside. Mrs. Sandecki is on her back, dressed in a blue nightgown. She seems to be sleeping. "Mama," her daughter shouts in her ear. "How're you feeling? I brought a gentleman with me. He wants to meet you."

The old woman opens her eyes and favors me with a weak smile. "God bless you," she murmurs.

Mrs. Hladek helps her mother sit up. "Mama, get up a little bit. Just move your feet down so they dangle."

While Mrs. Sandecki sits thus, we speak of her as if she were not present. "I try to let her do things for herself," the daughter says, "'cause if I don't, she gets annoyed. Otherwise she'd feel like an invalid. She waters the plants. She feeds herself. And she loves to clip those coupons—things on sale in the stores. Sometimes I take her for a ride, like to the cemetery in Brooklyn where my brother is buried. But mostly she don't do anything now 'cause she's kind of weak. Listen, at that age . . ."

I ask Mrs. Hladek if she feels close to her mother. Her reply is matter-of-fact: "Not really. She never had time for any of us. My father died long long ago—I don't even remember him—and then I guess my mother had to go to work. She'd keep running back to the apartment to check on us kids, to make sure we were all right, and then out again to work.

"My mother came over from Poland when she was twenty. She did office cleaning—all those big buildings down on Wall Street. I think she did some waitressing, too, and I *know* she took in boarders. They were always eating with us."

She looks at her mother, who still sits on the edge of the bed. "I don't remember any hugging or kissing. It wasn't like today when people have more hours for affection. I guess she had a tough time." She laughs. "But good hard work don't kill you. You see that."

Then Mrs. Hladek tries to answer the questions I have not asked. "You and me," she begins, "we have just boys. Too bad we don't have girls. Hopefully, we'll be able to take care of ourselves when we get old. Today your kids want to travel and go places. But as long as they're willing to pay to have someone take care of us, that's good enough.

"Me? I'm a daughter. This is my job. But I wouldn't mind somebody coming in once in a while and giving me a rest. You know what I need? A vacation."

We have been standing all this time in the middle of the room, on either side of the empty wheelchair. Now she goes to her mother. "Ok, Mama, you can lay down now. I'm going home to make you some soup." To me she says, "She gets Meals On Wheels five times a week, but on weekends I do all the cooking. Meals On Wheels is a wonderful service. So is the clinic downstairs. The doctors and nurses will come right up to your room. House calls, no less. I'm going to take her down there pretty soon to see about a hearing aid. I've had her ears cleaned out a few times, and it helped."

As we walk briskly back to her apartment, Mrs. Hladek points out some of the shabbier sights: the litter on the street, the boarded-up store windows. "You can see what kind of neighborhood this is. Beggars, pushers, muggers—we got 'em all. When I come this way nights I carry an umbrella for safety. It'll be better with the new apartment. I'll be able to sleep there."

Mrs. Hladek and her husband live in a three-story brick apartment building, one of a half-dozen that surround a paved courtyard. A plaque there provides a bit of history: "The Nation's First Public Housing Project, November 21, 1934." The Hladeks' apartment is on the top floor. "No elevators in these buildings," she says as we climb the stairs, "so my mother can't live here with us. She wouldn't like it anyway. She wants her privacy. The older ones in the project are like us: They've been here a long time. There are enough of us now to have a Senior Citizens' Club. I'm the vice-president, so I guess I'm a senior."

The five-room apartment is immaculate and dark. We sip coffee at a table in the small kitchen. "I'm sorry my husband isn't here," Mrs.

Hladek says. "He's a veteran—Second World War—and since he retired from work he spends a lot of time at the veterans' club. My husband used to be in maintenance for RCA. We aren't starving. The social security's about $1,100 a month. But you know, when you think of the money it would cost to hire nurses and homemakers, well, it's just cheaper for me to take care of my mother myself."

She looks at her watch and stands up. "Whaddaya know? It's past noon already. I better start lunch."

Late Dispatches

Gradually the news arrives, filling in our spotty picture of home-care practice nationwide. It appears that the death of the American family has been greatly exaggerated: The Mary Hladeks and Agnes Sullivans are more the rule than the exception. As Ethel Shanas reported, "the major finding of social research in aging in all Western countries has been the discovery and demonstration of the important role of the family in old age."[13] The 1981 White House Conference on Aging is equally explicit: "We recognize that the support system for older persons remains anchored in the family and extended family. Therefore, national policy should be redirected to provide greater resources for families who are caring for older members."

But national policy has not risen to the occasion; it has left most care-giving families to shift for themselves. Recent scholarly dispatches can tell us a good deal about family struggles in America's home-care trenches.

By Tacit Policy and in Actual Practice, Care-Giving Remains Women's Work. American women now spend more years caring for aging parents— eighteen years, on average—than they spend caring for their children.[14]

"Who are the caregivers?" asks Jane Porcino, a gerontologist at the State University of New York (Stony Brook). "They are predominantly female, with 50 percent having a spouse over 65. They themselves are often aging—with chronic health care problems. They know little about nursing care and less about the few available community services. An even higher proportion of non-white caregivers are female. This group has the highest rate of poverty."[15]

In her study on "parentcaring," Patricia G. Archbold concluded that the responsibility almost invariably "falls to the wife, the daughter, or daughter-in-law to provide the care and support necessary." She described such women as "living under extreme stress and hardship." They "should be viewed as an 'at risk' population."[16]

The double standard at work here seems beyond question. On the whole, society tends to disregard female sacrifices even as it encourages their spread. A "Gray Paper" issued by the Older Women's League demonstrated how a physician will often help a man find home-care assistance for his ailing wife but will not turn a finger when the spouses' conditions are reversed. Instead the physician will find words of encouragement for the wife, e.g.: "Isn't he lucky to have a wonderful woman like you to take care of him!"[17]

Along with other parts of our life-sustaining landscape—air, for instance—women caregivers remain invisible. The language we employ is oddly genderless, a point neatly analyzed by a spokesperson for the Older Women's League in testimony before the Senate Finance Committee: "Sometimes 'the family' is cited as the caregiver; other frequently used references include 'informal support systems,' 'community supports,' and simply 'relatives' or 'children.' But 'caregivers,' whether in institutional or noninstitutional settings, is a euphemism for women."[18]

Home Care Is a Lonely Enterprise, Especially for the Poor. "Research indicates that low income elderly are more isolated with less access to friends, neighbors, relatives and confidantes than high income elderly."[19] A. Golodetz and associates noted in an earlier study that "the sense of isolation in [caregiving] household units was palpable." Here are those researchers expatiating on the lot of the care-giving wife:

> She is not trained for her job, *a priori.* She may have little choice about doing the job. She belongs to no union or guild, works no fixed maximum of hours. She lacks formal compensation, job advancement and even the possibility of being fired. She has no job mobility. In her work situation, she bears a heavy emotional load, but has no colleagues or supervisor or education to help her handle this. Her own life and its needs compete constantly with her work requirements. She may be limited in her performance by her own ailments.[20]

Patricia Archbold writes of "the major costs of caregiving," putting "lack of freedom" at the top of the list. "All caregivers give up social activities with friends," she said. The women she interviewed had much to say on this subject, e.g.,: "I'm not going to have any friends when my mother dies. We gave up having people over to the house three years ago."[21]

A seventy-eight-year-old widow has written: "My husband had a stroke after 23 years of a wonderful marriage. For the next 17 years I was his 24-hour-a-day caregiver. Gradually friends and relatives dropped away, unable to bear the anguish of seeing this once strong, handsome, vital man so diminished. I was alone—his only life support system. There was no one to help with his care. I felt abandoned by the world."[22]

The Work Is Exacting, Frustrating, Relentless. In helping their bedfast spouses, Shanas writes, "Men take over traditionally female tasks as necessary, [and] women find the strength to turn and lift bedfast husbands."[23]

"The provision of care . . . entails intense physical and psychological stress," notes Chai R. Feldblum in a perceptive essay. "Much of the work, such as bathing and changing beds, is tiring and unenjoyable. It may be especially depressing if the caregiver was close to the elderly person when [that] person was once capable and independent. . . . It is not surprising that caregivers are . . . prone to intense feelings of frustration, disappointment, ambivalence, guilt and anger."[24]

"I prepare her food, do the bathing, lay out her clothes, put on pads for incontinence, watch her diet so she does not get loose bowels—everything."[25]

Many Caregivers Also Work for a Living. The Travelers Corporation in Hartford polled a random sample of its 7,000 employees over the age of 30 and discovered that 28 percent spent time each week taking care of elderly relatives or friends. Seven of every ten of the caregivers were women. One-third said they "had not had a vacation from care-giving duties for more than a year." Average time devoted to caregiving was 10.2 hours a week. Average age of those receiving care was 77.2 years, and 69 percent of them were women.[26]

In a study prepared by Elaine M. Brody of the Philadelphia Geriatrics Center, 28 percent of the working women interviewed "had reduced their working hours or were considering quitting" because of care-giving obligations. A similar percentage of women who stayed home to take care of elderly mothers, Brody said, had quit work for that purpose.[27]

Not everyone has a choice. Especially in rural areas, where the old farm-based economy is eroding, have women been forced to seek jobs outside the home. As a result, writes Millie Buchanan in a profile of Madison County, North Carolina, "The support system that once allowed older relatives to live out their lives at home has thinned. . . . The relatives and neighbors who once rallied to help when the sick or elderly needed full-time care are now either living elsewhere or leaving home at dawn to drive long distances to work."[28]

It Hurts to Be Poor. There was an old woman I met in Miami whose husband had suffered a stroke in 1978 and had been entirely in her care ever since. This woman recently was forced to sell her shared rights to a shack her family owned in South Carolina. The $1,500 she got will help keep her husband dry: Three times a week she must go to a supermarket and buy him Depends, a brand of adult diapers, at

$6.20 a package. That comes to $967.20 a year, or about one-fourth the couple's total income.

Home-Care Policy in Absentia

We turn now to the question of home-care policy, or rather to its shadowy surrogate in Washington. Policy implies commitment, and it is just such a sense of national commitment that has been oddly missing from the preceding accounts of care-giving. For reasons all too apparent, neither the cared-fors nor the cared-bys have evinced much faith in society's readiness to come to their rescue.

More than most commentators on this subject, Davis and Rowland have made clear what occurs in our communities when government lacks a plan to govern: "No single program provides the services or financing to accommodate the multiple long-term care needs of the elderly, and most are left to receive services at home from family and friends with little assistance from public programs."[29]

There is, to be sure, an appearance of busyness and concern. At least forty-three different federal agencies sponsor home-care programs of one kind or another. But in allocating such services they spend less than $7 billion a year, most of it for home health care reimbursed by Medicare or Medicaid.

The existence of so many different federal programs has sown disappointment at levels farther down the home-care hierarchy. For what at first appears to be a useful system meant to answer elderly needs is soon discovered to be something less promising: a collection of disparate measures with no binding rationale, no sensible financing mechanism, and no claim to universality. What we have here is a nonsystem shaped to the airy specifications of a nonpolicy.

The Medicare program is a case in point. In some respects it has been moving right along. The program's home-care expenditures between 1970 and 1980 rose from $61 million to $662 million, and the number of "covered visits" tripled during the same period. Since 1980 Medicare's at-home performance has been better still, thanks chiefly to a decision by Congress to liberalize restrictions on the number of home-care visits the program will cover.

Yet Medicare today remains essentially what it has always been: an insurance program for acute illness. "By law, Medicare pays nothing for home health care for chronic illness, leaving millions of elderly to choose between paying for it themselves, forgoing home health services, or entering nursing homes to obtain the care they need."[30] Only 2 percent of Medicare's budget goes for home care, which is viewed by the program as a marginal responsibility, albeit a medical one. As Davis and Rowland emphasize, "Services must be ordered by a physician and be delivered by a certified home health agency."[31]

Medicare's fussy definition of home care is further restricted by its neglectful notion of what hospital dischargees require in the way of follow-up assistance. During the first seven months of 1985, for instance, only 172,000 Medicare hospital patients—less than 4 percent of the total—were "discharged to home health services," while 3.7 million (79 percent) were "discharged to home *self-care*."[32]

Most of our current federal arrangements seem designed to *discourage* home-care services and to drive elders into subsidized exile. Medicare's home-care myopia is not the only handicap. The problem is made worse by Medicaid's peculiar rules, which render the elderly ineligible for long-term assistance as long as they choose to live in the community. Only when they consent to pauperizing themselves and entering a nursing home do the dollars begin to flow. The programs's institutional tilt thus conflicts with the prospective beneficiary's fiercest wish—to remain independent.

Medicaid's fiscal contradictions have not been entirely lost on a budget-conscious Congress. Hoping to reduce nursing home costs, the lawmakers in 1980 passed an amendment allowing states to apply for permission to include more home-care items on their Medicaid menus of reimbursable services. The fresh roster could encompass just about any service within reason—provision of homemakers and health aides, personal care, respite care, case management, and rehabilitation therapy, to name a few. Known as "the 2176 Waiver," the measure seemed to promise a more open-handed attitude on the part of Medicaid toward its clients' home-care needs, one that could make room for noninstitutional, even nonmedical, services.

But the states' response has been less than overwhelming. Rather than opt for statewide reforms, most have practiced extreme caution. Only in the smallest of ways and within the narrowest of geographical boundaries have they chosen to expand their Medicaid home-care programs. In consequence, as Feldblum has noted, "Although a number of states have submitted waivers . . . , there has not been a substantial expansion of home health care services for large numbers of Medicaid recipients."[33]

The 2176 Waiver reflects Congress's customary approach to home-care reform: It is atomistic, treating each federal program in splendid isolation, one from another. In the intellectual vacuum that currently characterizes Washington, the trick is to think small: Fine-tuning becomes preferable to redesigning, even when the social mechanism in question may be in need of a total overhaul. It is not that we don't from time to time make headway, only that for major varieties of distress we keep looking to minor forms of relief.

How Do You Spell Relief?

Any attempt at remedy ought to begin with our strongest assets. Those invisible caregivers—the wives and daughters who do nearly all the work and get none of the recognition—should be at the top of our list. They need respite; they need emotional and physical support; they need to know that as a society we are prepared to back up their efforts.

The public sector should pay for caregiver assistance and counseling—but the private sector can also be helpful. As Feldblum pointed out, most of the caregivers are middle-aged women, and most middle-aged women work for a living. In 1979, 58 percent of women between the ages of forty-four and fifty-four were in the labor force. By 1992 the proportion is expected to rise to 70 percent. Employers can make things easier for their care-giving workers. They can allow flexible work schedules and grant care-giving leaves without penalty. Not every form of human distress requires a government-inspired solution. Where the need is both widespread and urgent, many in the community can find a way to pitch in.

Withal, our second strongest asset is the federal health-care system already in place. Medicare and Medicaid together embody our most reasonable chance of transforming home care for the elderly from a casual concern into a major priority. For openers, Medicaid will have to kick the nursing home habit and start using home-care substitutes. At the very least, states should be pressed to wield the 2176 Waiver with more zest and compassion, not timidly here and there, but boldly everywhere. Meanwhile, Medicare needs to be redesigned in ways that will enable it to transcend its origins and its acutely narrow framework. Illness is illness, whether acute or chronic; and health care is health care, whether strictly "medical," as with an injection of insulin, or broadly therapeutic, as with an injection of TLC. Sooner rather than later, both Medicare and Medicaid will have to begin reimbursing a far wider range of essential home-care benefits, including transportation.

Most of the foregoing measures will require additional dollars, though it is not yet clear how many—or how few, for a shift from expensive institutional care to relatively inexpensive home care may not be so costly as some planners fear. Much of the needed money can be raised through a reasonable long-term-care insurance premium appended to people's Medicare contributions, while the rest will have to come from general revenues. In both instances the tax burden will be appropriately intergenerational. Each of us, in effect, will be ensuring our own future long-term care—at home or in nursing institutions—as well as the more imminent care of our parents and grandparents. We will also be assuring protection for family caregivers, a consideration not to be lightly dismissed. For we have met the caregivers, and in every sense that matters, they are us.

At least at community levels there seems no lack of natural sympathy for the many who are deprived of home-care services. The trick is to energize that sympathy by means of laws and dollars. All things considered, we require no more of those "great institutions" William James said he was done with. Medicaid and Medicare can probably be reshaped to complete much of the task; individuals and small local institutions can do the rest. The money will have to come from the top down. The caring, as always, will percolate from the bottom up.

We conclude the chapter with an imperfect illustration of that chemistry in action. Our transportation programs for the rural elderly have their flaws, but they do sometimes make a profound difference in the quality of older lives, and they suggest what can be achieved when the yeast of federal funds leavens the grain of local obligations: A few extra dollars, a dozen wheels, a handful of volunteers—and many a despairing citizen is suddenly able to seize the day, no matter how late in life that day happens to arrive.

Reinventing the Wheel

A person's hands can get awfully cold in the Berkshires. So when Mr. Larkin lost his gloves in Patricia Pixley's ten-seater van, the other passengers sprang to his assistance. They looked under their seats, behind the folded wheelchair, even in Mr. Larkin's jacket pockets. But it wasn't until Mrs. Turner, a ninety-year-old retired schoolteacher, stood up that Mr. Larkin spotted his gloves. She had been sitting on them.

For Pat Pixley it was all in a day's work. She had been driving that van—one of three operated by the nonprofit Community Corporation of Great Barrington, Massachusetts—for sixteen months, transporting older residents to the senior center, the clinic, the library, the supermarket, wherever riders wished to alight. If Basha lived in Great Barrington instead of Venice, California, her busing worries would be over and she'd feel less lonely to boot.

"Sometimes it's a soap opera in here," Pat Pixley tells me. "Everyone shares problems. Everyone helps each other. It's like a family."

Pat and the other drivers log about 40,000 elderly-passenger-miles each year, according to Thomas Rathbun, the program's executive director. Three-fifths of the riders have incomes below 125 percent of the poverty line, and most live in such out-of-the-way hamlets as Egremont, Otis, New Marlboro, and Monterey. "We have an eighty-six-year-old man in Otis," Rathbun marvels, "who lives a mile and a half down a dirt road. He's totally isolated—no car, no telephone. Once a week we pick him up in the van, and as soon as he gets in he starts talking a blue streak. He's been so *lonely*—nobody to talk to except his dog and cats."

Like the thrift shop with which it shares space in downtown Great Barrington, the Community Corporation runs chiefly on hope and volunteers. It keeps stitching itself together—a bit of local support here, a bit of federal or state funding there—all the while wishing for a patron more generous, a future more secure. The corporation's entire transportation budget in 1985 came to $68,000.

Yet this fragile enterprise reflects something new on the elderly landscape—a fresh determination in many places to reinvent the wheel. They are called "paratransit" programs, these scattered efforts, and they can be found in some 5,000 towns, where they operate more than 23,000 vans and minibuses.[34] From their struggles and strategies we can begin to respond to that difficult question concerning how to go about institutionalizing compassion. One answer seems to be *very gently*.

Peter M. Schauer, a consultant and close observer of these paratransit groups, has named "intimacy" as their chief characteristic. Most, he has said, "are friendly places to work, with employees being drawn together by a sense of mission and being motivated more by the 'cause' than . . . by any salary. . . . The drivers usually know their riders as friends, which may mean a batch of cookies at Christmas or a personal gift on a birthday." From his survey of such programs Schauer found that half used fewer than five vehicles and, like the one in Great Barrington, got by on annual budgets below $70,000. "A manager may have a problem keeping up with the paperwork," he noted, "but the scale of the operation never goes beyond an individual's grasp." The upshot is "a small group of employees with . . . a modest budget working closely together to meet the transportation needs of their clients."[35]

Not surprisingly, the paratransit people have to be ready to shift gears more quickly and frequently than their mass-transit counterparts. Their schedules are elastic, their itineraries inventive, and their routes both circuitous and far-flung. Not everyone who rides these hybrid vehicles—part buses, part taxis—is over sixty-five. The passengers may also include Head Start children, Medicaid patients, the handicapped— almost anyone, in fact, who needs a lift and can't pay much for it. But older citizens remain the most frequent users. Their growing demand for paratransit services is part of a larger transportation story having to do with the virtual abandonment of rural America, and of large stretches of urban America as well, by private carriers.

The tale could begin in 1914 when a former iron-mine worker named Carl Erie Wickman went into the bus business. He had sunk all his savings into a Hupmobile agency in Hibbing, Minnesota, but when he could find no takers for the lone Hupmobile in his dealership window, he made a bus out of it. Wickman squeezed ten seats into the seven-seat touring car and began making hourly trips from a saloon in Hibbing to the firehouse in a town named Alice, four miles away. A one-way trip cost fifteen cents; a round-trip, twenty-five cents. By 1925 Wickman's tiny caterpillar of a company had emerged as a butterfly. Its new owners called it the Greyhound Lines.

The word "bus," of course, comes from the Latin *omnibus,* which can mean "for everyone." In its formative years Greyhound lived up to that classical definition, dispatching buses to all corners of the land and traveling America's remotest byways as well as its busiest highways. The logic of the marketplace back then demanded comprehensiveness, making it unlikely that rural residents would miss the bus. But after World War II the country's commercial bus lines began to pull out of small communities. Instead of beefing up its busing efforts, Greyhound bought out Armour and became a leading producer of bacon and hot dogs. In 1983 the company finally shed its original cocoon: It canceled all service to Hibbing and the rest of the Minnesota Iron Range. Altogether that year, Greyhound dropped service in 1,313 towns in forty-three states.[36]

Rural citizens are familiar with the consequences of this nationwide exodus: isolation and costly dependence on automobiles. The burden has fallen most heavily on those approximately 5 million older rural residents who are either too poor or too disabled to drive a car. For want of wheels, many have become reluctant shut-ins. It is a rural form of house arrest.

Without a bus to take her where she needs to go, Hazel Johnson guesses she soon will be leaving Union City [Michigan] and the second-floor apartment in the quiet whitewashed boarding house where she has lived for fourteen years. At eighty-three, Johnson is not keen on moving, but she knows that if she wants to get around, there is no other choice. She has applied to a retirement home in Jackson, twenty miles east. Johnson doesn't relish the idea of sacrificing her independence. "It's a real disappointment," she said, "I don't want to leave here, but I have to be able to go places, don't I?"[37]

It took Congress a long time to concede that older Americans needed to go places. Not until 1973 did it authorize capital funds to nonprofit groups in the business of providing rides to elderly and handicapped citizens. The rural side of paratransit got going the following year, when Congress earmarked transportation dollars for projects "exclusively . . . in areas other than urbanized." Then, in 1975, a Comprehensive Service amendment to the Older Americans Act channeled minibus money to senior centers, again underscoring the critical role played by wheels in elderly lives.

There ensued the customary government gambit: an explosion of federal paratransit programs, most of them underfunded, overobligated, and unrelated to one another. A 1982 General Accounting Office study found no fewer than 114 federal programs dispensing transportation to a variety of constituencies, including the elderly. The resulting confusion uncannily mirrored the larger chaos afflicting home-care programs overall.

For local paratransit operators, the bedlam has created king-size administrative headaches. Patricia Flincbaugh, who directs the York Transportation Club in Pennsylvania, has described her all-too-typical ordeal to a congressional committee: "I prepared two budgets, attended a score of contract hearings, prepared statistics to meet 30 funding guidelines and met with at least 25 monitors and evaluators throughout the year. I calculated that 50 percent of my time . . . was spent in servicing the idiosyncracies of each contract."[38]

Withal, federal assistance to paratransit operations has never been bountiful. Some current dollars, about $100 million annually, trickle down from the Urban Mass Transit Administration, otherwise know as UMTA. But that sum, in 1985, constituted less than 3 percent of UMTA's $4.1 billion budget. An additional $900 million or so flow each year from different agencies within the Department of Health and Human Services. Most paratransit programs for the elderly draw sustenance from all these sputtering spigots as well as from a variety of state and local agencies and philanthropies.

Only recently has Congress attempted a serious examination of the wheels it helped to reinvent. In May 1985, rural transportation took center stage at hearings conducted by a subcommittee of the House Public Works and Transportation Committee. The occasion was tinged with anxiety: Earlier, the Reagan administration had recommended deletion of many rural paratransit projects from the budget. To add to the drama, the hearings were chaired by James Oberstar, a Minnesota Democrat who represented the very district in which Greyhound had gotten its start.

Oberstar opened the hearings with a comment about his father, who had died only a few weeks before. "My father never in all his 75 years owned a motor vehicle," Oberstar said. "He used to tell me, 'If you can't walk where you need to go, then you probably don't need to go there.' That is not true today. The nature of our society has changed dramatically."[39] As evidence Oberstar entered into the record excerpts from some of the one thousand letters people in his district had written to Congress and the White House. The writers were hoping to save their local paratransit project, Arrowhead Transit Service, from Reagan's axe.

A woman who identified herself as "Gladys" wrote: "I have heard the news that there is talk of discontinuing the local buses in rural areas. That would be a poor thing to do. . . . Many, like me, cannot walk far because of their age (80 yrs) or their health condition. Please. People who have never lived in rural areas do not realize what a bus means."

"I am very concerned about the prospect of having our rural bus service discontinued," wrote Ilene C. Pearson of Duluth:

> For some of the elderly, who are trying to live independently in their own homes, it will mean entering a nursing home earlier than originally anticipated, because they will no longer have a means of transportation to get medical attention, groceries and other basic necessities. When one considers the high cost of maintaining persons in nursing homes, it is difficult to understand how our present administration feels that they will be saving dollars by cutting out . . . transportation.

"Dearest President Reagan," began Doris Drake, writing from the Sunrise Nursing Home in Two Harbors:

> Ever since President Roosevelt, I have loved you both very much. You see I vote for the man and not the Party and I am not wrong. . . . I don't have much but I have love for everybody. . . .
>
> We stand a chance of losing our Mini-bus. Please don't let this happen, and all the other Mini-bus's all over these United States, Please let them be. . . .
>
> Sure, we need for defense, and lots of it too. Never will we let Russia or any other country take us. We need planes, Helicopters, Cars like your Limousines and hundreds of other things, but minibus's are essential, too.
>
> Good luck in all you do. I like to listen to you on T.V.

It was clear that the minibuses could mean more than transportation. For many of the letter writers they represented rare social opportunities—to visit a friend or relative, to mix with others at the senior center. Just riding the bus seemed a convivial experience. A woman from International Falls credited Arrowhead Transit with preventing her and her neighbors from becoming "woebegone, whining Senior Citizens." "With the very inexpensive bus service," she said, "and our great driver, Mr. Fleming, we can easily manage to get around. After all, we are the Survivors!"

Maybe the late newspaper commentator Simeon Strunsky was right when he remarked that "People who want to understand democracy should spend less time in the library with Aristotle and more time on buses. . . ."[40] I was thinking about that the day I visited the Community Corporation in Great Barrington—a chilly, rain-drenched morning—and rode around in Pat Pixley's van.

We began at the PriceChopper supermarket, where Mr. Larkin, Mrs. Turner, and a half-dozen others climbed aboard with their groceries. But our getaway was not the speediest. Muscles and joints were aching in the damp weather, and Pat had to do a lot of helping and hauling. She also took the time to introduce me to each rider by name.

"How do you do?" I said to one gentleman.

"You're welcome," he replied.

From the PriceChoppers we drove to the public library, where we let off a woman in her eighties who explained that she was partial to suspense novels. "Have been since I was a little girl. I also like to poke around the stacks," she said as she disembarked.

After that Pat started taking some passengers home and picking up new ones. It was getting near noontime, and most of the riders were bound for the senior center, where they ate lunch every weekday. Pat was right about the family feeling in the van. The talk that morning was relaxed and varied, the sort one hears around the dinner table. It ran to the wet weather ("Saps the vitality"), the situation in the Philippines ("Too much bloodshed"), the fact that Washington's birthday was no longer celebrated on February 22 ("Confusing!") and to the interesting patch Mr. Wright was wearing on his blue nylon jacket. It said, "Kiss me."

"Who's that message for?" a woman asked.

"It's for anyone who wants to volunteer," replied Mr. Wright.

Pat's last stop before reaching the senior center took an unusually long time. The new rider was a thin man with a cane. Even with Pat's patient help, it was slow-going over the snow and ice for this very frail gentleman.

At last he stepped into the van. "Well," he said to no one in particular, "I made it."

Mrs. Turner patted him on the hand. "That's all any of us can do is make it," she said. "When you get to be our age, it's one step at a time."

CHAPTER FIVE

◆

A Personal History

Now I may wither into the truth.
—W. B. Yeats,
"The Coming of Wisdom with Time"

She may have known she was slipping long before my brother and I found out. How could we tell? For us she was always "on." Our visits did more than brighten her hours—they sharpened her wits. But afterwards, when Phil had returned to Michigan and I to Connecticut and she was alone again in those silent rooms, she must have had plenty of time to think about it and to worry.

Once she gripped my arm and demanded: "Promise me one thing. No matter what happens, never condescend to me. I couldn't stand that."

"Mother, don't talk that way. What could happen to you?"

"Just promise," she insisted. And I promised.

We noticed it first with the bills. For as long as we could remember she had taken scrupulous care of her accounts, sitting at the maplewood desk and writing checks with her favorite pen, the kind you had to pump ink into. She had been proud of her rounded, graceful script, and of her bookkeeping talents. But now the script looked unfamiliar, *angular,* and the columns in the checkbook never seemed to add up.

More and more she found herself walking over to the Grand Avenue bank and asking Mr. Gottschalk—"that nice young man whose desk sits on a rug"—to balance her totals. To us she made a joke of it. "Poor Mr. Gottschalk," she would say. "Whenever he sees me toddling in he puts his head in his hands. I can just hear him muttering, 'Oh, God, here comes that crazy old lady again.'"

The walk to the bank was only three blocks, but for Mother that was a great distance. Her hip pained her—calcium deposits, her doctor had said—and she had to use a cane. In time a second cane became necessary, and then a walker. No more visits to Mr. Gottschalk. The bills accumulated. And they began to turn up in unexpected places—in kitchen drawers, inside magazines, beneath pillows.

Phil and I decided to take regular turns going to St. Paul. One of us would show up near the first of each month. We would stay long enough to help Mother write the checks, and to take her to "The Lex," her favorite restaurant. The next day, or even that same night, we would return to our wives and our children, plunging back into the main currents of our lives.

One morning I kissed Mother good-bye, got a taxi to the airport, and boarded a plane homeward. When I walked into the house six hours later, Diane was on the telephone. She gave me a funny look and handed me the receiver.

"Where ever *are* you?" Mother was asking. "You said you'd be here. I stayed up half the night waiting."

I reminded her of my visit, of our parting that very morning, and for a moment she seemed to get it all in focus. Then she lost it. "Naturally I'm disappointed," she informed me in rational tones, "but I do understand. I know how busy you are."

I shed tears that night on Diane's shoulder. They were mourner's tears, for I felt that a part of my mother had died. After that, when I went to St. Paul, I tried to stay an extra night or two.

My brother is a doctor. On one of his visits he took Mother to see a neurologist, someone my brother had gone to medical school with. The neurologist was very thorough. He took pictures of Mother's brain; he flexed her limbs and tested her reflexes. Then he asked her some questions: "What day is this?" "When were you born?" "Who is president of the United States?"

Phil called me the next day. "Her brain cells are dying," he said. "It happens sometimes. They say it's irreversible." I tried to picture a billion fireflies inside Mother's head. One by one they were winking out.

I hung up and dialed St. Paul. "How did it go at the doctor's, Mother?"

She laughed. "He asked me a lot of silly questions. Why would he care when I was born? Why would anyone care—it happened so long ago."

Our trips to St. Paul were taking on greater importance. It wasn't just the bills anymore; it was something harder to deal with—a mysterious change of rhythm, a turn in Mother's personal weather. She seldom went out now, not even to buy groceries. Sometimes the refrigerator was empty. Her Wednesday canasta game with "the girls," a social occasion she had relished, was a thing of the past. We guessed that the arithmetic of the cards had become too much for her. Once I asked her why she didn't play any more. "Oh," she snapped uncharacteristically, "they all talk too much."

Her life seemed to be shrinking before our eyes. We noticed that the telephone, which in our youth had seemed a veritable extension of Mother's personality, rarely rang. Why should it? Her closest friends were gone: Alice and Harriet dead; Rose in California, living with her daughter Phyllis; Josephine and Saul in a Florida condominium, and Saul dying of cancer.

Mother was spending a lot of time in her bedroom now, the room furthest back in the house. The living room remained dark, the drapes drawn tight. Mail and newspapers lay in a pile on the front porch. Phil or I sifted through them once a month.

Worse was to come. Suddenly Mother's daily routine, all the little domestic acts the rest of us took for granted, seemed freighted with danger. One evening she went to bed without turning off the oven. She might have died, but around midnight the tenants upstairs smelled smoke and banged on Mother's door. A close call.

Another time she was unable to climb out of the bathtub. She lay in the gray water for hours, until Anna, her occasional cleaning woman, let herself in with a key we'd given her and rescued Mother.

We knew that Anna's fortuitous appearance could not be counted on again. Something had to be done—but what? In situations like this wasn't the community supposed to help? What had become of all those caring organizations Mother had once been a part of—the auxiliaries, the sisterhoods, the charities that had kept her phone ringing all day? Wasn't it their turn to give something back?

Phil and I had grown up in that social-service milieu, yet now we did not know where to turn. We began telephoning our old friends, asking them to look in on Mother from time to time. They were sympathetic, and they tried their best; but they had much else to do. We called local agencies. Did they offer home-care services that Mother could use? Well, yes and no: yes for short-term care of the sick, no for long-term care of the frail; yes for once or twice a week, no for every day.

Phil called Mother's family doctor, Milt, another friend. "Your mother can't take care of herself," Milt said. "She belongs in 'The Home.' You boys have been putting it off too long."

The Home! People went there when they had nowhere else to go. Mother had served on its boards and committees, had raised money for it, had called on its residents many a Sunday. She and her friends were proud of the institution they had helped to build. It was thought to be the best in the state—the finest doctors and nurses, the most up-to-date services, the cleanest corridors. Still, Mother would return from those Sunday visits shaking her head. "Poor Della," she would say. "Poor Celia . . . Poor Mrs. Buxbaum . . ." The Home, I had learned early on, was nobody's happy ending.

Milt's advice jolted us into action. Against Mother's will, we ordered Meals On Wheels for her. At least she would not go hungry. Then we called a college in the area and got a graduate student, a woman from Israel, to live with Mother rent-free in exchange for a few services— shopping, cooking, just being there. The young woman seemed pleased to have found us. She smiled at Mother, who did not smile back. "I like my privacy," Mother told us. But she let us have our way.

Or did she? Early one morning I got a long-distance call from a St. Paul police sergeant. Mother had accused the Israeli woman of stealing her jewelry. They had been up all night, and the stunned woman had left the house at dawn, in tears. None of us ever saw her again.

There followed a sad procession of "companions"—practical nurses, teenage sitters, and part-time "homemakers" supplied by commercial enterprises we'd found listed in the *Yellow Pages*. At first we were very careful: We interviewed each applicant and sought Mother's opinion. But soon the circumstances overwhelmed us. From hundreds of miles away, by telephone, we tried to piece together the splintered logistics of home care. Our goal by then was to have someone in the house with Mother twenty-four hours a day, seven days a week. No single agency, it seemed, and certainly no one individual, sufficed to fill all the time slots. And if any had, would it have mattered? We knew, but never let on, that in the long run neither Mother nor we could afford the around-the-clock services we were so frantically seeking.

There was always the possibility that Mother would consent to live with one of us. It wasn't what she wanted—after more than half a century in St. Paul she couldn't picture herself anywhere else—but her choices were narrowing. Phil pressed harder than I. He went to St. Paul and took Mother back with him to Ann Arbor. She should try it, he told her. She could stay as long as she wished. The next morning he found her standing in the front vestibule, impatiently tapping her foot. Her bags were packed. Phil took her to the airport.

We went back to our scheduling circus and awaited the inevitable. It came one Monday morning. The homemaker had failed to show up Sunday night and Mother was alone. She must have walked in her sleep. The paperboy found her in her nightgown, lying in a puddle of vomit on the cement porch floor. It was March and still cold in

Minnesota. Fearing that Mother might have caught pneumonia, the police took her by ambulance to the hospital.

That afternoon my brother and I were back in St. Paul. We went first to the hospital. Mother was all right. Then we got into our rented car. Very slowly, as in a cortege, we drove out to The Home.

*   *   *

Mother lies in a coma now most of the time, her eyes wide open and childlike. Occasionally her eyelashes flutter and she wakens. Then Lorraine raises Mother's head and brings a glass straw to her lips. "Here's some water, dear. Aren't you thirsty?" It has been nearly a week since Mother has eaten anything solid.

Her breathing is slow and relaxed, though once in a while she emits a great sigh—of forbearance, perhaps, or of impatience. I have no way of knowing. Everything I am witness to here is a mystery.

The room has two other beds in it. One is empty and stripped down to its stained mattress. The other barely seems occupied. Rebecca, a tiny gray woman who never removes her pink anklets, sleeps all day atop the smooth Dacron blanket, her marionette legs and arms folded tight like a baby's. Rebecca is no bother to anyone, yet I resent her presence.

In the beginning, more than four years ago, Phil and I kept pestering the director and the head nurse to transfer Mother to a room of her own where she might enjoy a few modest amenities: an unshared bathroom, a telephone by the bed, more family photographs on the walls. But such luxuries at The Home were reserved for those who could still manage by themselves. Mother's very helplessness, her low "self-care index," consigned her from the start to a section where the smell of disinfectant mixed noisomely with that of urine.

"Now don't you worry," the head nurse told us with a smile that gave no warmth. "You *know* we'll take good care of your mom."

The director had his own way of handling our complaints: He complained right back. "You can't know what I'm up against," he'd say. "Everyone thinks they're special. Everyone wants a favor. Last night at dinner my wife asked me why I was smiling. Why shouldn't I be smiling? She'd caught me thinking about my retirement."

In truth, as the strands of Mother's life attenuated—as she found it more and more difficult to walk, to speak, to think—her privacy ceased to matter so much, or so my brother and I must have decided. Somewhere along the line we fell into step with The Home's own fateful scenario: We gave up the struggle.

Now Mother will have to die in semiprivate surroundings, as so many of her roommates have died before her. Over the years newly inked names have intermittently appeared on the wall outside the heavy bedroom door, signaling the presence of new occupants of the metal beds within.

Lorraine sits opposite me, on the other side of the bed, gently stroking Mother's veined hand. We are sweating out this vigil together, I the restless son, she the latest and most faithful of friends.

Everyone who works at The Home calls Mother by her first name, but Lorraine has earned the right. "Clara," she calls in a singing voice, "can you hear me, dear? I'm right here beside you. You don't have to be afraid." Did Mother blink just then, ever so slightly? Lorraine is certain of it. "You see?" she says to me. "Your mother can still hear us. She understands."

That has been Lorraine's assumption all along: If Mother could no longer speak, she could at least listen, and sometimes she could find ways to respond—by humming a tune, for instance, or by whistling. In recent months, with Lorraine's encouragement, Mother has done a lot of both.

Lorraine never gives up on anyone. "Your mother won't go," she assures me now, "until your brother gets here from Michigan. She's waiting to say goodbye to both her sons."

I am skeptical. My brother is due to arrive this very evening. "That's an interesting theory," I say politely.

Lorraine is a young artist who earns extra income as a part-time companion to residents of The Home. She and Mother have what the staff here calls "a special relationship." They fell in love at first sight. When Phil and I watched them together—when we heard Mother laugh as she let Lorraine brush the tangles out of her long, gray-black hair— we were sorry we hadn't found Lorraine sooner. In our helplessness we doted on the difference she made.

It wasn't that the staff had not been doing its job, only that the job itself was defined so mechanically, so bloodlessly. The nurses and their aides fussed and bustled. They kept Mother well scrubbed, put clothes on her back, gave her medicine, spoon-fed her, wheeled her through the corridors by day, and strapped her into bed each night. In the course of performing such chores they must have touched Mother with their hands hundreds of times, but rarely out of affection. Even the most well oiled of institutions, alas, shares with the Tin Man in *The Wizard of Oz* a fatal hollowness of spirit: It possesses everything but a heart.

Parked in her wheelchair in a TV lounge or in one of those long, antiseptic hallways lined with donors' plaques, Mother must have felt terribly alone. Life of a sort buzzed all around her, but it was a life as indifferent to her own as was the constantly flickering television screen—The Home's eternal light—to which no one ever paid the slightest attention.

Sometimes, when I look back now at Mother's fifty-two months in The Home, I see her trapped in the eye of a storm, inside an institutional whirlwind composed equally of bureaucracy and bedlam. If children in a sandbox engage in what psychologists call "parallel play," then the aged in nursing homes engage in parallel pain. At The Home they seemed always in full cry, pounding their trays and shouting their torments, while a staff clad in white went calmly about its business, dispensing pills, giving baths, mopping floors.

Out of all that commotion emerged nothing sufficiently real to engage Mother's feelings or to address her in ways she could comprehend and reciprocate. Where were the intimacies of yesteryear, where the connections of the heart?

There is a broader way of expressing this: Mother suffered from a type of emotional deprivation endured by nursing home residents everywhere. She was cared *for* but not, in most instances, cared *about*.

Mother fought back in her fashion, especially at first, when she still had the strength. Against the institutional frost she posited the gentlest of thawing agents—her warm and elegant manners. With her walker clearing the way, Mother in a flowing housecoat could inch through bedlam like some lame celestial hostess, conferring hospitality on sufferers and therapists alike.

Long after she had lost the greater part of her prodigious vocabulary, she retained a few useful phrases from the language she held dearest, the language of graciousness: "How nice to see you." "Where have you been keeping yourself?" "Oh, perish the thought—it is I who should thank you."

The rituals of civility that Mother never completely abandoned were more than a reflex; they were part of the emergency rampart she raised to make bearable a life that must have seemed beyond bearing. She would not lack for inventiveness, as I learned the very first time I telephoned her at The Home. (Incoming calls came through a pay phone in the hall, a few feet from the noisiest lounge.)

"I'm feeling much better, thank you," she informed me. "The doctor says I may be able to go home soon."

The next night I called and inquired again. "Well," she said, "the lake is beautiful and there's a nice clientele here, but the rooms are damp and the food is hardly up to . . . hardly up to . . ."

"Standards?" I suggested.

"Snuff," she replied.

The following night she seemed to be back in the hospital and feeling "a little under the weather." But a few days later she was apparently visiting her cousin Esther in Ohio. "Esther and I are sharing a room," she told me. "Esther snores."

"You mean Minnie?" I asked. Minnie was Mother's first roommate at The Home.

"Minnie who?"

Seldom did I have the heart to challenge Mother's fantasies. What good would it have done to insist that she was not visiting Ohio, or not luxuriating at some sunny lakeside spa of her youth? Indeed, it seemed to me she had chosen to sojourn at places more pleasant than any Phil or I could provide for her.

To be sure, the psychologists and social workers at The Home took the opposite tack. Their treatment of residents was "reality oriented," in accord with the latest gerontological theory. A blackboard in the lunch room got updated each morning to imbue elders with a sense of the here and now:

You are living at THE HOME
Today is TUESDAY
The date is SEPTEMBER 5
The temperature outside is 56

These were centripetal news items designed to keep residents from slipping off the mundane coil. But of what use was journalism when the news was always bad? For some like Mother, reality's strictures seemed far less appealing than imagination's privileges. As Dostoevsky's Underground Man observed, "the formula 'twice two make five' is not without its attractions."

Phil and I, meanwhile, entertained some fantasies of our own. Chief among them was our initial illusion that life at The Home need not be lived underground, that Mother in that place could stay connected to the quotidian world at large. Accordingly, we kept up her subscriptions to *Time* and the St. Paul *Pioneer Press;* we maintained her memberships in sundry organizations, both local and national; we even, in a moment of foolish hope, sent her a datebook.

My brother and I should have known better. We should have taken the hint from Mrs. Pollack, who supervised "housekeeping" at The Home, when she gently suggested that we buy Mother "some appropriate clothes"—shifts and robes rather than dresses, slippers rather than shoes. These were shut-in costumes, the raiments of people with no place to go.

Or, earlier still, we might have gotten the message from Banny Baer, an old family friend, after we told her that Mother was moving to The Home. "Damn!" Banny said, and that was all. The lone word assaulted our expectations. It seemed as peremptory, as final, as the slamming of a door. Yet we persisted in the charade; our wish was father to our fantasy.

Mother never did read the publications we sent her. Her reading skills had declined along with her memory. Once, as the two of us sat silently in her room, Mother pointed to a book I had written years before, a fable for children that I had dedicated to her. It had been one of the few things she'd brought with her to The Home, but now she seemed not to recognize it. "What is this?" she asked.

I picked it up and began reading aloud. The story, about a fish's comic attempts to persuade a hungry bear not to eat it, instantly delighted Mother. She took the book from me. Now it was her turn to read aloud, haltingly, her index finger sliding from one word to the next. It had been a long time since I'd seen her so utterly engaged, and so enchanted.

The next morning I sought out a floor supervisor to tell her how much Mother had enjoyed the story. I suggested that other residents might also benefit, and I offered to donate some children's books to The Home. The supervisor was most polite. "I must think about that," she said. "As you know, creativity is built into our daily program."

But I do not wish to be unfair to The Home, which after all pursued its own peculiar vision of excellence. The staff, by and large, was cheerful and considerate (even if the philosophy often seemed obtuse and authoritarian), and the activities offered were as varied and entertaining as one could reasonably expect. Bingo, group singing, lectures, concerts, and folk dancing were the regular fare. For the ambulant there were tours and bus trips to "outside events." For the confined there were visits by members of The Home's always-busy women's auxiliary, who in many instances had known some of the residents in happier circumstances.

The Home was not a business—it was a voluntary, nonprofit, enterprise whose lines reached back into the supporting community. Friends and relatives freely wandered in and out, adding a touch of reality amidst the ongoing madness. Some who served on The Home's board of directors had parents or other close relatives living there.

The Home's facilities included a beauty shop on the first floor, a chapel off the lobby, and a physical therapy unit in the basement. At one time or another Mother partook of all those services and more. There was a period, in fact—perhaps spanning much of her second year there—when Mother seemed remarkably in tune with The Home's institutional rhythms. I could almost believe she was content.

Phil and I traveled to St. Paul as often as we could. It didn't seem to matter which one of us went there; the routine seldom varied. We would take Mother to lunch at The Lex and then go for a long ride in Como Park or along the Mississippi River. Sometimes we would shop at her favorite stores in Highland Park, but never for very long. It wasn't just the walking that exhausted Mother, it was the people she kept running into, people who had known Mother for years. Try as they might, they could not keep from staring at the plastic identification bracelet The Home had fastened around her left wrist. It was a strangely disconcerting symbol, the jewelry of someone outside the pale.

Still and all, those outings were glorious occasions. To Mother they must have seemed like holidays; certainly they did to us. She would have a cream sherry before lunch and a chocolate sundae for dessert. Our ride through Como Park might be topped off with Cokes at the Pavillion or even with more ice cream.

Going back, of course, was another story. "I don't want to go to that place," she would say.

"I know, Mother, I know." But one afternoon the conversation took a surprising turn. We had parked as usual on the ambulance ramp in front of The Home. Through the front windshield Mother gazed wonderingly at the large brick building with its massive glass entranceway glinting in the sunset.

She turned toward me and touched my arm. "This is where I live, isn't it?" she said softly.

"Yes. This is your home."

It may have been the closest either of us ever came to glimpsing reality.

Our little excursions became more difficult as Mother's health deteriorated. The pain in her hip got worse, finally proving impervious to all the painkillers in The Home's capacious pharmacopoeia. We were not surprised when a nurse telephoned my brother one morning in Ann Arbor and told him that Mother could no longer get around with a walker. "We've requisitioned a wheelchair," she said.

At that melancholy juncture, it seems to me in retrospect, The Home simply gave up on Mother. The doctor stopped prescribing physical therapy for her hip; the nurses stopped encouraging her to eat in the congregate dining-room, preferring now to bring trays to her room; and the aides stopped taking her to concerts and other events in the main hall. (By then Mother lacked both the strength to take herself and the words to ask for a push.) To an extent we only half-recognized at the time, Mother had become a part of the general bedlam, another shapeless body to be deposited each morning in the TV lounge.

Withal, Phil and I persisted in taking Mother out. But now we brought along a nurse's aide to help Mother get in and out of the wheelchair and to assist with the food when Mother's hands became too shaky to wield a knife and fork.

One day in October, after a particularly trying lunch at the restaurant, the aide and I were unable to coax or carry Mother into the front seat of the car. Somehow she ended up in a heap on the leaf-strewn sidewalk, crying in panic and begging to be left alone. It took the generosity and muscle of three passersby to rescue her.

That was Mother's last outing. A few weeks later we found Lorraine.

"Tell me," Lorraine now asks, "what was your mother like when you were a child? She must have been a beautiful woman." I try to remember for Lorraine's sake. I am her charge now, her target of mercy, no less than Mother.

But remembering is not easy. Is the old woman lying here really my mother, the same angel-empress who anointed me a prince? How is that possible? My head is dizzy with this grievous disjunction.

Still, I must make an effort. I begin chronologically, as in an old-fashioned novel, the kind Mother used to enjoy reading. In the first place there were her parents—her merchant father, who died of diabetes when she was four, and her remarkable mother, who was part of our own family all those years and who became a third parent to Phil and me. In the second place there were Mother's public school days in Chillicothe, Ohio—where she was taught Latin, French, German, Spanish, and a smattering of Greek—and then her stint at Ohio State, which she cut short to marry Dad. In time there unfurled those sunny days in St. Paul, days the color of yellow grass or clean white snow, before our father took sick.

As I speak, the memories begin to flood my brain: the nifty veiled hats Mother wore; her handsome penmanship and the sepia ink she unaccountably favored; the way she felt my forehead for fever and held me when I had nightmares; the time I discovered her teenage diary and, against her wishes, read a few of the wonderfully frivolous entries (I was a teenager myself then); the secret, extrasucculent words we savored together: "hoopla," "hosanna," "lubricous," "litotes"; how she looked that stricken time I had to tell her Dad was dead, and how Phil and I at the funeral tried to quell her wrenching sobs; her faith, which I could never emulate, and her singing, which no one in the congregation could ever match: "May the words of my mouth / and the meditations of my heart / be acceptable in Thy sight, O Lord."

On and on I talk, for fear of drowning, while Lorraine just by listening keeps me afloat. And all the time I am drawing nearer, feeling closer, to the woman who has brought us together and now lies between us. My mother.

It turned out Lorraine was right as usual. My brother arrived at six o'clock, and less than two hours later Mother passed on, gently and without complaint. She was two months short of being eighty-two.

Incredibly, Mother had uttered a word, an affirmation, in our presence. "Clara," Lorraine had called, "do you know where you are going? It won't hurt, dear. It isn't at all painful."

And from the very edge Mother had whispered, "Yes."

It was not until days later that I realized Rebecca, the spectral roommate, was out of the room when Mother died. Perhaps a considerate nurse had found another bed for her. If so, I am grateful. In nursing homes, as in all final refuges, no kindness can ever be taken for granted.

CHAPTER SIX

Exile: The Perils of Institutionalization

*We need someone to hold our hand, kiss us on the cheek,
reassure us and commiserate with us. Please don't find fault
with us, ignore us or scream at us. We are not inanimate
objects. . . . Recognize our needs and desires.
Tomorrow we will be gone.*
—A nursing home resident in Boston

If you have tears, prepare to shed them now. We are in the presence of an institution society needs but does not wholly accept, an institution that many deplore but none can reform. It is a system grown remote from the people it was meant to protect and the communities it was supposed to serve. Its humane components, left over from an earlier era, have become endangered species, while its predatory elements thrive as never before.

The business enterprises this system spawns and supports can yield fabulous rewards to its stockholders but few consolations to its workers and fewer still to its customers. Profits are its daily quarry. Among the affluent it regularly courts favor; against the poor it routinely discriminates. And all this is made possible by an enormous, fragmented government bureaucracy created for the best of reasons and perpetuated with the worst of consequences.

In such a climate, social commentary seems awash in tears but empty of hope. One of the best of the commentators is Bruce C. Vladeck, who ended his sensitive study, *The Nursing Home Tragedy,* by pointing a finger at all of us—"not because we are unsympathetic to people's needs," he said, but because "there are certain things only government can or will do, and we have denied government the means to do them." In a nation that prizes the public sector chiefly for its weaknesses, "people who cannot make their way privately are out of luck." Vladeck must have encountered thousands of such luckless people in the course of his researches. His book's grim conclusion bespeaks their helplessness and his: "So they sit in their nursing homes, minds clouded by drugs, staring unfocusingly at daytime television, and soon, but not soon enough, they are dead."[1]

It is well to set the scene, which keeps ramifying, and to name the cast, which keeps growing. At present (1989) about 16,000 nursing homes with some 1 million employees provide shelter, care, and sustenance of varying quality to 1.5 million older Americans.

In contrast to the flimsy public superstructure on which home-care practitioners must rely, our nursing homes enjoy considerable federal and state support. But much of it seems as unfocused as were Vladeck's hapless residents, for no one in Washington ever pays much attention to nursing home issues. Vladeck is correct in noting that the formulation of nursing home policy has largely been "an afterthought, a side effect of decisions directed at other problems—mostly those of health care and poverty."[2]

One upshot has been a procession of debatable measures enacted without meaningful debate. Medicaid, brought forth with Medicare in 1965, has supplied the legislative matrix, but Medicaid was itself hastily conceived and improvidently passed. Viewed from the angle of a nursing home resident who is poor—that is, from the inside looking out—Medicaid fully justifies Wilbur Cohen's point that a program designed for the poor will probably be a poor program.

As a "partnership" between the federal government and the separate states, Medicaid is not one but fifty-one programs, and its lines of authority are tangled beyond extrication; as a means-tested subsidy system, it makes pauperization the price of rescue; and as an extension of national ambivalence, it is careful with its disbursements but careless in its role as watchdog for the aged.

Who will expound on the exact nature of our obligations to these fellow voyagers turned castaways? And who can say for certain that we shall not ourselves be one day set adrift? "The aged are not a class," observed I. M. Rubinow, who spent the greater part of his life fighting for the enactment of social security. "They are a stage of our own lives." It will probably take more than good intentions to make the best of the shared calamity we call institutional care. In the end it may require our utmost in social and political ingenuity. This, too, Rubinow foretold. "If we are really concerned with making the lives of all the old people as happy as possible," he wrote, then we must pay strict attention to "the problems arising out of proper organization of institutions for the aged."[3]

Those problems are what this chapter is mainly about. It includes two overviews, one a history, the other a here-and-now broadside examining the present performance of nursing homes. In both sections I take into account commerce as well as compassion, the marketplace and the mercy place. There follows an examination of the Medicaid program, its uses and its abuses. The chapter ends with an attempt to demonstrate the futility of fatalism and the benefits that can accrue from community commitment.

"Over the Hill": The Past as Prologue

Most of the shortcomings displayed by nursing homes and their governmental partners—the class favoritism, the neglect of poor people, the bottom-line mentality—stem from attitudes that have long been associated with the national psyche. They constitute the American nightmare as well as the American dream. The two, in fact, appear inseparable.

From the beginning we envisioned a kind of Puritan paradise, a stern utopia in which—to quote the Mayflower Compact—"willful poverty should find no lodgment." True, the helpless were to be helped, but never cheerfully or generously, and nearly always at a profit. Ethel McClure has described the process:

> As the number of poor persons increased and the giving of relief grew to be more and more of a burden, it became the aim to dispose of these people as cheaply as possible. Thus developed the public auction, where the pauper was awarded to the family who would care for him for the smallest amount or, if he were able to work, to the person who would bid the highest sum for his services.[4]

At such an auction, observed the historian Robert W. Kelso, citizens "could speculate upon the bodily vigor and the probable capacity for hard labor of a half-witted boy, a forlorn-looking widow, or a halt and tottering old man."[5]

Public auctions persisted into the nineteenth century, gradually to be replaced by methods only a scant less callous. In one arrangement, a town would contract with someone to take care of all the poor under a single roof. Here was the forerunner of today's proprietary nursing home, which from its inception seems to have relied on public funds. Kelso called it "a privately operated almshouse where the profit to the keeper was the object sought."[6]

Another approach was to have a city or county operate a "poor farm" at taxpayer expense, though the outlay in most instances could not have been substantial. Here, too, the past foretold the future. A legislative committee investigating county-run almshouses in the state of New York, for instance, reported in 1856 that most were "badly constructed, ill-arranged, ill-warmed and ill-ventilated." Furthermore, "the rooms are crowded with inmates; and the air, particularly in the sleeping apartments, is very noxious."[7]

Both the public poor farms and the private almshouses served as catchments for all kinds of sufferers: "the widow who was beyond self-support; the little child left orphaned; . . . the idiot who was the grinning butt of public ridicule; the maniac; the lame; the halt; the blind."[8] But as the nation grew older, so too did its poorhouse population. As early as 1851 a Rhode Island investigator named Thomas R. Hazard could complain that poorhouse overseers were often too young to understand elderly needs. Pointing out that more than one-fourth of the state's almshouse residents were aged, Hazard introduced a problem we are still trying to resolve—the dilemma of exile: "To separate an old person from a home that they have long been accustomed to . . . is very much like tearing an old tree from the ground in which it has grown. . . . They will both, in all probability, wither and die."[9]

At first imperceptibly, like the hands of a great clock, the separate ideas of poverty and of old age drew closer to each other in the public's mind. Then Will Carleton, a popular poet of his day, sped up the clock with his "Over the Hill to the Poor-House," published in *Harper's Weekly* during the summer of 1871. A first-person tale of woe and neglect, the poem presented a species of intergenerational conflict that in time would become all too familiar, as would the sad conclusion:

Over the hill to the poor-house I'm trudgin' my weary way—
I, a woman of 70, and only a trifle gray—
I, who am smart an' chipper, for all the years I've told,
As many another woman that's only half as old.

This spry widow, it seemed, had been nudged out of her home by her youngest son Charley and his new wife; her only recourse had been to move in with another of her married offspring. First she tried Thomas, her oldest son:

But all the childr'n was on me—I couldn't stand their sauce—
And Thomas said I needn't think I was comin' there as boss.

Then she wrote to Rebecca and to Isaac, both of whom lived "out West." But—

> one of 'em said 'twas too warm there for any one so old,
> And t'other had an opinion the climate was too cold.

In the end, betrayal begot tragedy:

> So they have shirked and slighted me, an' shifted me about—
> So they have well-nigh soured me, an' wore my old heart out;
> But still I've borne up pretty well, an' wasn't much put down,
> Till Charley went to the poor-master, an' put me on the town.

Carleton's rhymed lament so captured the public's imagination, and perhaps its conscience as well, that "over the hill" soon became a synonym for "poorhouse." But the demographics of old age seem over time to have altered the phrase's meaning. According to Eric Partridge's *A Dictionary of Slang and Unconventional English* (1984), current definitions of "over the hill" include "getting on in years" and "long in the tooth."

By the turn of the century the public-poorhouse approach to human helplessness had been widely discredited but not wholly discarded. In many places there were appearing fresh alternatives in the form of charitable institutions, precursors to our voluntary nursing homes. The new altruists, mostly local religious groups, tended to be more selective than their predecessors. As their institutional names suggested, age and gender were deemed paramount: the Lutheran Orphans Home and Asylum for the Aged and Infirm; the Home for Aged Indigent Females; the Widows and Old Men's Home.

The sponsors' emphasis on age was timely to say the least. By 1923 more than half the country's public almshouse residents were over 65 and another 20 percent were between 55 and 65. Most were disabled, and all were compelled to live in excruciatingly close quarters with some of society's most difficult "rejects." In the words of the U.S. Department of Labor, "insanity, feeble-mindedness, depravity, and respectable old age are mingled in haphazard unconcern."[10]

The charitable homes' strict entrance requirements could be counterproductive. Writing in 1930, Florence E. Parker of the Bureau of Labor told of "a home of considerable size, beautifully situated and tastefully furnished, which accepts only Presbyterian ministers who do not use tobacco in any form. The home has had no occupants for several years."[11]

Parker and her colleagues at the bureau had recently completed a pioneering nationwide survey of homes for the aged. The count was 1,270 institutions and some 80,000 residents; all but 55 of the homes studied were under charitable auspices. Then, at a University of Chicago conference on problems of the aged (called by the indefatigable Rubinow), Parker summarized the bureau's findings. To anyone even modestly acquainted with nursing homes today, her major points will sound oddly up-to-date.

To begin with, Parker cited "the problems of idleness in old people's homes" and "the obvious effects of lack of mental occupation." Many of the "matrons" who answered the bureau's questionnaire, she said, "feel pride in the fact of the inmates' having 'nothing to do but enjoy themselves,' and fail to see that that very condition is in itself bad for the old people who are still active."

Next she noted that the survey had brought to light a surprising shortage of beds: "That they cannot begin to meet the need existing is shown by the fact that practically 90 percent of the homes visited had long waiting lists—so long that it may take years for an applicant to obtain admittance to the home."

But what struck Parker most powerfully about the homes were their class disparities. At one extreme, she observed,

is a home lavishly endowed under the will of a rich man, which stands in large landscaped grounds, in a beautiful residential suburb. The living rooms are the last word in comfort and luxury. Each inmate has his own bedroom which is furnished with soft, thick carpet, easy chairs, several floor and wall lights, individual telephone, four-poster bed, chiffonier, bookcases, fireplace, and a clothes closet equipped with both shelves and drawers.

The entrance requirements to such homes, Parker made clear, were unusually strict, while

At the other end of the scale are the homes which usually have no requirements except age and destitution. . . . These furnish only cleanliness and the barest necessaries of existence—the plainest food, and sleeping accommodations in large dormitories holding as many as thirty to thirty-five beds. In such homes there is practically no privacy, practically nothing in the way of comforts, and in some institutions of this type a splint rocker is regarded as a luxury.

Although Parker understood that beggars could not be choosers, she was not amused: "For the class of persons admitted, the assurance of food and shelter even of the poorest sort must be a blessing, but one visiting these homes cannot help but pity the old, tired bodies that must rest themselves in hard straight chairs, especially when the dormitories are locked during the day, as was found to be the case in several instances."[12]

Both the Bureau of Labor's survey and the University of Chicago's conference heralded something new on the sociopolitical landscape: an awakening to the presence of an older population on the rise and to its many unaddressed problems. The elderly in 1920 made up 4 percent of the overall population; by the time of the conference, a decade later, they had topped 5 percent and were climbing fast. Their institutional needs became more pressing, more visible, as their numbers grew.

In addition, the bureau's initiative represented an early significant effort on the part of a federal agency to stake out a role for itself in the emerging nursing home drama, albeit only as a collector of data. From such seedlings would eventually spring a whole forest of federal programs and subsidies; and, intentionally or not, many of those programs would promote the profitability of private nursing homes as surely as pauper auctions had once promoted the profitability of private residences for the poor. Even the Social Security Act of 1935 would play a part in the proceedings—with surprising results.

From Social Security to Medicaid

Most of those pushing for a federal old-age pension system expected the benefits eventually to render almshouses and homes for the aged all but obsolete. They based the prediction on a shaky supposition— that poverty, not decrepitude, was the leading cause of elderly institutionalization. Rubinow, of course, thought otherwise. He labeled such optimism "careless and . . . damaging to the movement," and he cited the many aged persons "for whom perhaps a complicated apparatus of continuous nursing and medical care is necessary."[13]

The event fully justified the warning. In the 1940s, as monthly social security checks began to flow in earnest, more and more retired workers applied them against the costs of long-term care in homes for the aged. In consequence, business picked up for quite a few benevolent homes.

But it was not those benefits alone that lent new life to the homes, nor was it only the nonprofit enterprises that would register gains. Another part of the Social Security Act, Title I, established a federal program for matching grants-in-aid to the states for old-age assistance (OAA). Congress authorized about $25 million for the means-tested program the first year—but it specifically barred from participation any "inmate of a public institution."

The prohibition seemed a good idea at the time. Public poorhouses were notorious for the shabby services they provided; no one wished to support them at national expense. It was assumed, moreover, that the elderly inmates would soon abandon those scorned institutions: They would simply go home, where they could be eligible for OAA support.

In fact, something quite different occurred, as became clear in the very first issue of the *Social Security Bulletin,* the official publication of the Social Security Board in Washington. Most of the older almshouse residents, reported the *Bulletin* in 1938, "require institutional care and hence cannot be removed." Vladeck has summed up the lesson, echoing Rubinow: "Pensions, it turned out, were *not* a substitute for indoor relief, at least not for the elderly who were infirm as well as poor."[14]

But pensions could do wonders for another, less conspicuous kind of indoor relief. The proprietary "nursing homes"—still mainly boarding houses and convalescent homes—which had been struggling through the Great Depression, now started to thrive and to multiply. They were accidental beneficiaries of federal measures that had never taken them into account. Both the social security checks and the OAA payments heated up elderly demand for institutional care, while Congress's ban on subsidies to public almshouse residents deflected much of that demand toward homes run for profit.

The ban, to be sure, was lifted in 1950, but by then its consequences had, literally, been set in concrete, in the form of some 7,000 private, profit-making nursing homes. When the Public Health Service conducted its first national survey of skilled nursing homes in 1954, it found that of the 9,000 extant, 86 percent were proprietary and only 4 percent were public. The remaining 10 percent operated under nonprofit auspices.[15] (Those proportions have held more or less true to this day.)

By then, moreover, nursing homes had already assumed their characteristic hospital-like shape and ambience. Form followed function in the long, dreary corridors, the strategically placed nursing stations, the narrow beds with their squared blankets; and mood followed process in the stentorian loudspeakers on every floor, and in the staffs' crisp white uniforms that seemed to mock the residents' own drab, convalescent garb. Such now-familiar hallmarks placed most of the emphasis on "nursing" and hardly any on "home." The overall effect was to turn active residents into passive patients, blurring their identities and discouraging their participation in the life around them.

Meanwhile, a new payments process—specifically, a new way for OAA dollars to reach health-care suppliers—added to patient passivity.

OAA checks had always gone to the beneficiaries; now a 1950 amendment to the Social Security Act permitted states and local welfare agencies to short-circuit nursing home residents and hospital patients by sending payments directly to the "vendors." This was the start of a third-party reimbursement system destined to become the multi-billion-dollar centerpiece of U.S. health care.

All this may have been inevitable—or so it seems in retrospect. In some measure, at least, the need dictated the response. For what was society to do with its elderly "who were infirm as well as poor"? To whose care could they be commended? At the University of Chicago conference in 1930 a Massachusetts welfare administrator named Francis Bardwell had taken up those very questions. By far the greater number of long-term hospital patients, he'd observed, "are found among those suffering from chronic and incurable disease, old men and old women who need nursing care." Consequently, "we are little by little converting portions of various infirmaries into wards with chronic patients."[16]

At that early juncture it did seem likely that voluntary hospitals would ultimately shoulder the major responsibility for long-term institutional care of the aged. The likelihood increased with the close of World War II, when Congress began passing measures aimed at rebuilding the nation's rickety network of charitable and public hospitals. Most important was the 1946 Hospital and Construction Act, commonly known as Hill-Burton (after its Senate sponsors, Lister Hill of Alabama and Harold Burton of Ohio). Over the next twenty-five years Hill-Burton helped transform the U.S. health-care system, channeling more than $2.5 billion in construction loans to about 6,000 hospitals, and making possible 350,000 new beds. When all was spent and built, the hospitals emerged as the main attraction in American medicine, the prime healer and also the chief repository of health-care dollars.

Note, however, that initial Hill-Burton dollars went only to hospitals. The omission was corrected in a 1954 amendment, which provided grants for the construction of public and nonprofit nursing facilities as well. This was the first time lawmakers had singled out nursing homes for federal largess, and it reflected a growing recognition that hospitals were not, after all, going to fulfill the rising demand for elderly institutional care. As Rubinow had foreseen, the times called for "a complicated apparatus of continuous nursing and medical care"— in short, for nursing homes.

The extension of Hill-Burton to include voluntary nursing homes radically altered the picture. For one thing, it brought nursing homes into the jurisdiction of the Public Health Service (PHS), which administered the program, and thus transformed them into medical facilities. The PHS officials who drew up construction requirements, says Vladeck, "were heavily affected by their hospital orientation, which is why . . . most nursing homes look so much like mini-hospitals."[17]

For another, the program helped galvanize a new lobby in Washington, the American Nursing Home Association (ANHA), which represented proprietary interests but which had failed to get those interests included in the 1954 amendment. Now the ANHA turned to more friendly federal arenas. In 1956 it succeeded in obtaining authorization for construction loans from the Small Business Administration; better still, in 1959 it was able to tap into the lush programs of the Federal Housing Administration. That agency would, in due course, make available to profit-making nursing homes more than $1 billion in guaranteed mortgages.

But much more was in the offing, thanks mainly to Wilbur Mills, who chaired the House Ways and Means Committee, and to Robert Kerr, Mills's counterpart in the Senate. Together they managed to get passed a new program of "medical assistance for the aged," which included vendor payments via the states for "skilled nursing home services" to the "medically indigent," that is, to anyone who could not afford the cost of institutionalization. For nursing homes the measure seemed heaven sent. Their vendor payments increased almost tenfold in the five years before Medicaid. It has been estimated that more than half of all nursing home residents were beneficiaries of Kerr-Mills subsidies.[18]

The years immediately preceding Medicaid, then, represented a watershed for nursing homes in general and for the proprietaries in particular. Opportunities for huge profits abounded, and in hot pursuit came all manner of speculators and entrepreneurs. Some no doubt hoped to do good; others merely hoped to do well, and they did not care who suffered the consequences. The decade was rife with scandals— with tales of unsanitary conditions, tragic fires, widespread neglect, and abuse of residents—the sort of revelations, in fact, to which we have now grown accustomed.

Whatever had been the intent of federal policy over the past quarter century, it ended by placing proprietary nursing homes in the catbird seat, from which perch they enjoyed a steady flow of federal capital and a growing assurance of state vendor payments. The money, moreover, arrived virtually free of strings, for neither Congress nor the states had taken the trouble to introduce effective regulatory restraints. Thus did a somewhat unsavory industry profit from a largely unsaved clientele.

The Way Things Are Now

Under Medicaid all has changed, yet all has remained the same. For the most part the program has simply enlarged on old mistakes. Profits and class disparities keep expanding against a backdrop of deteriorating conditions inside many institutions. Commerce has gained new power and sophistication, further removing it from the reach of compassion. The shortage of nursing home beds, meanwhile, continues apace, creating a seller's market and often a buyer's nightmare. Finally, just as in colonial days, official policy aims "to dispose of these people as cheaply as possible." We begin with the industry and its profits, proceed to the residents and their woes, and conclude with Medicaid and its consequences.

The Fast-Care Industry

The business of nursing homes is chiefly business, and in recent years it's been booming. Gross income soared to $35 billion in 1985, exceeding by nearly three times what it had been a decade earlier. If the dollar deluge has whetted Wall Street's appetite, it may also have dulled the public's sensibilities. The very fact that journalists now refer to these care-giving institutions collectively as "the industry" suggests the extent to which they have been accepted as a branch of big business. Accounts have largely eclipsed accountability.

Not surprisingly, fewer than one-quarter of the nation's nursing homes today are operated by philanthropic organizations or by public agencies. Seventy-eight percent are run for profit, and a growing proportion of these consists of large, national chains—the caregiving equivalents of Sears and McDonalds. The chains control an estimated two-fifths of the total market; in many communities they already enjoy virtual monopolies. By the year 2000, Wall Street analysts have said, the chains will have increased their market share to at least 60 percent, a degree of concentration approaching oligopoly.

The market's bright prospects have already attracted companies with no previous experience in health care. Avon Products and the Marriott Corporation are two recent entries; so is the container manufacturer Owens-Illinois, whose subsidiary—the Health Retirement Corporation of America—has already become the nation's seventh largest investor-owned nursing home chain. The AFL-CIO could not have been far off the mark when, in a 1984 monograph on corporate takeovers, it concluded that the United States was "already well down the road to becoming the only country in the world with a health care system dominated by large, corporate . . . chains in the health business solely for profit."

In 1985 the top 50 nursing home chains took in $5 billion, more than half of which went to just two corporations, a pair of West Coast behemoths known as Beverly Enterprises and the Hillhaven Corporation. Beverly is the larger of the two, and its story is instructive. In 1963, the year the corporation opened for business, it owned just 3 nursing homes, with only 245 residents. Today it operates more than 1,000 homes and 115,000 beds. Beverly's heaviest concentration is in the South, but it also controls some 9,000 nursing home beds in California and nearly 5,000 in Michigan, or about 8 percent of the total in each. In Texas it owns 10 percent of the market, in Georgia 11 percent, and in Arkansas a whopping 25 percent.[19]

The astonishing growth of fast-care chains does not appear to have improved conditions in nursing homes. There are such things as chain-linked deficiencies, chief among them a tendency to maximize profits at the expense of services. What the chains usually do with their profits is of no use either to the residents or the general public. Instead of upgrading services, they increase dividends to stockholders; instead of building new facilities, they swallow up existing ones, thereby adding not a single bed to the nation's inadequate pool.

It is true that not all fast-care facilities are obsessed by profits, just as not all charitable homes are guided by altruism. In general, however, philanthropic nursing homes deliver better care than do commercial ones, and for obvious reasons. It is a question of ends and means: In philanthropic enterprises, care is the end and money is the means; in proprietary homes, the philosophy is reversed.

We can sense the latter approach at work in the testimony of Judy Moser, a former nursing home director in Madisonville, Tennessee. She told a Senate committee what happened when her employer sold out to a regional chain that owned fourteen other nursing homes. For openers, the staff-patient ratio jumped from one to ten to one to thirteen. "And all the good aides started quitting, because they could not provide the care that was needed; they did not have time." One day, remembered Ms. Moser, her bosses called a staff meeting: "They said they knew how to make money, and they were in it for the money, and that in order to make money they would have to cut the staffing, so they were going to cut it again, and the care was going to go down even worse." Ms. Moser's reply was to resign her position. "I told them that this was the people's home and that I would not be a part of making it a business."[20]

The chains, to be sure, take a more sanguine view of the matter. They argue that economies of scale and other corporate efficiencies actually improve the quality of care, that what is good for business is also good for residents. Beverly Enterprises in particular has been at pains to emphasize this putative connection between human welfare and corporate profits. "It is our dedication to the delivery of quality healthcare and our immense concern for the well-being of the elderly," the corporation has told its shareholders, "that has built our company into the most respected in its field today. . . . We can all continue to take pride in what we do. We do it better than anyone else."[21]

But pride may not be an entirely appropriate response—not in Michigan, at any rate, where Beverly's behavior has been closely scrutinized by the Department of Public Health and also by labor unions trying to organize the company's workers. A 1982 state-sponsored pilot project ranked nursing homes there on a three-step scale: better, average, and worse. Twenty-three percent of Beverly-controlled homes fell in the "worse" category, compared with 16 percent of nursing homes statewide. In the "better" category, 22 percent of Michigan's nursing homes but only 13 percent of Beverly's met the study's standards.

The AFL-CIO analysis went further still. Among other things, it examined what happened to the quality of care in seventeen homes that Beverly had acquired in 1981 from a smaller company named Provincial House. The evidence, culled from reports of state Public Health inspectors, suggested that "care deteriorated when Beverly Enterprises took over homes in the state." Excerpts from the notebooks of inspectors who investigated Beverly nursing homes about a year after they'd been acquired from Provincial House revealed heavier patterns of patient neglect. The notations do not make pleasant reading. Here are just a few:

> A patient with a feeding tube was not receiving adequate oral care as evidenced by parched lips and tongue and oral residue. Other patients were observed with sticky saliva stringed between their teeth. Fourteen bedside stands in Units A and B failed to contain a complete set of oral care equipment such as brush and paste. . . .
> 4 of 5 accidents involving bodily injury to the patients were not reported to the family, next of kin or legal guardian. . . .
> A total of 119 man-hours per day is not sufficient supportive personnel for a 360-bed facility, as evidenced by lack of acceptable sanitation practices and the poor nutritional care rendered.
> Three patients had contractures of the hands with one nail grown in flesh and one with skin breakdown from nails. Bed patients are not provided with padding between skin surfaces.[22]

The Michigan experience with Beverly Enterprises is hardly reassuring. At bottom it may reflect the limits of commerce in helping us make life easier for the oldest and frailest among us. That the "McDonalds-ization" of the nursing home system may be dangerous to society's health seems implicit in our apparent inability to intervene. Corporate care, like corporate control, can appear bafflingly remote; often it discourages traditional forms of community participation and thus deprives residents of protections once gained from citizen vigilance.

For most of us now it may be easier to buy stock in a nursing home corporation than to discover what goes on in one of its facilities.

A Surplus of Disabilities

It is possible to speak here of disabilities in two spheres, for many nursing homes—and not just the chains—seem at least as incapacitated as their residents; that is, they display an "absence of competent physical, intellectual or moral power, means, fitness or the like"— which happens to be my dictionary's definition of *disability*. For an illustration the dictionary cites John Milton concerning "disabilities to perform what was covenanted," a fair if unintended summation of the nursing home tragedy.[23]

As for the residents, their infirmities keep piling up. The gerontologist Dorothy P. Rice has provided a partial synopsis:

> In general, elderly residents . . . suffer from multiple chronic conditions and chronic impairments. About two-thirds are senile, 36 percent have heart trouble, and 14 percent have diabetes. Orthopedic problems . . . are common. About a third are bedfast or chairfast and about a third are incontinent. Almost half the elderly in nursing homes cannot see well enough to read a newspaper regardless of whether they wear glasses; one-third cannot hear a conversation on an ordinary telephone; and one-fourth have impaired speech.[24]

So disabled a clientele requires constant attention. Federal government surveys indicate that more than half of all older residents need help with using the toilet, two-thirds with walking, two-thirds with dressing, and more than four-fifths with bathing. "Many have to be spoon-fed like babies," an aide in a New York City nursing home told me. "Without us they'd starve to death."

A visitor unaccustomed to the sights and sounds of amassed impairments among the aged may be in for some discouraging moments. The toothless crone weeping in her wheelchair and pounding the wall with a rolled-up newspaper; the cadaverous old man rocking fetus-like atop his bed; the patients with tubes in their noses and needles in their arms—such scenes can feed a visitor's suspicion that to enter here is to abandon all hope.

But in nursing homes things are not always what they appear to be. That rolled-up newspaper, for instance, is the *Christian Science Monitor,* which the weeping woman reads carefully every morning; the fact is, she is starved for news and conversation. The man who rocks on his bed likes to listen to Mozart and to hum along; he "responds well to music therapy," a nurse tells the visitor. Even the dying—perhaps especially the dying—cherish small favors: an aide's gentle hands, a cool sponge bath, the raising of a shade so that light streams through a window. Who at the Medicaid office can set a price on such "services"?

In nursing homes loneliness is a constant companion. One of every five residents has no living relatives; 85 percent are widowed, unmarried, or divorced. Many have outlived their siblings, their friends, even their children—everyone, in fact, who might come to their rescue. Can diagnosticians distinguish between the chemistry of the brain and that of the heart, between cellular decay and psychic bereavement? The symptoms may look remarkably similar.

Some of our novelists have probed these mysteries. In May Sarton's *As We Are Now,* the elderly protagonist has been placed in a nursing home by her brother and his new, much younger wife; and there, to hold on to her sanity, she keeps a diary. "The fact is," this woman writes at a particularly melancholy juncture, "that I am dying for lack of love."[25]

The best nursing homes take such insights into account. They run on the humble premise that no resident, however venerable or vulnerable, is beyond reach of help or affection. What these homes chiefly dispense, for all their sophisticated medicines and therapies, is custodial love, the same gift my friend Lorraine conferred on my dying mother. But in the nursing home wilderness such cases are hard to find.

"Descent into Hell"

The endemic shabbiness of elderly institutional care has long been recognized; it casts a familiar shadow over our social landscape. "The best governmental estimate," Vladeck noted in 1980, "is that roughly half the nation's nursing homes are 'substandard'"—a mild enough opprobrium, all things considered.[26] In 1986, after an exhaustive study, a special committee appointed by the Institute of Medicine concluded that "the poor-quality homes outnumber the very good ones."[27]

Others have resorted to stronger language. John Heinz, then chairman of the Senate Special Committee on Aging, told a press conference in 1986 that "for tens of thousands of our oldest, sickest citizens the hope for a haven for care becomes instead a sure descent into hell." To jaded journalists the Dantesque rhetoric may have seemed exaggerated, but Heinz's committee had just completed a major two-year quality-of-care investigation of U.S. nursing homes, and now he was trying to do justice to the dismal findings.

This study is noteworthy on at least two counts—for the thoroughness with which it was conducted and for the truths it uncovered. Not only did the staff examine hundreds of nursing homes firsthand, it analyzed thousands of state inspection reports that the Health Care Financing Administration (HCFA)—the federal agency that manages Medicaid and Medicare—had apparently never bothered to read.

The results justify netherworld analogies; and they explicitly challenge a favorite American myth—the one that assures us things are getting better all the time. Committee researchers concluded just the opposite: "Horror stories in nursing homes are thought by many to be rare occurrences, isolated in number and, for the most part, relegated to history. Unfortunately, this is an untrue perception; an alarming number of nursing homes continue to provide grossly inadequate care resulting in humiliation, suffering and premature death."[28]

Thanks to those state inspection reports, the researchers were able to trace over time certain violations of federal rules for caregiving. They found, for instance, that the 1982–1984 period saw a 75 percent increase in nursing home "failures to provide adequate supervision"; another 75 percent increase in "cases where residents were subject to mental, physical and/or chemical abuse"; and a 61 percent increase in the number of nursing homes that deprived residents of around-the-clock services.

All the examples Heinz cited seemed related to a single problem— inadequate staffing. "We find," he said, "more elderly residents strapped into wheelchairs all day, fed a diet of tranquilizers, . . . going month to month without a doctor's visit or a review of medications, . . . having heart attacks in the middle of the night with no nurse to call."[29]

The sour joke revealed by such investigations is that our nursing homes employ remarkably few nurses. More than 70 percent of the "nursing" personnel is made up of unlicensed aides, and these account for as much as 90 percent of the care delivered. To put it another way, aides in nursing homes provide six times as much care as do registered nurses and five times as much as practical nurses. Federal regulations permit aides to dispense all the care most of the time—from 3:00 P.M. to 7:00 A.M. every day—without licensed supervision.[30]

An index of one's perceived worth in society can be the wages one earns. Perhaps a more telling index is the wages one's caregiver earns. In 1986 a nursing home aide's average wage was less than $4.00 an hour, considerably below that paid for comparable work in clinics and hospitals. The nursing homes take whomever they can get for the price they are willing to pay. As the Institute of Medicine pointed out in its report, "aides usually are not experienced or adequately trained for their jobs. . . . In some places they speak English poorly and . . . are new to the job as well."[31] The turnover rate among aides can be as high as 75 percent at a single nursing home within a single year.

But there is another side to the story. If one reality of the nursing home business is how little its workers receive, one miracle is how much they give. Whatever acts of kindness these enterprises generate, whatever moments of tenderness or affection they make possible, come directly from this bottom echelon of servitors, a contingent more generous and steadfast than we have any right to expect.

An official of the Service Employees International Union, whose job is to organize low-level nursing home workers, complained to me of strikers who returned to work as "volunteers" because they could not bear to neglect their elderly charges. "That's a hell of a way to conduct a strike," growled the union leader.

*　　*　　*

In general, then, the picture that emerges is of an industry whose obligations have outrun its capacities, a system either unable or unwilling "to perform what was covenanted." The fault is not in the chains alone. It appears to lie everywhere, and thus chiefly in us and in the sort of society we have chosen to tolerate. We reached this impasse in part via the imperatives of private enterprise but mainly, as will become clear, via the dictates of public policy.

The Use and Abuse of Medicaid

In nursing home circles Medicaid is the measure of all things, paying for at least some of the costs incurred by more than two-thirds of the residents. Only a small proportion of homes, about a thousand in all, have not been "Medicaid certified," meaning that the rest can, and in theory must, accept patients who are on Medicaid. In consequence, almost half the industry's annual revenue comes via those channels. Although a bare majority of homes admits *only* Medicaid-supported residents, these account for 63 percent of all nursing home beds.

The states and the federal government share expenses about equally. In most state budgets Medicaid is the second largest item, just behind education, and it has been growing faster than any other category. Still, nursing home operators frequently complain that the costs of caring for Medicaid-assisted residents exceed the state's reimbursements. "In some cases," concedes the Institute of Medicine, "the Medicaid rate may be too low to provide adequate care for certain individuals."[32]

The more a state contributes, the more nursing home beds it seems to spawn. California and Massachusetts, for instance, boast 63 and 72 beds, respectively, for each 1,000 of their elderly citizens; in Florida, where the Medicaid subsidy is much lower, the ratio is just 21 beds per 1,000 elderly. Ironically, the states with the highest ratios are usually among those with the longest waiting lists. The Medicaid enzyme apparently creates its own "supply side" shortages of nursing home beds.

The shortages are widespread and persistent. In nearly every state there are more people seeking admission to nursing homes than there are beds available. Occupancy rates often exceed 90 percent and waiting periods can run as long as two years. The supply squeeze makes it possible for nursing homes to be very finicky about whom they admit: Medicaid prospects are generally eschewed, as are patients who may require "heavy care." ("Bed-fast or severely demented residents are examples of heavy-care residents," explains the Institute of Medicine.) In other words, Medicaid and the market have stood commonsense priorities on their head, steering assistance away from those in greatest need.

Equally distressing, the shortages have made states reluctant to come down hard on offenders. Just as building inspectors in tight housing markets hesitate to condemn tenements for fear of promoting homelessness, state nursing home inspectors hesitate to "decertify" even the most blackguardly of institutions. Decertification deprives a nursing home of Medicaid payments; more often than not, that is tantamount to putting the home out of business. In checking federal files full of state inspection reports, Senator Heinz's committee found that "almost 1,000 certified skilled nursing homes . . . fail year after year to meet critical quality standards," yet few are ever penalized with more than a slap on the wrist. In 1985, the states and HCFA actually shut down just 27 nursing homes nationwide.

Since the mid-1970s Congress has been trying to get the Health Care Financing Administration to install a system of "intermediate sanctions" less drastic than decertification but strong enough to hold the respectful attention of offending nursing homes. HCFA's response was first to do nothing and then, in 1986, to pretend to do something. The intermediate penalties it wrote into its new procedures apply to only about one of every sixteen nursing home violations committed. For all other violations there remains no form of legal redress other than decertification, which has proven useless.

Enforcement of the rules is also discouraged by the strange solicitude some state inspectors show nursing homes. Senate investigators found that in many instances "nursing homes know when the inspectors are coming and are able to present to inspectors conditions that are not representative of an average day at the facility."

Here is what the daughter of one resident, "who visited her mother in the nursing home two or three times a day," told the committee:

"They seem to know when the inspections are coming. I could tell . . . just by the way they were making preparations." Her bedridden mother had a bad back. Therapy was supposed to include one hour each day in a wheelchair, where her mother had to be supported by a back brace and by a device called a "posey restraint." But they wouldn't use the restraint. "I told them, 'Use the restraint, it's in the record.' They checked the record, then put a *strap* on her! There was no brace. They left her that way for three hours. She was really hurting when they put her in bed. But when the state was coming in, all the patients would be up in wheelchairs, and my mom would be up with a posey on properly."[33]

This daughter understood more than most about nursing home procedures, yet even she did not know where to turn. In matters pertaining to Medicaid there appears to be no ultimate authority on which one can rely, no place for the buck to stop. It keeps getting passed between HCFA and the states. (Every state has a nursing home ombudsman program, paid for by the federal Administration on Aging [AOA], but these have been largely unassertive. AOA's attitude, noted Vladeck, "has run the gamut from mild support to total indifference."[34])

In theory the buck is supposed to stop in Washington. A federal Court of Appeals said as much in a 1984 decision arising from a suit that nursing home residents in Colorado had filed a decade before. The judges ordered HCFA to issue regulations to ensure "high quality care" in nursing homes, and added that failure to do so "is an abdication of the Secretary's duty." The regulations HCFA eventually promulgated, however, seem no better than those the judges rejected. The new cask contains the same old watery wine.

Nursing homes are not the only item on Medicaid's crowded agenda. The program reimburses other providers of health care for the poor, and it assists the young as well as the elderly. But nursing homes receive almost one-third of Medicaid's total outlays and about 70 percent of all its disbursements on behalf of the aged. The program and the industry are thus joined in symbiotic matrimony. When Medicaid catches cold, the industry sneezes.

Medi*care,* in contrast, plays a lamentably minor role in these proceedings, accounting for only 2 percent of annual nursing home revenues.[35] Thus, whereas it is mainly Medicare that serves the middle-class elderly in their pursuit of affordable health care, it is chiefly Medicaid that abets their financial struggles in nursing homes. But by that time they are no longer middle-class—they are destitute. For a salient feature of Medicaid is that it does nothing to dispel poverty; it manufactures it.

What Antonio in *The Merchant of Venice* says about "Fortune" can here as justifiably be said about Medicaid: ". . . it is still her use / To let the wretched man outlive his wealth, / To view with hollow eye and wrinkled brow / An age of poverty."

Medicaid is a crucible for downward mobility, compelling families to "spend down" before the program will consent to prop them up. "Spending down" is a government euphemism for parting with one's social security and life savings, and in most cases the process is not lengthy. Davis and Rowland reported that 30 to 40 percent of all nursing home residents enter as privately paying patients and later convert to Medicaid. For two-thirds of those, according to the Institute of Medicine, the descent takes less than two years. To those who have no spouses, poverty comes sooner still. A 1985 study by Massachusetts Blue Cross found that 63 percent of the unmarried residents ran out of money within thirteen weeks.[36]

In the tangled skein of Medicaid regulations there is a place in some states reserved for "nondirect" nursing homes. These have federal and state permission to reject applicants who require Medicaid support from day one of their nursing home stays. The "nondirects" look instead to the *prospective* poor, those who still have enough money to spend down with. Nondirect nursing homes generally make more money than do the "directs," which are required to accept applicants already destitute.

For the prospective poor, of course, the extent of the charges determines the pace of impoverishment. The average annual cost of living in a skilled nursing facility in 1986 exceeded $25,000. Prescription drugs, medical equipment, and a variety of treatments and amenities— physical therapy, for instance, or a shave—often cost extra, so that a yearlong tab of $30,000 or more was not unusual.

In New York City, as I had occasion to learn, the bill could run as high as $60,000, or about $5,000 a month. That was what an administrator said his nursing home would have to charge my ninety-two-year-old father-in-law when we took him there one chilly day in November 1986. To my stunned mother-in-law, the administrator explained that her husband's social security payments would probably not be enough to satisfy state spend-down requirements. Their joint savings might also have to be tossed into the Medicaid maw, depending upon how the state of New York in its wisdom chose to interpret certain complex regulations and court decisions.

Then the administrator, a not unkind man, surprised us. "My advice," he said to my mother-in-law, "is to get a divorce."

"At my age?" she asked in disbelief.

"If you're not married," he said, "the state can't take your money to pay for your husband's care." (By now the administrator may have changed his tune: In 1988 Congress moved to keep a bigger share of the spouse's income and assets out of Medicaid's reach.)

Caste and Class

Medicaid reimbursement levels vary from state to state. In all but one, however, the amounts nursing homes can collect for services rendered to Medicaid residents are lower—sometimes *much* lower—than those they can collect from private-paying residents. (A Minnesota law keeps the two rates equal.) The shortfall has added several new wrinkles to the two-class system of care that Florence Parker discovered six decades ago. Increasingly now at nursing homes throughout the nation the affluent are flying first-class while the poor are going air freight.

Often it is easy to tell when you are in one part or the other of a two-fare nursing home. The atmosphere in the air-freight wing is likely to be cramped. As many as four residents may share a room and bath in surroundings that are relentlessly functional—metal beds, plastic utensils, linoleum floors. Over in the first-class wing, life appears more gracious: The halls are usually carpeted and the dining room tables may gleam with real china and glassware; each resident has a room and bath to herself, often with space enough to accommodate sitting-room as well as bedroom furniture. What we have here is an old story of class division, but we can give it a new name—geriatric gentrification.

A proprietary home in Rockville, Maryland—the Potomac Valley Nursing Center—provides an example that may not be extreme. Private-paying residents there must shell out about $30,000 a year, which entitles them to all the customary services. But for a few extra dollars a day they can join the "Potomac Club Plan" and reap many additional benefits, or what the nursing home's brochure describes as "over 120 different life-style options." These include a private dining area and "entertainment center," tickets to plays and concerts, "fresh, in-room flower arrangements provided every month," transportation to "outside events" in "club stretch limousines," bedside color television, and a "direct hot line" to the nursing director's office.

It is not clear whether the "club concept," as its promoters like to call it, is waxing or waning. The nursing home industry seems of two minds. As some see it, the clubs appeal to precisely the sort of up-scale clientele the nursing homes yearn to attract—aged yuppies with go-go bank accounts. "At long last," rhapsodized a Nevada marketing man, "nursing homes . . . have the ability to end their abject dependence on Medicaid."

This man's testimonial appeared in a trade-journal advertisement for a firm known as Marketing and Merchandising Associates, based in Erie, Pennsylvania. The company sells "club packages" to nursing homes nationwide, and as the ad copy made clear, M&M's big selling point is its resolve to separate Medicaid chaff from high-yield wheat.

"We devote time," the ad proclaimed unsyntactically, "to detect and correct the almost unbelievable mistakes being routinely made in the admissions process." For instance, M&M consultants discovered that nursing home administrators "were engaged in 'Negative-selling'! They were actually pushing Medicaid! They volunteered to help fill out Medicaid forms!"[37]

But in the nursing home business even the power of positive selling has its limits. The bittersweet news is that the clubs may be offering a good deal more than most residents are in a position to enjoy. As one admissions director, a gerontologist, explained to me, "The great majority of our residents are too ill to entertain graciously or to take advantage of all those other alleged amenities. Here, we're ecstatic when one of our patients just eats with her family in the main dining room."

I cannot name this administrator because she was unaware she was being interviewed. On the telephone I told her I was representing an elderly gentleman who was thinking of moving to a nursing home and wanted to learn more about the club associated with hers. "The club went down the tubes before I got here," she said. "It was a terrible idea, one of those marketing gimmicks that was supposed to make millions." Quite a few clubs, she added, have foundered for a shortage of prospects whole and hearty enough to take advantage of the proffered luxuries: "They were thought to be the wave of the future, but now I hope the wave has passed. No self-respecting gerontologist would have anything to do with them." The marketing experts should have read Rubinow, in which case they might have known that what most residents required was not the easy illusion of sumptuousness but the hard reality of service—"a complicated apparatus of continuous nursing and medical care."

Maybe there is nothing wrong with class distinctions. Why shouldn't people be allowed to use their hard-earned savings to purchase a few niceties, a bit of modest elegance, in their declining years? But the clubs betray some unpleasant truths about many nursing home operators—not only their nervous solicitude for the rich but also their profound contempt for the poor.

Medicaid is what keeps many nursing homes in business, yet those eligible for the program's benefits are often those most shunned by its vendors. The industry's tacit rating system consigns such as they to the lowest of castes. In the fall of 1984 Senator Heinz's committee devoted a day of hearings to the plight of Medicaid untouchables and their families. The committee concluded that "in some areas of this country up to 80 percent of what are called federally certified nursing homes . . . actively discriminate against Medicaid beneficiaries in their admission practices."

Those were the same sessions at which Judy Moser, the Tennessee nursing home administrator who'd resigned her job in protest, gave strong testimony, and she had something to say about her former employer's discriminatory habits. When the new managers took over, she recalled, they warned her, "You have too many feelings to work here," and they ordered her to "keep patients out of the front lobby."

"We had several patients that just refused to go anywhere else and sit. I told the new owner that this was their home and they should be allowed to sit where they wanted to. He said, 'It is not their home. It is an institution and just a place to live.'"

The ban on lobby sitting was intended to spruce up the home's image and thereby enhance its attractions for private-paying prospects. At the same time the company took steps to keep out the poor, each of whose Medicaid payments would fall short of private fees by $150 a month.

"These people, unless they had money for private pay, the new owners would not let me admit them. You know, you have got somebody that you know needs to be there, and you know they do not have money. . . . I just could not tell people, 'You cannot come here, even though you need a room.'"

The Tennessee owners were hardly the cleverest of miscreants cited. Toby S. Edelman, a staff attorney at the National Senior Citizens Law Center, described for the committee several commonplace gambits that Ms. Moser's employers had apparently overlooked. "Sometimes," Ms. Edelman testified, "nursing homes offer to put the [poor] applicant's name on a waiting list. The waiting list may not exist at all, or it may simply be thrown into the trash can at the end of the month. People usually never hear again from the facility."

Other nursing homes, she said, "ask for contributions to a building fund before they will admit a Medicaid recipient"; or they may restrict Medicaid residents to a single floor or wing; or they may sign an agreement with the state agency that limits their number of Medicaid beds to, say, one of every ten; or "facilities will require people to sign private-pay contracts which obligate them to pay personally for their care for specified periods of time . . . before they will be permitted to apply for the public benefit they are entitled to. . . . Discriminatory practices such as these occur throughout the country."

Federal and state regulations are supposed to protect families from nearly all such tricky expedients, but the pursuit of justice can be chancy to say the least. Consider the testimony of Robert B. Snook of Bayville, New York. His mother suffered a stroke in May 1982 that left her partially paralyzed, "and the course of her recovery was very slow." After six weeks in the hospital, she was admitted to a nursing home owned by the Glengariff Corporation in Glen Cove, Long Island. It was then, said Mr. Snook, that "I signed an agreement which stated that she would remain a private-paying patient for a period of eighteen months. At that time, I had no idea how long she would remain in the nursing home, or any knowledge of my mother and father's personal financial situation."

A Glengariff administrator told Mr. Snook that his mother was not eligible for Medicare assistance, when in fact she was entitled to one hundred days of post-hospital care in a skilled nursing home.

The bill at Glengariff came to about $3,000 a month, and in addition the corporation demanded a two-months' security deposit. With help from their mother's personal savings Mr. Snook and his brother managed to make the deposit and to pay the first few monthly bills. But it soon became clear that "some other means would have to be found, . . . as her funds were rapidly being depleted." Mr. Snook consulted a lawyer, who advised him to apply for Medicaid on behalf of his parents and to make no further payments to the nursing home. He applied on October 8; a Medicaid caseworker assured him his mother would be eligible.

The application, however, did not please Glengariff. "One day while visiting my mother," Mr. Snook remembers, "I was called into the business director's office, and he told me that I had signed a contract and that he was going to hold me to the contract and sue me." The business director was as good as his word. He had Mr. Snook served with a summons for breach of contract. A follow-up letter threatened to "discharge . . . your mother from our Skilled Nursing Facility" and to collect "the sums due Glengariff from the security account. . . . It is our sincere wish," the administrator concluded on a friendly note, "that . . . Mrs. Snook will remain an inpatient here."

In late November Mr. Snook got another unpleasant surprise: "I received a notice that Medicaid had been denied because I signed an agreement with Glengariff Nursing Home to pay for private care for eighteen months. We requested a fair hearing on the denial."

There followed a protracted series of legal confrontations, from which Mr. Snook and his family emerged bloodied but ultimately victorious. In February 1983, an administrative law judge reversed Medicaid's denial and ordered the county Department of Social Services to start making nursing home payments, retroactive to November. (The county got around to doing that in June.) Later, a second administrative law judge ruled that Mr. Snook's mother had been entitled all along to Medicare support for her first hundred days at Glengariff. Then, in January 1984, a New York State Supreme Court judge dismissed the Glengariff Corporation's suit against Mr. Snook on grounds that the contract between them was unenforceable.

What looms as unusual in Mr. Snook's testimony is not the financial catastrophe he and his family faced—that happens to many—but the legal battle they waged and won. Few such stories have happy endings, chiefly because few such families can summon the requisite tenacity. People trying to place a loved one in a nursing home are unlikely to think clearly or to resist resolutely. Much of the fight may already have been wrung out of them. In their guilt and desperation they may at first view the nursing home as an angel of mercy that cares deeply about their anguish; only later do they begin to see it as something else—as a business like any other. But by then it may be too late: The contract has been signed; the patient has been put to bed.

The impression one gets as one reads each sad family scenario—and there are thousands—is of a vast social helplessness to match the physical or mental helplessness of the institutionalized loved one. Technically, the law may be on the family's side; but that very technicality is part of the problem. How are folks to make use of the law when it speaks in riddles; or worse, as in the initial stages of Mr. Snook's struggle, when it speaks as if it were a hireling of the industry?

"In pursuing your rights under federal or state law," Senator Heinz asked Mr. Snook, "did you ever receive any assistance from the state or federal governments?" The answer was "No."

The Triumph of Jargon

There may be a hidden formula at work in every government welfare program: The weaker its commitment to the poor, the more vague its procedures and the less accessible its bureaucracy. From the beginning, vagueness has been a peculiar feature of the Medicaid program, virtually its signature. The very idea seemed to materialize overnight as an afterthought tacked onto Medicare; it was something Wilbur Mills had shrewdly guessed the Congress could live with. No one on the Hill or in Lyndon Johnson's White House ever took time to think through the enormous technical difficulties that lay ahead.

The original Medicaid measure mentioned "skilled nursing homes" just once, as one of five "basic" services Medicaid patients would be entitled to. On all related matters Congress maintained a sphinxlike silence. How were reimbursement rates to be set? To what standards of care might nursing homes be held, and who would stick up for the residents when the standards were violated? Such questions, it was casually assumed, would be answered by each state in separate negotiations with the nursing home industry.

The arrangement seemed convenient, although—or perhaps precisely because—it left federal power largely out of the picture. As the social analysts Robert and Rosemary Stevens have observed, "Congress had passed a program of massive proportions and minimal federal accountability."[38]

Much of what has occurred since can be seen as a series of fitful efforts to introduce federal accountability into the Medicaid program. Under pressure from Congress, the courts, and the public, succeeding administrations in Washington have revised Medicaid nursing home regulations at least once every decade, but each fresh version has turned out as toothless as the last. In consequence, the Medicaid program today bears the Scarlet Letter borne by all welfare programs in America: It is a second-rate endeavor for persons perceived as second-rate citizens.

Everything the federal government does betrays its reluctance to make a firm commitment to those who must live in nursing homes. The monotonous parade of studies and reports, the mountebank regulations, the careful neglect of its own data, all these reveal a bureaucracy paralyzed by indifference and mesmerized by its own jargon.

Is it any wonder that state agencies and inspectors often seem as confused as their elderly constituents? A private consulting firm hired by HCFA in 1985 to analyze nursing home inspections reported "a wide variance in how individual states decided upon what to cite. . . . Several states cited deficiencies that in other states were presented as recommendations."[39]

The Institute of Medicine's study on the quality of care in nursing homes was aimed primarily at government and nursing home administrators, yet the institute felt called upon to include a fifteen-page "Glossary" in which it defined 118 different terms used in extended-care circles. In another section the writers decoded 34 "Acronyms and Initialisms." These were eloquent tributes to the triumph of jargon over accountability, which has pervaded every level of the national care-giving enterprise.

To be ignorant of the lingua franca is to live in a foreign country. My family and I got that feeling when we took my father-in-law to the nursing home in New York. The administrator there did his best to explain to my mother-in-law the kind of care her husband, a very sick man, was slated to receive. "We're a combination SNF and HRF," he told the perplexed woman, "so we're able to place your husband in a swing bed." (An approximate translation: "We've been certified as both a skilled nursing facility and a health-related facility; that's why we're putting your husband in a room where he can get both kinds of care.")

My mother-in-law asked if her husband would be eligible for Medicaid assistance. "Certainly," replied the administrator, "but you'll have to take the PRI to the District Office to get Prior Approval. They'll tell you how much to spend down."

Just about everyone who lives in a nursing home is old enough to remember Bob Hope's wartime quip: "Where does an alien go to register?" It seemed funny at the time.

A Few Suggestions

How did we reach this odd impasse whereby an intimate interpersonal obligation—the care of our elders—has become a remote mystery wrapped within an alien language? It is easy to blame "the government," but since the government is ultimately us, we must be the responsible party as well as the unhappy victim. Through Medicaid we set out to rescue the most fragile of our compatriots and somehow created the most heavy-handed of institutions.

Vladeck has tried to explain how we achieved this nonmiracle: "There are certain things only government can or will do, and we have denied government the means to do them."[40] But Vladeck's just assessment only begs the question, which is, Why haven't we done better? Besides, given the present system, it remains unclear whether money alone will assure older Americans decent long-term institutional care. Too much of the money now goes into profits, acquisitions, and mergers; not nearly enough is used to increase staffing, to improve facilities, to sharpen care-giving skills.

What we have denied government, in addition to dollars, is the sense of urgency needed to get the job done. That may be because we have both underestimated and overestimated the task, and in the end the two miscalculations have amounted to much the same thing. If a part of us pretends that long-term institutional care is a routine matter requiring no more than a routine response, another part of us despairs of ever doing the job right: We assume that most nursing home residents have deteriorated to a point beyond reach of whatever quality of mercy we might muster.

In either mood, then, we do what Lorraine would have considered unthinkable: We give up. The case against giving up, like the quality of mercy, is not strained; it cannot be found in government guidelines or in economics textbooks. Its power to persuade depends less on logic than on people, who above all must sense the unnaturalness of giving up.

Even with the best of will, however, the road seems anything but smooth, paved as it is with corporate intentions. Medicaid's weak federal commitment, its built-in reluctance to carry a big stick, has strengthened the marketplace at the expense of the mercy place. Increasingly now in the nursing home business the private sector sets the standards and reaps the profits while the public sector pays the bills and wrings its hands.

The old benevolent homes—where decent instincts can still flourish— play but a minor role in these multi-billion-dollar proceedings. While investor-owned chains in 1985 were increasing their number of beds by some 27,000, the not-for-profits were augmenting theirs by just 3,500. The difference reflects a strain of rot that is permeating our entire health-care system, what the sociologist Paul Starr has called "the decomposition of voluntarism."[41] In effect, we have transferred momentum and power from altruism to commercialism, and the transfer has been costly: Not only have we failed to get our money's worth, we have also failed to take due note of our elders' worth.

Still, for those uneasy about giving up, three useful approaches come to mind. One seems achievable right now, another within the foreseeable future. A third approach, concerning federal entitlements, is for long-distance runners.

To begin with, we can remind ourselves that most older Americans will go to any length to stay out of a nursing home, and they might appreciate some help. Home care is one kind of help; day care is another. Both can be important stages in a gentler, more cushioned slide toward the vale of dependence. A number of nursing homes have, in fact, established day-care programs that go far beyond what most senior centers offer—not just a few hours of respite around lunchtime, but an all-day menu of recreation and therapy under guidance of a trained staff. In many cases, even Alzheimer victims and their families have chosen this intermediate form of assistance over institutionalization. Both day care and home care in the long run may be less costly to the public than institutional care. At present, however, only institutional care—the final stage—gets substantial federal and state support.

Second, we ought to rely less on free enterprise (which in any case is not free but heavily subsidized) and more on community-sponsored efforts. The fast-care chains will not go away, but there are things we can do to help the smaller nonprofits compete more effectively. For instance, our Medicaid reimbursement policies can encourage nursing homes to reinvest earnings in staff and services rather than in acquisitions and dividends. The idea would be to penalize excessive acquisitiveness while rewarding exceptional caregiving. Nowadays we are doing just the opposite.

Nor would it be amiss at this juncture for Congress to dust off the old Hill-Burton legislation as it pertained to nursing homes, again restricting construction dollars to nonprofit and public sponsors. A renewed building initiative might at last end the bed shortage, shaking us free of a seller's market and its attendant evil—discrimination against the aged poor.

Finally, we must look at ways to take the sting out of Medicaid assistance. When the price of rescue is pauperization, the rescue itself becomes compromised. The practice of compulsory "spending down" is a throwback to the days of almshouses and public auctions. It makes no sense in a civilized modern society, much less in the world's richest nation.

If we wish to make headway here, then what the Stevenses have called "a program of massive proportions and minimal federal accountability" will have to shift its administrative weight from the states to Washington, where it has always belonged. The federal giant, so long asleep at the wheel, can still be roused and placed in the Medicaid driver's seat. Only then will we be ready to begin moving the program away from means-testing and toward something nearer to a universal entitlement. The entitlement in that case would assure older Americans a step-down progression of long-term-care services—delivered at home, at day-care centers, and in nursing homes.

The ultimate goal should be a national long-term-care insurance plan financed in part through payroll premiums and in part through appropriations by Congress. Its price may be high, but unlike the price of today's Medicaid program, it will not be exorbitant, the difference being that under a universal plan all of us will stand a better chance of getting our money's worth.

*   *   *

There is yet something more we can do: We can pay careful attention to the better nursing homes in our midst, for they have much to teach us about the delicate art of dispensing long-term care. To an extent that might have surprised even Rubinow, these homes appear to have mastered many of "the problems arising out of proper organization of institutions for the aged." Such places may be relatively rare, yet I found examples wherever I took the trouble to search, including one in my own community. We close now with a look at that nursing home—the Jewish Home for the Aged in New Haven, Connecticut. The purpose of looking is both to cheer us up and to egg us on.

The Virtues of Not Being Up-to-Date

"Believe me," says Miriam Parker, associate director of the Jewish Home for the Aged, "no one wants to go into a nursing home—not even this one." Parker and her colleagues do everything possible to postpone the moment of entry. Their "updated philosophy"—to quote from the home's 1986 annual report—envisions "an expanding geriatric center with a variety of in-patient and out-patient services for our elderly frail." One thing a nursing home should not be, says the report, is "the 'last stop' for the very ill."

Accordingly, the home has opened an adult day-care center on the premises, to which some twenty-five elderly clients—most of them still living independently—are bused each day. The care provided is lengthy (nearly seven hours a day) and lavish. It includes meals, baths, exercises, music, and lectures. In 1986 an additional aide was hired to take care of the Alzheimer participants.

Yet the home's vision of becoming a caregiver for all elderly seasons remains unfulfilled. The day-care center is costly—about $35 daily for each participant—and the sliding-scale fees do not meet expenses. A home-care program, meanwhile, is still on the drawing board, as are plans for an elderly outpatient clinic. More by necessity than by choice the institution's energies continue to focus on last-stop services to its 210 residents.

The services are a story in themselves. They constitute an imaginative blend of the technological and the tender—X-rays and podiatry alongside hugs and commiserations. The secret of the home's success appears to lie less in its "updated philosophy" than in its old-fashioned fidelity to certain care-giving precepts. For residents, the idea is to make life worth living; for staff, to make the work worth doing. "Don't be sorry for any of us, . . ." cautions a resident, a ninety-year-old woman, who appears in a brief promotional film the staff likes to show visitors. "All the doors are open to help us."

The key here, as in all superior nursing homes, is adequate staff. One way to measure the home's generous staffing practices, particularly in regard to licensed nurses and their aides, is to compare them with the state's requirements. In many nursing homes these mandated minimums, inadequate as they are, turn out to be absolute maximums. At the Home for the Aged they are routinely surpassed.

The requirements vary with the type of care to be provided and also from shift to shift (more workers by day, fewer by night). Here

I cite the state's cumulative minimums for all three shifts in a skilled nursing facility that serves 150 residents, and compare these with the home's daily totals.

	Connecticut Requires	*Home Provides*
Licensed nurses	15	22
Aides	20	39

The differences are more than digital. They pay off, as Miriam Parker has pointed out, in ways that do not always get counted. For instance: "Our residents get more baths; they have more chances to get dressed up, to look good and to feel good about themselves; we don't have anyone sitting for hours on a toilet crying for an aide who never comes." On the night shift, says Parker, the home uses more than twice as many aides as the state requires: "Let me tell you, those aides are on their feet all night. Patients have to be constantly turned and changed. The aides have to make beds with people lying on them. It's a very busy time."

Two full-time general physicians run the medical department, backed up by several part-time specialists (including a psychiatrist and a dentist) and a small army of physical and recreational therapists, social workers, and dieticians. Sometimes the home's sophisticated health-care component can keep sick residents out of the hospital. A case in point was Mrs. Cohen, who did not have to move after she suffered a stroke at the home—she could be treated right there. And when she began to get better, the home's rehabilitation supervisor, Sandra Steingard, could help Mrs. Cohen regain the use of her legs.

"There's an incredible spirit and drive in elderly clients," says Steingard. "They give you their all." Within two months Mrs. Cohen was taking steps with a walker.

The condition of each resident is regularly discussed at staff meetings, and everyone is consulted—the aides and the food-service people as well as the doctors and therapists. "We're the eyes and ears of this place," an aide told me. "We see the danger signs first—like someone who suddenly won't eat or won't get out of bed in the morning, or who stays in her room all day. Those are things I tell the doctors about."

The home seems lucky in its aides, though luck may not in fact be the explanation. It is one of just twenty unionized nursing homes in Connecticut and its beginning workers earn $7.35 an hour, about $2.00 more than the wages commonly paid by competing proprietaries. "If you invest in your staff," says Parker, "you get good care and less turnover." Half the staff has been working there for at least five years.

Life Begins with Volunteers

All this got under way in 1914 when the Sisters of Zion, a small voluntary group in New Haven, decided to risk their entire nest egg of $300 on efforts to establish a home for the aged. The Sisters were not entrepreneurs; they were do-gooders responding to a social emergency.

The first wave of Jewish immigrants from Eastern Europe was growing old, and some had no place to turn other than the city poorhouse on Spring Street. It was a fate to be avoided at all costs. A story still recited by that generation's great-grandchildren—the people responsible today for the Jewish Home for the Aged—has the early immigrants preferring starvation to the poorhouse. Some simply refused to eat.

Two years of fund-raising netted the Sisters enough for a down payment on a small house on Davenport Avenue, in the old Jewish neighborhood and not far from Yale University. There a few elderly immigrants took up residence, though by present-day standards they may not have been all that old. The home's original motto—Life begins at 60—signifies a difference between then and now: Among today's residents the average age is just under 85. (The youngest in 1986 was 59; the oldest, 101.)

"Sometimes," marvels a current staff member, "I mistake the visiting son for his resident parent. What I keep forgetting is that many of today's children are actually older than the so-called old people who first lived here."

The home still stands on Davenport Avenue, but now it covers a square block and operates on an annual budget in excess of $9 million. A few gross totals will suggest the size of the present enterprise: In 1986 the home's food service prepared more than 300,000 meals, its physical therapy unit provided 5,800 separate treatments, its 276 full-time and part-time workers drew wages amounting to more than $6 million, and its volunteers put in about 25,000 hours of unremunerated labor.

This last may be the most telling of all numbers, for it reflects an ongoing community interest, stretching back to the Sisters of Zion, that no proprietary nursing home could hope to inspire. Generally speaking, the volunteers come in two guises—a thirty-person board of directors and a women's auxiliary of some five hundred members. The directors, of course, shape the policies—but that is the easy part; then they must go out and find the funds. In the nonprofit world,

Medicaid and private fees are not the whole revenue story. Any year at the Jewish Home for the Aged the board and staff are able to raise at least a half-million additional dollars, nearly all of which go into the building fund.

Contributions from the auxiliary are less lucrative but everywhere in evidence. Among other things, the members decorate the dining room with flowers, provide orchestras for special events, do errands for the residents and take them shopping, run the gift shop, help out at the residents' new coffee shop, and, like the Sisters before them, raise money through all the customary devices of local philanthropy— raffles, dances, and theater benefits. The events attract many residents as well as relatives and friends; such activities have been known to yield as much as $80,000 at a single shot.

The auxiliary also forges links with the larger community, including New Haven's children. An annual "Portrait of a Friend" contest, for instance, invites schoolchildren citywide "to think about the elderly" and then to submit a poster or an essay about one special relationship with an older person. Several hundred students enter the contest every year, competing for two $25 prizes.

The things these volunteers do in New Haven are the things volunteers do everywhere. Yet their work at the home makes a critical difference: Besides attracting essential dollars, the work generates within the community a vital stake in the institution. Money and communal pride can do wonders for a nursing home. They can assure it an infrastructure that allows staff the luxury of diligence in its daily handling of "a complicated apparatus of continuous nursing and medical care." A postulate worth considering here is that traditional forms of voluntarism make possible effective forms of care-giving.

"Stamp Those Feet. . . . Do What You Can"

We are walking through the New Building, completed in 1985, which houses sixty of the home's residents. Susan Yolen, a staff member and my guide this morning, explains how the addition has freed up the institution. "We used to have very long waiting lists," she begins. "People would have to go to other nursing homes while waiting their turn here. Some of them died before we ever got a chance to take care of them; others spent all their money at the first home, so by the time they came here, they were on Medicaid. Now at least a few can afford to pay us private fees."

Since the new units were added, the proportion of Medicaid residents at the home has dropped from 80 to 70 percent, and the difference, says Mrs. Yolen, may have put the home in the black this year "for the first time in recent memory." The state pays about $110 per day for each Medicaid resident, whereas those who can still afford private fees pay about $140.

"But we don't discriminate against Medicaid residents," she assures me. "They get exactly the same services and the same rooms that everyone else gets. Our staff doesn't even know who's on Medicaid and who isn't."

Unlike the many nursing homes that segregate residents by their ability to pay, this one divides them by their ability to function. Two of the seven units specialize in giving "total care" to those who are very confused or very disabled, or both. (There are 30 residents in each unit.) But as Susan Yolen warned me ahead of time, "You'll see very frail people in all the units. There are people here with minds intact but with bodies impaired. Some can't walk or talk. They need lots of attention." A 1986 census of residents has enumerated some of their needs: 55 need help walking and 49 others are confined to chairs or beds; 140 require assistance in eating, 158 in dressing; 80 are listed as incontinent.

Here in the new building the inhabitants are said to be relatively alert and robust. For them the home's planners hoped to fashion something rare in contemporary nursing homes—a decor emptied of clinical content. "This particular unit," Mrs. Yolen explains, "was designed to look less like a hospital than the older units. Residents on the other floors tend to crowd around the nursing stations; sometimes they have no other place to congregate. But here we've put the nursing station off to one side and left a much larger space for sitting and talking. We think it's a more comfortable setting."

Actually, the setting reminds me of certain small-town airports I have passed through—very modern but oddly quiet. It is a large, brilliantly lit commons, mainly white, where the "passengers" sit and wait, and then sit and wait some more. One of them, strapped in a wheelchair, appears to be crying. With the back of a bony hand she wipes tears from her cheek, while an old gentlemen sitting beside her pats her shoulder.

"Are they married?" I ask.

"No, just good friends."

Like Susan Yolen and me, some of the residents seem out for a stroll. We overtake a well-dressed man (tie and jacket) bent low over his walker, which he grips tightly in both hands. In tiny steps he paces the wide, shining floor. This man greets us with just a suggestion of a wave of the hand. In nursing homes the battle for balance never ceases; communication can come down to the subtlest of gestures.

There is music here, too, but not by Musak. Right now a tape is softly playing Tommy Dorsey's rendition of "Thanks for the Memory." Dorsey's sweet trombone is soothing as always, but the words—if anyone can recall them—may be rather too much to bear. (The stereo system was a gift of the auxiliary.)

Most of the bedrooms in the new building, as in other sections of the home, are for single occupancy, though each occupant shares a large bathroom with her next-door neighbor. All open out to the commons, and the first thing one notices is the way each door has been numbered. The white digits are at least a foot tall, visible to the dimmest of eyes.

Nearly everyone seems to have a private telephone and TV set. The furnishings are not opulent, but here and there are loving touches added by residents and their families—a flowering plant, family photographs, a favorite desk or rocker plucked from earlier surroundings and cherished still. A surprising number of nursing homes forbid such niceties; the Jewish Home for the Aged goes out of its way to encourage them.

It is easy to peek into the rooms because they are all empty. "Where is everybody?" I ask. "Here and there," I am told. The answer becomes clearer as we make our way from floor to floor. Everybody is in the corridors, or at the doctor's, or in the beauty shop, or attending an activity. This is a place where no one wants to be alone.

We visit an exercise group, where fourteen women are sitting in a circle. Some are in wheelchairs and some have walkers beside them. All are watching Jodie Gross, the home's music therapy specialist, who stands inside the circle strumming a guitar. "Point those toes," she sings as she plays. "Use both feet. . . . Don't forget your ankles."

She pauses for a brief lecture: "Now remember, I'm not looking to see who's doing better than who. I'm watching for *movement.*" She returns to the music, a version of "Jada": "Jada, jada, jada jada cha cha cha. . . . Down and up and down and up. . . . Jada, jada, stamp those feet. . . . Do what you can." The women tap to the rhythm, some feebly, some vigorously. Sunlight pours through the wide window. Jodie's dog Susie, a tan-and-white mini-collie, wanders from person to person, wagging her tail. A woman in a wheelchair smiles down at the dog. "Cha cha cha," she says.

"You just happened to come in while we were working on the feet," Jodie tells me afterwards. "I go through the total body. I might play 'High Hopes' to get them to stretch their arms high, or 'Dark Town Strutters' Ball' to get them to kick. The idea is to stimulate movement in all the limbs, to get their blood going better and improve their breathing.

"When I first came here five years ago, no one wanted to participate. They were afraid of looking foolish. Now, just about everyone comes except the new residents. I have to go to them one at a time and work out their misgivings. They're so depressed and full of grief. They don't think anything good can happen to them anymore."

Sometimes, said Jodie, she relies on theater to make good things happen. There was that puppet play she wrote, the one that nine of the residents performed for schoolchildren. The play was based on the biblical story of Purim, wherein Queen Esther and her Uncle Mordecai manage to save their fellow Jews from destruction at the hands of the infamous Haman. Haman was an "enemy of the Jews" and adviser to a powerful Persian king, "who reigned from India even unto Ethiopia, over a hundred and seven and twenty provinces," including Judea. In our time the tale has taken on new meaning. It has become a metaphorical response to the Holocaust: The wicked Haman gets hanged from the very gallows he built for Mordecai.

Jodie said there were lots of things to consider when writing a script for the elderly: "I wrote this one all in rhyme so it would be easier to read and remember, and I printed it in very large type. The average age of the cast was eighty-one; at least one member had been in a concentration camp, so the story really meant a lot to them.

"We rehearsed for months and months. Then, just a week before opening, our narrator passed away—such things happen in nursing homes—and we had to find a replacement right away. There was a woman in the cast who stuttered badly. She didn't want to be the narrator but finally we talked her into it.

"The day of the show I went around and pasted big gold stars on all the actors' doors. Everyone was excited; everyone was *very* nervous. But you know what? They were terrific. The kids kept shouting for encores. You have no idea how proud we all were. We smiled and smiled.

"The funny thing was, the narrator didn't stutter once. In fact, she's been fine ever since. I think the play cured her."

In the drama some call "the nursing home tragedy," we are all actors with gold stars on our doors. The cast never stops rehearsing or hoping; the stage never empties; and the play, for all its risks and sorrows, never closes.

Epilogue

If out of this conference . . . there should develop
any material for wholesome propaganda,
I for one shall have no occasion to regret it.
—I.M. Rubinow (opening address
to the Deutsch Foundation Conference
on the Care of the Aged, 1930)

"Everything begins in sentiment and assumption," observed the turn-of-the-century French writer Charles Peguy, "and finds its issue in political action and institutions." The actions and institutions described in the foregoing chapters did not magically materialize: They were emanations of the civic heart, the imperfect outcomes of our sentiments and assumptions regarding old age and poverty.

There is, to be sure, something unsatisfactory about singling out the old for social analysis. The process tends to blur some sharp truths concerning present-day America, where the erosions of poverty can be found at every age level, including infancy. It is true that old age presents itself as a biological condition distinct from all others and replete with its own set of disabilities; but old age is also a cultural artifact that we can alter simply by changing our attitudes—or with the stroke of a pen, as Congress did when, at the late Claude Pepper's urging, it banished some forms of mandatory old-age retirement.

What we have been investigating all this time turns out to be not old age per se but a certain species of helplessness exacerbated by retirement or deterioration, or both. For many older Americans helplessness is not a novel condition; it has been the story of their lives. Their earlier poverty has in large measure determined their later dependency.

183

The lesson then is long-range and intergenerational: One way to reduce the future incidence of helplessness among the old is to reduce it now among the young. Nothing that has been said here about the risks of old age should obscure the risks of poverty at any age; and nothing said about federal programs for the elderly should divert us from working for a family income–support program, a universal health-protection plan, and a humane minimum wage.

One-fifth of America's children live below the poverty line. Four of every ten poor Americans over fourteen years of age *hold jobs.* There were 6.5 million working poor in 1979; there are 9 million today. Such figures underscore the widening gap in this country between rich and poor. We shall have to work hard to close that gap, to redistribute more of our wealth; and how generously we succeed will profoundly affect the condition of the elderly in decades to come. Without our political intervention, today's underpaid workers and their families are virtually certain at some point down the road to join the ranks of the elderly poor. We have the resources to head off the next scheduled social catastrophe. Do we have the will?

Here and there one sees signs that Congress may be coming to terms with some intergenerational truths. As I write this (in the summer of 1989) both houses are considering a five-bill Medicaid package that could benefit the poor of all ages. It would bring more home care to the elderly and more medical care to pregnant women and their children. Although one bundle of bills does not make a policy, the Medicaid package gives us reason to hope that lawmakers have begun to learn how to view dependency along a lifetime continuum.

The late Michael Harrington, a man who never forgot the poor, liked to observe that there was nothing wrong with America's heart. "It's our head that gives us problems," he once told me. "If we consider ways to fight poverty, our minds get muddled. We become lazy thinkers."

To a nation that runs more on instinct than on intellect, *elderly* poverty may be the sternest cerebral challenge of all. For it has to be acknowledged that we Americans have never been much good at endings. When we look into a national mirror, we are less likely to see the wrinkles of time than the glosses of youth. What delights and excites us is the "fresh, green breast of the new world" (evoked by F. Scott Fitzgerald in *The Great Gatsby*) "that flowered once for Dutch sailors' eyes" when they first glimpsed the Long Island shore. We have been hooked on beginnings ever since.

Nor have we been especially diligent in counting and preserving our blessings. The preferences we often display bear the mark of eternal adolescence: to acquire, consume, discard—and then to acquire once more and begin the cycle anew. A taste for commerce may be what underlies our disposable ways, our habit of throwing out whatever seems old and unmarketable. Yet the values of commerce in the face of human frailty cannot suffice. They make life particularly difficult for the very old, each of whom represents a striking example of built-in obsolescence.

Must our attitude toward the needs of the aged, asked Rubinow some sixty years ago, "be left to chance, to luck, or to individual philanthropic motive? Is that the most efficient way in which our highly organized society can face a problem of such magnitude and importance?"[1]

Our response to Rubinow's cry in the night—he was speaking before the dawn of social security—has been remarkably ambivalent. At our worst, we have let commercial principles overwhelm humanitarian ones. With Casca in *Julius Caesar* one could say, "the bird of night did sit, / Even at noonday, upon the marketplace, / Hooting and shrieking."

We turned Medicare and Medicaid into cornucopias for the health-care and nursing home industries, driving the cost of decent doctoring beyond the means of just about everyone, even the government. Of the social security system we made a meritocracy, whereby a profitably spent youth and middle age could alone ensure an adequately supported old age. Hoping to ease the housing shortage for old and young alike, we relied for the most part on a private-profit system unprepared to deliver affordable shelter. Then, in our confusion over what constitutes sensible public assistance and who merits it, we demanded pauperization as the price the elderly must pay in exchange for help with their escalating nursing home bills.

As if all that were not enough, we kept erecting new benefit barriers and inventing fresh indignities to impose upon the elderly welfare queue. Medicare and social security may have been the sole exceptions, and even Medicare, with its opaque explanations and its unanswered telephones, could frequently sting.

Still, given our aversion to government spending and our devotion to private enterprise, perhaps we did better than anyone had a right to expect. We have come a long way since Rubinow's times. There have in fact been moments in our social development when our heart and our head have shown signs of cooperating with each other. At those moments compassion has soared unexpectedly to the top of the national agenda.

In the 1960s we became temporarily committed to providing decent shelter to the many in need, especially the elderly; in the 1970s, with Supplemental Security Income, we created the first guaranteed income-support program in U.S. history. Then, by liberalizing social security and inventing Medicare, we cut the elderly poverty rate to one-third of its 1960 level. Millions of older Americans continue to benefit from those breakthroughs. Such programs can serve to remind us, in a deficit-ridden post-Reagan era, that social progress is not so wild a dream.

Perhaps the most powerful dream-tamer of all is simply the human condition, for a characteristic that distinguishes old age from every other "minority" status is its universality. There is, in fact, only one way to escape its travails—and who wants that? As taxpayers we may fret about the broad demographic consequences of an aging population—all the human depreciation and the fiscal burdens that go with it—but not, truth to tell, about our own personal prospects. Never mind the possible hardships lying in wait for us; never mind the long-term care we shall one day require: Longevity is a state to which most of us instinctively aspire.

More than most aspects of politics of the elderly, the long-term-care dilemma challenges our basic values and thus invites the most imaginative social response we can summon. For if we genuinely believe in individualism, we have our work cut out for us. Here, after all, are millions of aged, the most determined individualists among us, for whom each day is a fresh contest. It is one of the many ironies of longevity that in order to sustain our independence we must sometimes depend on strangers. With one hand we cling to autonomy; with the other we beckon for assistance. What Americans have been seeking all along, albeit in piecemeal fashion, is a worthy communal response to the legitimate claims of elderly individualism.

As we have seen in Part 2 ("The Struggle for Independence"), however, the responsibilities imposed by an aging America remain more personal than communal. In the fullness of time and attrition each of us may be asked to play parent to his or her parents and grandparents. The risks of old age have thus become the risks of middle age as well.

Family obligations derive from those shared sentiments and assumptions Peguy spoke of, and such feelings have already begun to find their issue in political action. Young parents are not the only ones demanding subsidized day care; that concern now cuts across all generations. It falls with particular force upon the elderly's offspring, an invisible army of caregivers, nearly all of them women, who find themselves in desperate need of the respite that community support might bring.

All the evidence suggests that the public is more alert to, and alarmed by, the long-term-care emergency than is the present administration in Washington. A public opinion survey commissioned by the American Association of Retired Persons and the Villers Foundation tells the voters' half of the story. "Long term care," the researchers concluded after polling a nationwide voter sample, "is a growing issue of nearly universal concern. . . . Americans not only want a comprehensive federal long term care program, they are willing to pay for it with increased taxes." More than three-fourths of those polled said they were willing to pay higher taxes—as much as $60 more each month—for a "Federal Program of Long Term Care."[2]

But the administration's half of the story has yet to be computed. No comprehensive long-term-care policy has been proposed; no fresh vision of social progress—of what we can achieve on behalf of our parents, our grandparents, and ourselves—has been presented to the American people. Facing a blank policy screen, Congress frets and spins dreams of its own.

In 1988 more than a dozen long-term-care bills were placed in the congressional hopper, all aimed at creating some sort of social insurance program capable of covering long-term care at home and in institutions. That none of the measures came close to getting passed testifies to the well-known sluggishness of democracy's gears: The procedures that carry us from debate to consensus, and then to enactment, can be exasperatingly slow.

Yet here we have one of the classic conditions preceding social reform, namely, a rising demand by families for assistance in taking care of their own. It was a similar demand that eventually led to passage of the Social Security Act of 1935.

There are some striking parallels between the 1930s and the 1990s—and some striking differences. Then as now, the prime incentive for reformers was to keep the aged out of institutions. What Eleanor Roosevelt told a U.S. Chamber of Commerce audience in January 1934 applies today with equal force. "The community," she said, "owes to its old people their own home life as long as they possibly can live at home. Old people love their own things even more than young people do. It means so much to sit in the same chair you sat in for a great many years; to see the same picture that you always looked at. . . . And that is what an old age security bill will do."[3]

The purpose of the Social Security Act was not to replace the family but to enhance its role as caregiver of the first resort. "By funneling money back into the American family," observes the historian William Graebner, "social security promised to restore the primacy of home and family."[4]

The differences today lie chiefly in our leaders, who lack social imagination, and in our own attitudes, which lack faith in the miracles that politics can achieve. If widespread fear was the mental plague of the Great Depression, widespread fatalism may be considered the hex of the Great Deficit. The enormous debts incurred in the Reagan years weigh down on our hopes, engendering something very close to legislative paralysis. "It might be called 'the deficit-made-me-not-do-it' approach to politics," noted a reporter for the *New York Times*. "So far," he added, "it seems to be working for Mr. Bush."[5]

But is it working for the rest of us? Given some new global realities, are we not missing a rare and remarkable opportunity to put our house in order? For much of this century, professing to fear military attack, our leaders have thrown billions of dollars at deterrence. Now both our enemies and our friends have signaled a desire to lay down their arms. They are inviting us to do the same. What's keeping us? One needn't possess a Ph.D. in economics to perceive the enormous social benefits that could accrue from mutual disarmament: universal long-term care, to name just one, instead of long-range nuclear warheads.

Alexander Pope had a piece of the truth. "He's armed without that's innocent within," Pope wrote in *Imitations of Horace, Epistle I*. We Americans could use some of that armor. For if innocence implies a strong sense of optimism, a faith in one's capacity to leave the world a better place than one found it, then it may be that we temporarily lost our innocence in the cold war arms race.

Still, it's never too late to be born again. FDR helped us to overcome our fear. Who now will rouse us from our fatalism? Perhaps we shall have to do it ourselves—and hope that our leaders will follow. Call it a reordering of priorities. Call it *perestroika*. Whatever name we give it, may our hearts and our heads be equal to the task.

NOTES

◆

Notes to Introduction

1. Alvin L. Schorr, *Common Decency* (New Haven: Yale University Press, 1986), p. 1.

2. "The Old Folks," *Forbes,* February 18, 1980, pp. 51–56.

3. "Gray Power!" *Time,* January 4, 1988, p. 36.

4. *Washington Post,* January 5, 1986, p. D1 (Outlook section).

5. "Consuming Our Children," *Forbes,* November 14, 1988, pp. 222–28. Census chart, p. 225.

6. Vance Packard, *The Ultra Rich* (Boston: Little, Brown, 1989), pp. 4, 15.

7. Robert Lekachman, "A Mystery Readily Solved," *The New Leader,* October 5, 1987, p. 20.

8. Irving Howe, "Social Retreat and the *Tumler,*" *Dissent,* Fall 1987, p. 409.

9. Robert Hunter, *Poverty* (New York: Macmillan, 1904), p. 83.

10. Michael Harrington, *The Other America* (Baltimore: Penguin, 1969), pp. 101–18.

11. Cited in Villers Foundation, *On the Other Side of Easy Street,* Washington, D.C., 1987, p. 24.

12. Stephen Crystal, *America's Old Age Crisis* (New York: Basic Books, 1984), p. x.

13. U.S. Bureau of the Census, Series P-60, August 1988.

14. Mollie Orshansky, "Who's Who Among the Poor: A Demographic Review of Poverty," *Social Security Bulletin,* July 1965, p. 27.

15. Mollie Orshansky, "Counting the Poor: Another Look at the Poverty Profile," *Social Security Bulletin,* January 1965, p. 26.

16. Robert N. Butler, *Why Survive?* (New York: Harper & Row, 1975), p. 145.

Notes to Chapter One

1. Alvin L. Schorr, *Common Decency* (New Haven: Yale University Press, 1986), p. 28.

2. *Economic Security Bill, H.R. 615,* 74th Cong., 1st sess., April 15, 1935.

3. Quoted by Paul Light, "Social Security's Cash Squeeze," *Wilson Quarterly,* New Year's 1985, p. 131.

4. "U.S. Pensions Found to Lift Many of Poor," *New York Times,* December 28, 1988, p. 1.

5. Cited by Schorr, *Common Decency,* p. 29.

6. Italics added.

7. Robert M. Ball, *Social Security Today and Tomorrow* (New York: Columbia University Press, 1978), p. 33.

8. House Committee on Ways and Means, *Background Material and Data on Programs Within the Jurisdiction of the Committee on Ways and Means,* 101st Cong., 1st sess., 1989.

9. Villers Foundation, *On the Other Side of Easy Street,* Washington, D.C., 1987.

10. Cited by Robert Lucke, "Options for Financing Long Term Health Care," charts and oral presentation (undated), p. 1.

11. Karen C. Holden, in *A Challenge to Social Security,* ed. R. V. Burkhauser and Karen C. Holden (New York: Academic Press, 1982), p. 47.

12. Martha Derthick, *Policymaking for Social Security* (Washington, D.C.: Brookings Institution, 1979), p. 348.

13. James H. Schulz, *The Economics of Aging* (New York: Van Nostrand Reinhold, 1985), p. 103.

14. Quoted in "Meanwhile, Back at the Deficit," *New York Times,* March 9, 1988, p. A30.

15. "Why Subsidize the Monied Classes?" *New York Times,* July 18, 1985, p. A23.

16. *New York Times,* Letters, March 29, 1988.

17. Quoted by Mollie Sinclair in "The Challenge to Social Security," *50 Plus,* May 1986, p. 28.

18. House Committee on Ways and Means, 1986, p. 79.

19. Schulz, *The Economics of Aging,* p. 93.

20. Executive Order 6757, June 29, 1934.

21. Cited in Villers Foundation, *On the Other Side of Easy Street,* p. 15.

22. Theda Skocpol, "Legacies of New Deal Liberalism," *Dissent,* Winter 1983, p. 59.

23. Vincent J. Burke and Vee Burke, *Nixon's Good Deed* (New York: Columbia University Press, 1974), p. 191.

24. Cited in ibid., p. 200.

25. See, for instance, the Villers Foundation study, "SSI Aware: Why the Elderly Poor Don't Get the Help They Were Promised," Washington, D.C., 1989; Mimeographed.

26. Burke and Burke, *Nixon's Good Deed,* pp. 196–97.

27. "Buses Warm Elderly at Social Security," *New York Times,* January 10, 1974, p. 41.

28. Social Security Administration, "Study of Burnout Syndrome among SSA Field Public Contact Employees," Division of Personnel Policy, Data and Research, 1979.

29. Quoted in Schulz, *The Economics of Aging,* p. 82, from Wilbur Cohen and Milton Friedman, *Social Security: Universal or Selective?* (Washington, D.C.: American Enterprise Institute, 1972).

30. "Federal Dunning: Social Security Agency Is Seeking Repayments from Overpaid Clients," *Wall Street Journal,* July 20, 1982, p. 1.

31. Ibid.

32. "Debt Collection Activities," *Commissioner's Bulletin,* Social Security Administration, No. 8, January 6, 1983.

Notes to Chapter Two

1. House Select Committee on Aging, 1988 figures.

2. Villers Advocates Associates, "Special Report," Washington, D.C., 1988. As I write this, the act is itself threatened with repeal, the target of a taxpayers' revolt among the elderly affluent.

3. Richard Harris, *A Sacred Trust* (Baltimore: Pelican Books, 1969), p. 214.

4. Quoted by Paul Starr, *The Social Transformation of American Medicine* (New York: Basic Books, 1982), p. 368.

5. Quoted in Harris, *A Sacred Trust,* p. 207; italics added.

6. U.S. General Accounting Office, *Medicare,* Washington, D.C., April 1986.

7. Villers Foundation, *On the Other Side of Easy Street,* Washington, D.C., 1987, p. 50.

8. Ibid., p. 42.

9. "Study Says Medicare Blurs Cost of Treatment," *New York Times,* July 4, 1985, p. A15; the study appeared on the same date in the *New England Journal of Medicine.*

10. Quoted in press release, "Elderly Forced Out of Hospitals Sicker and Quicker," University of California at San Francisco, Institute of Health and Aging and Institute for Health Policy Studies, February 5, 1986.

11. "Out 'Sooner and Sicker': Myth or Medicare Crisis?" Hearings before the House Select Committee on Aging, Comm. Pub. No. 99-591, April 10, 1986.

12. Anne R. Somers, "Why Not Try Preventing Illness as a Way of Controlling Medicare Costs?" *New England Journal of Medicine,* September 27, 1984, p. 855.

Notes to Chapter Three

1. Denise Hinzpeter and Anita Fischer, *Graying in the Shadows,* New York City Service Program for Elderly People, 1983.

2. Roberta Youmans's testimony, "Homeless Older Americans," Hearing before the Subcommittee on Housing and Consumer Interests, House Select Committe on Aging, May 2, 1984, pp. 101–09.

3. Low Income Housing Information Service, "Special Memorandum," Washington, D.C., March 1989.

4. Unless otherwise noted, the source for all numbers cited here is Department of Housing and Urban Development, *American Housing Survey for the United States in 1985* (Washington, D.C.: Government Printing Office, December 1988).

5. J. P. Zais et al., *Housing Assistance for Older Americans* (Washington, D.C.: Urban Institute Press, 1982), pp. 44–45.

6. The Grier Partnership, "Cold—Not by Choice," National Consumer Law Project, Washington, D.C., April 1984; Typewritten.

7. "Energy and the Aged: The Impact of Natural Gas Deregulation," Hearing before the Senate Special Committee on Aging, March 17, 1983, p. 92.

8. Ibid., pp. 109–10.

9. *Orlando Sentinel* [Fla.], March 16, 1986.

10. "Living at Home Program," Commonwealth Fund, 1985.

11. S. Newman, R. Struyk, and J. Zais, "Housing for Older America," in *The Physical Environment and the Elderly* (New York: Plenum Press, 1982).

12. Roger Sanjek, "Federal Housing Programs and Their Impact on Homelessness," Coalition for the Homeless, New York, 1982, p. 1; Typewritten.

13. Coalition for the Homeless, "An Embarrassment of Riches," New York, 1985, p. 9; Typewritten.

14. Mary Ellen Hombs and Mitch Snyder, *Homelessness in America,* Community for Creative Non-Violence, Washington, D.C., 1983, p. 4.

15. "Homeless Older Americans," pp. 33–48.

16. "Developments in Aging," Vol. 1, A Report of the U.S. Senate Special Committee on Aging, February 26, 1988, pp. 269–75.

17. Quoted in Irving Bernstein, *A Caring Society* (Boston: Houghton Mifflin, 1985), p. 4.

18. Quoted in Harold Wolman, *Politics of Federal Housing* (New York: Dodd, Mead, 1971), p. 31.

19. Chester Hartman, "National Comprehensive Housing Program," working paper, Institute for Policies Study, 1986, p. I-12.

20. Nathan Glazer, "Housing Problems and Housing Policies," *Public Interest,* Spring 1967, p. 37.

21. Jon Pynoos, "Setting the Elderly Housing Agenda," *Policy Studies Journal,* September 1984, p. 175.

22. Moses Gozonsky, "Senior Citizens," *New Jersey Municipalities,* June 1965, p. 27.

23. Senate Special Committee on Aging, "Section 202 Housing for the Elderly and Handicapped: A National Survey," Information paper prepared by committee staff, December 1984, p. 4.

24. R. J. Struyk, N. Mayer, and J. A. Tucillo, *Federal Housing Policy at President Reagan's Midterm* (Washington, D.C.: The Urban Institute, 1983), p. 4.

25. Low Income Housing Information Service, "Special Memorandum," Tables 1 through 4.

26. Hartman, "National Comprehensive Housing Program," p. I-19.

27. Low Income Housing Information Service, "Special Memorandum," Table 6.

28. *Orlando Sentinel* [Fla.], March 16, 1986.

29. Robert N. Butler, *Why Survive?* (New York: Harper & Row, 1975), p. 134.

Notes to Chapter Four

1. Barbara Myerhoff, *Number Our Days* (New York: Simon and Schuster, 1978), p. 1. The subsequent quotations are from pp. 1–2.

2. "Independence Is Soon Lost to Old Age," *Boston Globe,* March 6, 1985.

3. "First Portrait of the Very Old: Not So Frail," *New York Times,* January 5, 1985, p. A1.

4. Ibid., p. C8.

5. Ibid.

6. Quoted in "When Age Doesn't Matter," *Newsweek,* August 11, 1980, p. 73.

7. Beth J. Soldo, "A National Perspective on the Home Care Population," Center for Population Research, Georgetown University, Washington, D.C., 1983, pp. 5–7.

8. Adapted from ibid. Soldo's figures are based on the 1979 National Health Interview Survey (NHIS) and its Home Care Supplement published by the National Center for Health Statistics.

9. Karen Davis and Diane Rowland, *Medicare Policy* (Baltimore: Johns Hopkins University Press, 1986), p. 69.

10. National Center for Health Statistics, reported in "Developments in Aging," Vol. 1, A Report of the U.S. Senate Special Committee on Aging, 1984.

11. All figures but the last adapted from Chai R. Feldblum, "Home Health Care and the Elderly: Programs, Problems and Potentials," *Harvard Journal on Legislation,* Winter 1985, pp. 195–96; final figure from interview with George Rucker, research director, Rural America, Inc., Washington, D.C., 1986.

12. Feldblum, "Home Health Care and the Elderly,"p. 195.

13. Ethel Shanas, "The Family as a Social Support System in Old Age," *Gerontologist* 19, No. 2, 1979, p. 169.

14. Older Women's League, "Failing America's Caregivers: A Status Report on Women Who Care," Washington, D.C., 1989, p. 1.

15. Quote from transcription of testimony, Public hearing of New York State Governor's Task Force on Aging, 1985.

16. Patricia G. Archbold, "An Analysis of Parentcaring by Women," *Home Health Care Services Quarterly,* Summer 1982, p. 6.

17. Vanda Colman, "Till Death Do Us Part," gray paper, Older Women's League, 1982, p. 2.

18. Senate Finance Committee, Hearings on Long-term Care, 1983.

19. Alfred P. Fengler and Nancy Goodrich, "Wives of Elderly Disabled Men: The Hidden Patients,"*Gerontologist* 19, No. 2, 1979.

20. Quoted in ibid., from A. Golodetz et al., "The Care of Chronic Illness: The 'Responsor Role,'" *Medical Care* 7, 1969, pp. 385–94.

21. Archbold, "An Analysis of Parentcaring,"pp. 18–19.

22. Letter to Jane Porcino.

23. Shanas, "The Family as a Social Support System," p. 171.

24. Feldblum, "Home Health Care and the Elderly," p. 221.

25. A daughter quoted in Archbold, "An Analysis of Parentcaring," p. 14.

26. "Many in Work Force Care for Elderly Kin," *New York Times,* January 6, 1986, p. B5.

27. "Business and Health," *New York Times,* July 1, 1986, p. D3.

28. Millie Buchanan, "Health Care Choices," *Southern Exposure,* March-June 1985, p. 108.

29. Davis and Rowland, *Medicare Policy,* p. 62.

30. "Medicare: Coming of Age," working paper, Harvard Medicare Project, 1986.

31. Davis and Rowland, *Medicare Policy,* p. 65.

32. Telephone interview with researcher for Health Care Financing Administration who asked to remain anonymous. Italics added.

33. Feldblum, "Home Health Care and the Elderly," p. 206.

34. "Rural and Specialized Transportation Fact Sheet," Rural America, Washington, D.C., 1985, p. 1.

35. Peter M. Schauer, "The Typical Elderly Transportation Provider," reprinted by House Subcommittee on Investigations and Oversight, Committee on Public Works and Transportation, Hearings May 14 and 15, 1985.

36. *ruralamerica,* July-August 1983, p. 4.

37. Steve Braun, "Without the Buses, What's to Become of Union City?" *ruralamerica,* July-August 1983, p. 11.

38. Her testimony was reprinted by the House Subcommittee on Investigations and Oversight, Hearings May 14 and 15, 1985.

39. Author's notes from House Subcommittee on Investigations and Oversight, Hearings May 14 and 15, 1985.

40. Simeon Strunsky, *The Rediscovery of Jones* (Freeport, N.Y.: Books for Libraries Press, 1967, reprint of 1931 ed.), unpaged.

Notes to Chapter Six

1. Bruce C. Vladeck, *Unloving Care: The Nursing Home Tragedy* (New York: Basic Books, 1980), p. 266.

2. Ibid., pp. 30–31.

3. I. M. Rubinow, "The Modern Problem of the Care of the Aged," in *The Care of the Aged,* ed. I. M. Rubinow (Chicago: University of Chicago Press, 1930), pp. 4, 7.

4. Ethel McClure, *More Than a Roof* (St. Paul: Minnesota Historical Society, 1968), p. 3.

5. Ibid.

6. Quoted in ibid., p. 3.

7. Quoted in ibid., p. 5.

8. Quoted in ibid., p. 4.

9. Robert W. Kelso, quoted in ibid., p. 5.

10. Vladeck, *Unloving Care,* p. 34.

11. Florence E. Parker, "Institutional Care of the Aged in the United States," in *The Care of the Aged,* ed. Rubinow, p. 36.

12. Ibid., pp. 35–38.

13. Rubinow, "The Modern Problem of the Care of the Aged," pp. 5–6.

14. Vladeck, *Unloving Care,* p. 37.

15. Ibid., p. 43.

16. Francis Bardwell, "Public Outdoor Relief," in *The Care of the Aged,* ed. Rubinow, p. 58.

17. Vladeck, *Unloving Care,* p. 43.

18. Ibid., p. 46.

19. "*CLTC* Corporation Survey," *Contemporary LTC,* June 1986, p. 33.

20. "Discrimination Against the Poor and Disabled in Nursing Homes," Hearing before the Senate Special Committee on Aging, October 1, 1984, pp. 3–4.

21. Beverly mailing, January 31, 1983.

22. "Beverly Enterprises in Michigan: A Case Study of Corporate Takeover of Health Care Resources," Food and Beverage Trades Department, AFL-CIO, undated.

23. *Webster's New International* (Springfield, Mass.: G. & C. Merriam Co., 1928).

24. Dorothy P. Rice, "Home Care Needs of the Elderly," in *Long Term Care of the Elderly,* ed. C. Harrington et al. (Beverly Hills, Calif.: Sage Publications, 1985), p. 45.

25. May Sarton, *As We Are Now* (New York: W. W. Norton, 1973), p. 116.

26. Vladeck, *Unloving Care,* p. 3.

27. Institute of Medicine, *Improving the Quality of Care in Nursing Homes* (Washington, D.C.: National Academy Press), p. 11.

28. "Nursing Home Care: The Unfinished Agenda," staff report for Senate Special Committee on Aging, 1986, pp. 3–4; Mimeographed.

29. Press release, Senate Special Committee on Aging, June 26, 1986.

30. Institute of Medicine, *Improving the Quality of Care,* p. 101.

31. Ibid., p. 90.

32. Ibid., p. 195.

33. "Nursing Home Care," p. 4.

34. Vladeck, *Unloving Care,* p. 200.

35. Based on Karen Davis and Diane Rowland, *Medicare Policy* (Baltimore: Johns Hopkins University Press, 1986), p. 67.

36. "Officials Warn of Gaps in Insurance for Aged," *New York Times,* January 16, 1987, p. A10.

37. *Today's Nursing Home,* 1984 [clipping of ad otherwise undated]; italics in original.

38. Robert and Rosemary Stevens, *Welfare Medicine in America* (New York: Free Press, 1974), p. 74.

39. Report by Rehabilitation Care Consultants, Inc., cited in "Nursing Home Care: The Unfinished Agenda," p. 14.

40. Vladeck, *Unloving Care,* p. 266.

41. Paul Starr, *The Social Transformation of American Medicine* (New York: Basic Books, 1982), p. 446.

Notes to Epilogue

1. I. M. Rubinow, "The Modern Problem of the Care of the Aged," in *The Care of the Aged,* ed. I. M. Rubinow (Chicago: University of Chicago Press, 1930), p. 12.

2. R. L. Associates, "The American Public Views Long Term Care" (Princeton, N.J., typed and bound monograph, October 1987).

3. Quoted by William Graebner, *A History of Retirement* (New Haven: Yale University Press, 1980), p. 200.

4. Ibid.

5. E. J. Dionne, Jr., "Politics," *New York Times,* August 7, 1989, p. A12.

INDEX

◆

AAPS. *See* Association of American Physicians and Surgeons
Administration on Aging (AOA), 165
Aetna Insurance, 60
Ageism, 8–9
Alms. *See* Charity
Almshouses, 149–150, 151–154
AMA. *See* American Medical Association
American Medical Association (AMA), 56, 57
American Nursing Home Association (ANHA), 156
America's Old Age Crisis (Crystal), 10
Anderson, Grace, 118–119
Anderson, Melody, 115–116
ANHA. *See* American Nursing Home Association
AOA. *See* Administration on Aging
Archbold, Patricia G., 122, 123
Association of American Physicians and Surgeons (AAPS), 57
As We Are Now (Sarton), 161
Aten, Michael, 86–87
Atkins, Jeanne Paquette, 41
Auden, W. H., 3, 8
Avon Products, 157

"Balanced billing," 66
Baldwin, Leo, 85, 103
Ball, Robert M., 29, 30–31, 36
Bardwell, Francis, 155
Bauer, Carol, 93
Beverly Enterprises, 157–159
Bipartisan Budget Appeal, 33
Blacks, 23, 39, 82, 113–114

Blue Cross and Blue Shield, 60
Bradley, Bill, 36
Bratter, Bess, 61–62
Brody, Elaine M., 124
Buchanan, Millie, 124
Bureaucratism, 14
Burke, Vee, 36, 42
Burke, Vincent J., 36, 42
Burton, Harold, 155
Bush, George, 188
Butler, Robert N., 13, 104

Caregivers, 111–125, 127. *See also* Nursing homes, staffing; Women
Carleton, Will, 150
Carter, Jimmy, 45, 99, 100
Charity, 21, 23–25. *See also* Almshouses
Chriswell, William, 38
Church, Frank, 42
Churchill, Winston, 59
"Civic heart," 3–4
Cohen, Wilbur, 23, 24, 29, 32, 44, 148
Commercialism, 184–185. *See also* Nursing homes, for-profit
Congregate Housing Services Act of 1978, 103
Crystal, Stephen, 10–11
Cushing, Harvey, 56

Davis, Karen, 114, 125, 126, 166
Day care, 174, 176
Demographics, 5, 10
Department of Agriculture (USDA), 12

Department of Housing and Urban
    Development (HUD), 78, 98–99,
    100
Dependency, 109, 110
De Voto, Bernard, 72
Diagnostic related groups (DRGs),
    68–69, 74
Dickens, Charles, 21
Digging in, 85–90, 102. *See also*
    Housing
DRGs. *See* Diagnostic related groups
Dublin, Louis I., 51

Edelman, Toby S., 169
Eliot, T. S., 14
Enoff, Louis, 43, 44
Entitlements, 14, 21, 23. *See also*
    Social assistance
EOMBs. *See* Explanations of
    Medicare benefits
Equitable Insurance, 60
Estes, Carroll, 69
Explanations of Medicare benefits
    (EOMBs), 60, 75

Family, 117–122, 187. *See also*
    Caregivers
Family Assistance Plan (FAP), 39
FAP. *See* Family Assistance Plan
Farmers Home Administration, 94
Farrell, William, 50
Federal Housing Administration, 156
Feldblum, Chai R., 124, 126, 127
Flincbaugh, Patricia, 131
Food, 12–13
Forman, Maxine, 41
Fuller, Ida, 28

Gamber, Julie, 88
Glazer, Nathan, 95
Glengariff Corporation, 170–171
Goldwater, Barry, 57
Golodetz, A., 123
Goodman, Ellen, 112
Gozonsky, Moses J., 98
Graebner, William, 187

Greenspan, Alan, 32–33
Greyhound Lines, 130
Gross, Jodie, 181–182
Gutierrez, Alfonso, 84
Gutierrez, Elizabeth, 84

Hardesty, T. Frank, 47
Harper, Eileen, 61–62
Harrington, Michael, 9, 184
Harris, John D., 44
Harris, Louis, 75
Harris, Richard, 55
Hart, Orson J., 33
Hartman, Chester, 94, 101
Hazard, Thomas R., 150
HCFA. *See* Health Care Financing
    Administration
Health, 53–76, 114
Health Care Financing
    Administration (HCFA), 60, 74–
    75, 162, 164, 165
Health Retirement Corporation of
    America, 157
Heinz, John, 161, 162, 164, 169, 171
Helplessness, 183–184
Hill, Lister, 155
Hill-Burton Act. *See* Hospital and
    Construction Act
Hillhaven Corporation, 157
Hispanics, 23
Hladek, Mary, 119–122
Hoang, Ve, 37–38
Hombs, Mary Ellen, 93
Home care, 102, 109–134, 174
    aged-to-aged, 116–117
    federal policy, 125–127
    reform, 126–128
    See also Caregivers
Homelessness, 77, 92–93
Hospital and Construction Act
    (1946), 155, 175
Hospital stay, 68–71
House of Representatives
    Public Works and Transportation
        Committee, 131–132
    Select Committee on Aging, 69

Housing, 77–105, 185
  conditions, 82–85
  "congregate," 102–104
  costs, 82–85, 101–102
  federal programs, 93–101
  gentrification of, 78
  low-income, 82–85, 93–101
  reform, 102, 104
  "social ownership" of, 101
Housing Act of 1959, 98
Housing and Community
    Development Act (1974), 99
Howe, Irving, 8
HUD. *See* Department of Housing
    and Urban Development
Huddleston, Cindy, 49–50
Hunter, Robert, 8–9

Incrementalism, 54, 72, 75
Independence, 112–113, 186
Inflation, 101
Institutionalization. *See* Nursing
    Homes
Insurance
  comprehensive, 55
  "medigap," 58

Jackson, Adeline, 38
Jewish Home for the Aged, 176–182
Johnson, Helen, 47
Johnson, Lyndon, 57, 98, 171

Kelso, Robert W., 149
Kennedy, John F., 57, 98
Kerr, Robert, 156

Landon, Alfred M., 22
Lekachman, Robert, 7
Letting go, 90–92. *See also* Housing
Life expectancy, 5, 65
"Life-span analysis," 113
Locke, John, 24
Loneliness, 103–104, 161
Longino, Charles F., 112
Long-term care (LTC), 114–115. *See
    also* Home care

LTC. *See* Long-term care
Lykes, Dorothy, 92

McClure, Ethel, 149
McIntyre, Ross, 56
Magier, Leora, 115–116
MaGuire, Marie C., 95–98, 99
Mainstreaming, 22
Marketing and Merchandising
    Associates, 168
Marriott Corporation, 157
Means testing, 22, 23, 24, 34, 39
Media images, 6–7
Medicaid, 4, 9, 17, 173, 174, 185
  creation of, 67
  home care and, 126, 127
  nursing homes and, 148, 156, 163–
    173, 180
  reform, 128, 174–175, 184
  reimbursement policies, 175
Medicare, 4, 9, 15–16, 17, 53–76, 185
  assignment, 66
  benefits, 58, 73, 75
  carriers, 60, 74–75
  Catastrophic Protection Act, 54,
    67, 72
  coverage, 58, 66–67, 73–74, 75
  creation of, 55–57, 67
  deductibles, 65, 66
  home care and, 125–126, 127
  nursing homes and, 165
  Part A., 58–59, 65
  Part B., 58–60, 65, 66
  physicians and, 55, 56–57, 58, 66,
    68, 73, 75
  reform, 72–76, 127, 128
  reimbursements, 68–69, 74
  shortfalls, 66
  vendor payments, 156
"Medigap," 58
Mills, Wilbur, 32, 37, 156, 171
Milton, Harold, 25–26
Minorities, 10, 23, 39, 82, 113–114
Morrison, Edna, 78–81, 105
Moser, Judy, 158, 169
Myerhoff, Barbara, 109

Neugarten, Bernice L., 113
Nixon, Ethel F., 112–113
Nixon, Richard M., 39, 98–99
"Nonmarrieds," 34
Nursing homes, 139–143, 147–182
    chain, 157–158, 174
    class disparities of, 152–153, 167–
        168
    conditions of, 158–163, 167
    decertification of, 164
    for-profit, 157–160, 174–175
    government policies and, 148,
        153–156, 163–173
    Medicaid and, 148, 156, 163–173,
        180
    quality of, 175–182
    shortages of, 164
    social security and, 153–155
    staffing, 162–163, 176
Nursing Home Tragedy, The
    (Vladeck), 147
Nutrition, 13

OAA. *See* Old-age assistance
OAI. *See* Old-age insurance program
OASDHI, 28
OASDI, 28
OASI, 28
Oberstar, James, 131–132
Old-age assistance (OAA), 153–155
Old-age insurance (OAI) program,
    28
Older Americans Act (1965), 9, 131
Olson, Minnie, 116
Orshansky, Mollie, 12, 13
Other America, The (Harrington), 9
"Out 'Sooner and Sicker': Myth or
    Medicare Crisis?" 70
"Over the Hill to the Poor-House"
    (Carleton), 150–151
Owens-Illinois, 157

Packard, Vance, 7
Paine, Thomas, 22, 24
Paratransit programs. *See*
    Transportation

Parker, Florence E., 151–152, 167
Parker, Miriam, 176, 177, 178
Partridge, Eric, 151
Pearson, Ilene C., 132
Pensions, 35
Pepper, Claude, 183
Peterson, Ivar, 83–84
Peterson, Peter G., 33
PHS. *See* Public Health Service
Physicians, 55, 56–57, 58, 66, 68, 73,
    75
Pixley, Patricia, 128, 133
Poor houses, 149–150, 151–154
Porcino, Jane, 122
Poverty, 184
    gap, 22
    line, 10, 11–13, 22, 35
    rates, 35
    See also Vulnerability
PPS. *See* Prospective Payments
    System
Preventive care, 73–74
Privacy, 104
Prospective Payments System (PPS),
    68, 69, 73
Provincial House, 159
Prudential Insurance, 60
Public Health Service (PHS), 155–
    156
Pynoos, Jon, 95

Rathbun, Thomas, 128–129
RDAs. *See* Nutrition
Reagan, Ronald, 5, 22, 45, 99–101,
    131, 132
Required Dietary Allowances
    (RDAs). *See* Nutrition
Ribicoff, Abraham, 42
Rice, Dorothy P., 160
Riemer, Jerry, 85
Roosevelt, Eleanor, 94, 187
Roosevelt, Franklin D., 22, 35, 56
Roosevelt, Theodore, 56
Rothschild, Edwin, 83
Rowland, Diane, 114, 125, 126, 166
Rubinow, I. M., 148, 152, 153, 154,
    155, 168, 175, 185

Russell, Robert M., 13

Sarton, May, 161
Savings, 35
Schauer, Peter M., 129
Schorr, Alvin L., 3, 22, 94
Schulz, James H., 32, 34
Self-employment, 35
Self-respect, 4, 9
Shanas, Ethel, 122, 124
Sisters of Zion, 178
Sisu, 86–87
Skocpol, Theda, 36
Slusser, Charles E., 103
Small Business Administration, 156
Smeeding, Timothy, 10
Snook, Robert B., 170–171
Snyder, Mitch, 93
Social assistance, 3–4, 7–8, 21, 35.
    See also Medicaid; Medicare;
    Social security; Supplemental
    Security Income
"Social insurance," 21
Social security, 4, 7, 15, 17, 22–23,
    24–25, 28–36, 185, 187
  benefits, 9, 22, 29–31, 32
  nursing homes and, 153–155
  payroll tax rate, 30
  third-party reimbursement, 155
  trust fund, 33
  "work connection," 28–30, 32
Social Security Act (1935), 28, 153,
    187
Social Security Administration (SSA),
    12, 15, 24
  "Debt Collection Action Plan,"
    44–50
  SSI and, 43–50
Soldo, Beth J., 113
Solidarity, 21–23, 36
Somers, Anne R., 73–74
"Spending down," 166
SSA. *See* Social Security
    Administration
SSI. *See* Supplemental Security
    Income

Starr, Paul, 174
Steingard, Sandra, 177
Stevens, Robert, 172, 175
Stevens, Rosemary, 172, 175
Struyk, R. J., 100
Studies of the Aged and Aging, 97
Sullivan, Agnes, 117–118
Supplemental Security Income (SSI),
    4, 9, 15, 17, 23–25, 35, 37–50,
    83, 185
  benefits, 39, 43
  nonparticipation rate, 41–43
  regulations, 39–42
  SSA and, 43–50
Supplementary Medical Insurance.
    See Medicare, Part B.
Svahn, John A., 47–48

Taxation, 7, 30–31
  of benefits, 31
  long-term care and, 187
  social security rate, 30
Temporary Emergency Food
    Assistance Program, 1
Transportation, 104, 111, 114, 128–
    134
"2176 Waiver," 126, 127

Ultra Rich, The (Packard), 7
UMTA. *See* Urban Mass Transit
    Administration
Unemployment, 35
Urban Mass Transit Administration
    (UMTA), 131
USDA. *See* Department of
    Agriculture

Veterans, 35
Villers Foundation, 29
Vladeck, Bruce C., 147–148, 154,
    156, 161, 165, 173
Voluntarism, 33–34. *See also*
    Medicare, Part B.
Volunteers, 178–179
Vulnerability, 10–11

Wagner-Steagall Low Rent Housing Act, 94
WEAL. *See* Women's Equity Action League
Wealth distribution, 6, 7
Welfare. *See* Health; Social assistance
Whitman, Walt, 5
Wickman, Carl Erie, 130

Williams, David, 84–85
Williams, Susan, 84–85
Women, 10, 23, 24, 31, 34, 39, 41, 113–114, 115–116, 117–123, 124, 127
Women's Equity Action League (WEAL), 41

Yolen, Susan, 179, 180
Young, Peter, 33–34